DREW PLUNKETT

CONSTRUCTION AND DETAILING FOR INTERIOR DESIGN

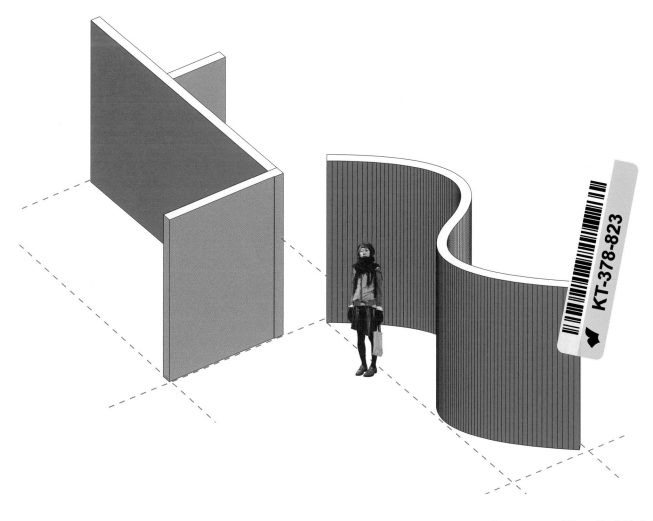

KT-378-823

Laurence King Publishing

Contents

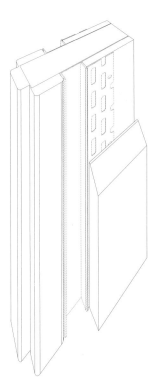

CONSTRUCTION AND DETAILING
FOR INTERIOR DESIGN

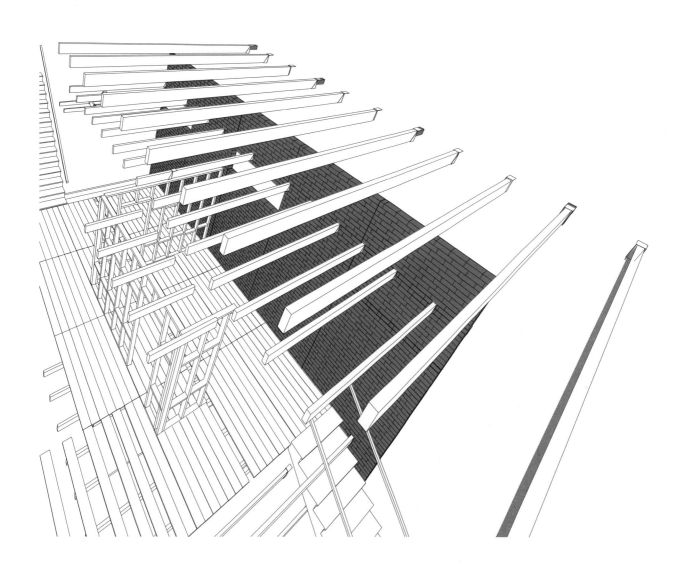

Published in 2010
by Laurence King Publishing Ltd
361–373 City Road
London EC1V 1LR
Tel +44 20 7841 6900
Fax +44 20 7841 6910
E enquiries@laurenceking.co.uk
www.laurenceking.co.uk

This book was designed and produced by
Laurence King Publishing Ltd, London

A catalogue record for this book is available from the British Library.

ISBN 978-1-85669-689-0

Designed by Olga Valentinova Reid

Printed in China

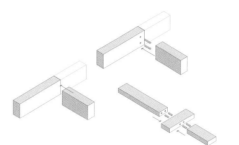

Related study material is available on the Laurence King website at
www.laurenceking.com

Introduction

Basic principles

Successful interior design depends on sound construction and beautiful detailing. A strong concept has to be carefully nurtured through the stages of its development and its success depends, ultimately, on the right decisions being made about the materials used and the way they are put together. Creative conceptual thinking needs creative practical thinking if the spirit of a project is to be successfully expressed in the finished building.

It is often said that interior design is 'about space', and undoubtedly the proportions of an interior volume are critical to its success. Ultimately, the appreciation of that volume will be determined by the colours and textures of the materials that define its planes and, as crucially, by the details of its construction – the junctions and fixings that fine-tune the perception of its proportions.

Designers, perhaps inevitably, develop a personal 'style', the result of preferred ways of expressing the elements – walls, floors and ceilings – that enclose a space. To achieve this, they evolve a personal vocabulary of construction details that determine how these elements are joined physically and visually. A good designer will constantly aspire to modify these preferences, to respond to the particular context and content of each new project. In addition, the particularities of a project should prompt new ideas and variations on old ones. However, the basic principles of sound detailing remain constant and it is these that this book will explain. The most visually diverse construction details will, if they are successful, have been built on an understanding of these basics.

Practical solutions and aesthetics

The engineer Peter Rice, probably best known for his work on the Centre Pompidou in Paris, maintained that a structure should not only be capable of fulfilling its load-carrying responsibility but should also appear to be so, to satisfy the instinctive expectations of anyone looking at it. This was an argument not for traditional or lumpen structures, but for clear visual expression of rational thinking in radical design – a recognition that practical solutions should inform and, in turn, be informed by aesthetic decisions. The outcomes of such creative fusion may initially surprise or disconcert those who encounter them but their inherent logic should ultimately communicate with and convince all those who see them. The same rule applies for all scales of detailing. If the interaction of the aesthetic and the practical is honestly assessed, the integrity of the result will be persuasive.

Technological advances

Another engineer, Auguste Choisy, writing in 1899, argued that significant shifts in architectural style had in the past depended on technological advances – the column and beam shaped Greek Classicism, the arch defined Roman structures, the dome was a key element in Byzantine architecture. If one considers the development of interior detailing, it becomes clear that what were essentially practical considerations shaped the conventions of interiors. It also becomes clear that these practical solutions were, in turn, shaped by human beings' instinct to embellish their habitations. It is enlightening to see that familiar decorative elements all have an essential practical role to fulfil, and, while that role determined their location, the recognition that they should be visually resolved and enriched became the primary aspiration of their makers. The practical was taken for granted, hidden behind visual extravagance.

Production and construction methods defined the potential, and therefore the character, of interior components. Simpler elements such as flat, plastered walls and ceilings were most conveniently made on site. However, there were limitations to the quality of finishing that could be achieved under site conditions and there were areas of every building that were particularly vulnerable to wear.

Skirtings evolved to conceal the necessarily untidy junctions of floors and walls, difficult to finish precisely and vulnerable to foot damage. Cornices smoothed over the angles between wall and ceiling – again, difficult to finish perfectly and also liable to cracking as the floor above flexed. To ensure the desired level of perfection, these protective, masking elements were normally manufactured away from the site and, as hand skills evolved and machine production became more refined, they became vehicles for the increasingly intricate moulding that could be achieved in workshops and came to characterize all styles of building that pre-dated Modernism.

Detailing today

What may now be perceived as the decorative excesses of the pre-Modern have largely disappeared from the vocabulary of building, but the obligation to deal aesthetically with the mechanics of construction – the junctions and fixings of the range of standard and innovative materials – continues to be the critical consideration in the creation of any interior. It might be argued that the Modernist reaction against applied ornament created fundamental detailing problems. Tried and tested solutions were rejected because pioneers of the new style failed to see behind their decorative façade, but enough time has now passed and enough evidence of relative performances has been accumulated to encourage a more inclusive attitude.

The traditional principle of the cover strip, which generated skirtings and cornices, architraves and thresholds remains valid but is now augmented by the Modernist 'shadow gap', a space between elements that creates the illusion of floating planes while, at a practical level, minimizing the perception of misalignments. Both may be applied, equally effectively, to the familiar problems that occur, inevitably, in similar locations.

Using this book

This book illustrates strategies and tactics for successful interior construction but it does not suggest that these are the only answers. Good interior detailing is bespoke, an informed response not only to the practical demands of a new interior but also to the physical characteristics of the existing structure that will enclose it. However, only knowledge of essential construction principles and techniques will ensure that innovative responses to context and content are soundly constructed.

In each chapter, detailed drawings demonstrate generic solutions to the construction of new elements, and these are offered as starting points from which the designer may begin to evolve personal and project-specific variations. While the simple fundamental sequences of construction and methods for connecting and fixing are likely to remain relevant for all proposals, materials and dimensions can and will vary. Those materials and construction techniques most frequently encountered in existing structures will be described, and the implications of amending them examined. Techniques for repair and restoration will be identified, and the practical and aesthetic implications of joining and juxtaposing old and new elements will be discussed.

In each chapter, text and diagrams will amplify the principles and considerations that should underpin all developmental design thinking, demonstrating and explaining rational, economic underpinnings for the most ambitious proposals and suggesting previously unconsidered aesthetic opportunities.

THE COVER STRIP
Traditional detailing used applied elements, which became progressively more ornamental, to cover components and locations that were difficult to finish well and were vulnerable to wear.

THE SHADOW GAP
Modernist theory rejected traditional applied ornament and favoured the visible separation of elements to eliminate awkward junctions, such as here between a plastered wall and timber skirting.

First principles

The raw, practical considerations that shape interior detailing are not demanding. Designers need not worry about the demands of weatherproofing that burden those designing the exterior skins of buildings with an inflexible repertoire of obligatory solutions and a restricted range of materials. However, as comparative freedom from the most stringent practical considerations means that decisions about interior details must primarily be made for aesthetic reasons, it can be argued that this makes the process more challenging – there are fewer practical priorities to inform and focus decision-making. Materials may effectively be nailed, screwed, bolted or glued together; the mechanics of construction need not be complicated but practicalities must be scrupulously refined to withstand close and sustained scrutiny.

Simplicity

It is probably safe to suggest that the best details are simple ones. Simple detailing is also likely to result in financially viable construction. Simple work, however, does not mean simplistic work, which is the result of lazy or shoddy thinking. The fixing on site of the most ornate traditional mouldings, almost invariably prefabricated in specialist workshops, was, and is, an essentially simple, utilitarian operation; the end result is extravagantly complex and highly refined.

Specialist knowledge

Most designers have an instinctive understanding of the capacities of familiar building materials to meet the practical demands made on them, and this intuition will be refined progressively as they see their work built on site, but part of the skill of being a designer is knowing when to consult specialists. Often it is enough to follow established practice, rules of thumb or one's instincts, but sometimes, as with complex structures or lighting installations, it is necessary to have a specialist consultant to provide precise calculations and proposals. The designer's role is to make an initial proposal and then to orchestrate the input of specialists so that the sum of their contributions makes for a successful whole that respects the designer's first intention but is also enriched by expert advice. Every designer should try to find consultants who will bring their own creativity to the process; it is usually foolish to ignore their advice.

New materials, and techniques that relate to their installation, are continually evolving. It is logical to consult manufacturers about the performance of their innovative products, or fabricators about the potential of their processes. Both are usually keen to collaborate in the hope of extending their market and their expertise. Manufacturers, who once had to rely on brochures, are increasingly developing websites that provide extensive and updated information about the performance and installation of their products.

A designer must have the core of practical knowledge that ensures sound detailing, but it is not possible or necessary to acquire specialist understanding of the entire range of materials and techniques relevant to interior construction. There is often no single practical answer and it is legitimate, and prudent, to take specialist advice. It is foolish to invent something from scratch when there is almost certain to be a tried-and-tested precedent that eliminates the inevitably awkward details of the prototype. A collaborative solution will be more efficient and effective. The designer can concentrate on ensuring that the visual refinement of the proposal survives the rigours of production.

Working methods

Increasingly, the hand tools associated with traditional building skills are being superseded by electrically powered alternatives; these progressively offer greater mobility as batteries replace cable connections to inconveniently situated sockets. Power tools not only speed up the time-consuming processes of cutting, drilling and screwing but, for many operations, provide a significantly improved degree of precision. Since the greater portion of the cost of any project tends to be for labour, any acceleration in working methods must be welcomed, with the proviso that an emphasis on speed does not lead, in the comparative chaos of building sites, to mistakes and a compromise in quality.

Where feasible, elements of a project are likely to be constructed off site in the workshops of contractors and specialist subcontractors. This generally ensures a high standard of work, and such items are generally brought to site and installed late in the construction process to avoid damage. It is important to remember that restrictive door heights and widths, narrow stairs and tight corners may compromise delivery; it is not unusual for elements to be delivered in manageable sections. It then becomes important to identify acceptable locations for visible joins and to design appropriate fixing techniques so that the assembled components read as a single unit.

Since much of this pre-fabrication will be carried out by specialist subcontractors, chosen for their expertise, a designer should try to discuss proposals in some detail with them before issuing drawings. It has become common practice for designers to define the form, dimensions and materials of their proposal and to leave decisions about construction methods to specialist fabricators who will produce their own drawings. These will, in turn, be sent for approval to the designer before work begins.

Sustainability and sizing

The designer's approach

While the greatest contributions to sustainability are made in the external skins of buildings, there are significant steps that an interior designer can take to improve performance. They may appear modest, but if some fundamental principles are integrated into design thinking then the accumulative effect will be considerable. Insulation of external planes, walls, floors and ceilings, and the insertion of double glazing where possible, will reduce fuel consumption. This is no more than any conscientious individual could, and should, do – in many countries it is a legal requirement except for historic interiors. It is in the careful consideration of construction and detail that the interior designer may make a specialist contribution. Simple detailing, if combined with economical use of materials, will go a long way towards satisfying concerns about depredation of natural resources. While it is important for designers to become knowledgeable about the sustainable status of the more exotic building materials, it is perhaps more important to use familiar options intelligently and sparingly to minimize a greater cumulative effect.

Standard sizing

Components in the building industry tend to conform to a range of standard sizes. For example, most sheet materials such as plasterboard, plywood and chipboard are around 2400 x 1200mm. This is beneficial for both manufacturers and designers as it creates compatibility and makes repair and replacement easier, minimizing the need for new elements and components. If fixings that allow dismantling with a minimum of damage, such as nails and screws, are used then elements may be recycled. Even this damage may preclude reuse as a finishing material but this will not affect reuse if the item is to be re-finished or used as substructure.

Standard sizes also provide a useful first reference point in decision-making. It always makes sense to reduce the labour and material used, so it is logical, for example, to cut a sheet of 1220mm-wide plywood into 305mm-wide strips, resulting in three cuts and four units, rather than 310mm strips, resulting in three cuts and a 290mm-wide strip of waste material, along with an additional cut from another sheet. Waste may be unavoidable but costs money, particularly if a wasteful module is repeated frequently.

There are two principal measurement systems in the building industry: metric (metres, millimetres) and imperial (feet, inches). The latter prevailed in English-speaking areas, but in all countries other than the United States, Liberia and Myanmar, there has been a decisive shift to the metric system, and even in these countries metric is used in some professional work. Direct translations of old imperial dimensions into metric equivalents has resulted in what may appear to be arbitrary sizes – the ⅜ standard thickness for plasterboard translates precisely to 9.5mm, but this is often rounded down to 9mm, while the standard 8 x 4 feet sheet translates to 2440 x 1220mm. This is used for most timber-based sheets, but plasterboard is often rationalized to 2400 x 1200mm. There are also many local variations, so it is prudent to check with suppliers before specification.

Materials and techniques

A designer can be selective in the materials specified, and there is increasingly detailed information available about relative performances – although, given the vested interests involved it is difficult to get a definitive view. The judgement is seldom simple as transportation can have an impact as great as production processes. Decisions about materials and techniques will often depend on financial considerations and, ultimately, belong to the client. However, since sustainable building methods tend towards the economical, a designer can, from the earliest stages of project development, set an appropriate course. In the end, however, the greatest contributor to sustainability is longevity. Sound construction and detailing can eliminate the need to repair and replace.

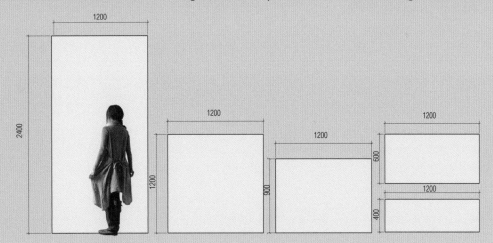

STANDARDIZATION

If designers use, from the outset of the design process, the standard dimensions of components manufactured for the building industry as a basic module in their planning, waste is minimized. Widths of sheets are multiples of 400mm, which is the standard spacing for framing and joists. The 2400mm height of a sheet determines the optimum height for new rooms. Lengths of timber come in multiples of 300mm.

Communicating information

Designers explain their intentions for the construction of interiors with a comprehensive set of drawings that describe in detail their intentions to all the trades involved in the building work. While the need to deal with the construction of larger elements is obvious, ultimately even the simplest instructions must be clearly communicated because it is precision of execution that determines quality. What may seem obvious to the designer who has been absorbed in the development of a project will not be clear to the contractor called in after the formative thinking is done.

Design feasibility

It is important when evolving methods of construction to consider the feasibility of carrying out instructions on site. Drawings made in the well-lit warmth of the design studio have to be implemented in the chaotic environment of the building site; it is easy to draw idealized proposals that are impossible to build. A designer must be able to visualize the process of construction so that its stages may be appropriately sequenced – for example, surfaces cannot be finished properly if they are inaccessible, but finishes are liable to be damaged if applied too early in the proceedings.

It is easy to overlook in the design studio considerations that are embarrassingly evident in the reality of the site. Dimensions of the entrance, for example, which are likely to be no bigger than a standard door, will determine the size of everything that is brought on to the site.

Designer–contractor relationship

Production information drawings, also referred to as 'production' or 'working' drawings, provide the building contractor, and anyone else involved in the construction process, with a comprehensive description in drawings and words of the full extent and quality of the work necessary to complete the project satisfactorily. They should describe the materials to be used, their sizes and the method for their assembly. They also provide a formal record of the details of the contractual agreement between a client and builder, describing in comprehensive detail the extent, and the quality, of the work to be carried out for the money agreed.

It is always desirable that the designer should take responsibility for approval, on behalf of the client, of the standard of work carried out on site, if quality is to be assured and the unforeseen difficulties that may come to light during construction are to be dealt with successfully.

Ideally, the construction process should be seen as a collaboration between designer and contractor. It is in the interest of both that work proceeds efficiently and quickly. Both should be capable of fulfilling their own responsibilities efficiently, and have a sympathetic understanding of the problems that may affect the other's performance. However, when difficulties arise the designer must act as an arbitrator to ensure, on the client's behalf, that the extent and quality of the work matches that quoted for, while also ensuring, on the contractor's behalf, that payment is made for completed work and for extra, unanticipated work that may have become necessary during the course of the contract. Such 'extras' are often the result of site conditions not apparent during initial surveys, made before any exploratory demolition. Sometimes they are the result of a client's requirements changing. Sometimes they are due to a designer's error: it is usually sensible to admit to these, since responsibility will be obvious and arguing otherwise can only lead to a loss of credibility and trust.

A completed set of production information drawings allows a contractor to estimate the cost of building work and to produce a 'tender' – the estimated cost of all necessary work, including labour and materials. A client may nominate a single contractor, often on the basis of a previous successful collaboration, to carry out the work. If this is done before, or early in, the design process it is usual for designer and contractor to discuss the most effective and economical way of constructing the work. Where collaboration during the design process has not been possible, the designer must advise the client on the fairness of an uncontested tender.

It is more usual for at least three contractors to tender and for the one offering the lowest price to be given the work. When the successful tender has been identified it is the designer's responsibility to check that the contractor is capable of carrying out the work to a satisfactory standard. This is particularly important if the tender is lower than anticipated, which can suggest that they have miscalculated or are too anxious to get the job – they may not have the reserve resources to carry out work to the required standard or to deal adequately with complications that may arise.

Cost

It is often hard to establish the cost of an interior project accurately. When operating in new buildings the nature of the work may be clearly defined and estimated, and unanticipated work or significant amendments to the contract should not occur. The estimating of costs in existing buildings is more difficult. Complications are often unforeseeable and emerge during the course of the work, as existing finishes are stripped and difficulties exposed.

It is also in the nature of interior work that finishes and construction details will be unique to a particular project, and therefore an accurate price depends on a contractor's perception of the intrinsic difficulties involved in meeting unfamiliar demands. Contractors inevitably prefer to work with familiar materials and techniques and are likely to submit an expensive quote for a complicated job, to ensure that what may potentially be more difficult work will be adequately rewarded and unforeseen costs covered.

The simple project will almost invariably prove cheaper. One that strays from the familiar will require extra commitment from a client, who may be inspired to agree to an expensive option by a seductive presentation but whose initial enthusiasm will weaken if there are a succession of expensive, unanticipated or unacknowledged complications. If creative ambition creates problems it is appropriate that the designer be blamed for the practical inefficiencies and overspending that result. A designer persuading a client to commit to an ambitious or innovative project must be prepared to spend more time detailing and supervising the quality of its construction, probably for the same fee as would be earned for a more conventional proposal.

Clients always have a budget beyond which they cannot or will not go. While they often have some capacity to extend this, there is usually a point when it becomes apparent that it will be necessary to negotiate details of the work with the contractor to reduce the overall cost. The designer is crucial to this process because decisions must be made about how savings will least prejudice the aesthetic and practical efficiency of the finished work, and only the designer has the overview and knowledge to resolve compromises in materials and construction successfully.

Presentation of drawings

There is no room for ambiguity in production information drawings. They should be clear and, as far as possible, simple. Even for the most complicated project, simple drawings will usually signify well-resolved thinking: an economical and effective solution, easily built and robust. They will reassure contractors that the extent of the work is clear, and should reduce the factor of financial safety built into a tender.

Project information can be distributed digitally, reducing delays that affect price or completion times. The disadvantage is that the designer is under greater pressure to respond quickly to unanticipated complications, and given that such revisions can have a significant, but not immediately apparent, impact on the whole project and its cost, it is sensible to agree a reasonable amount of time for consideration of each development. If a designer has given evidence of general efficiency, been sympathetic to the contractor's problems and is confronting an unforeseeable dilemma, it is reasonable to expect understanding in return.

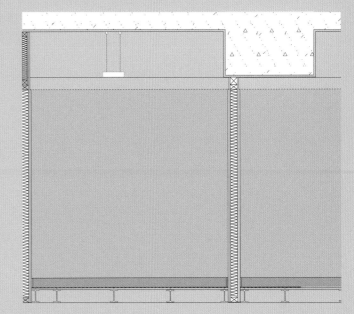

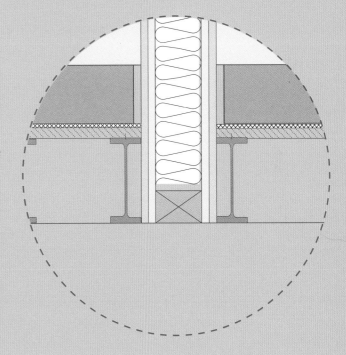

LAYOUT DRAWINGS
Plans and sections, at scales of 1:200, 1:100, 1:50 and perhaps 1:20, indicate the overall layout, materials and finishes, and the location of elements that will be dealt with in greater detail elsewhere.

DETAIL DRAWINGS
The precise methods of construction must be clearly indicated to a builder if the finished work is to conform accurately to a designer's intentions. These plans and sections are drawn at 1:10, 1:5, sometimes 1:2 or full size.

CHAPTER 1 EXISTING WALLS

Basic principles

Existing walls may be loadbearing or non-loadbearing. Before making alterations to them, it is crucial to consider the implications of any change. This is particularly important in buildings with multiple occupancy, where mistakes may result in damage to the property of neighbouring owners that must be paid for. Loadbearing walls divide spaces, but are also responsible for supporting the construction above them. Non-loadbearing walls are responsible only for the subdivision of spaces.

Construction techniques

Both types of wall can use techniques of monolithic or framed construction. In the first case, the wall – probably made of standardized units such as brick, block or stone bonded with mortar – will have an equally distributed loadbearing capacity across its length. In the second, framing elements located at regular intervals along the length of a wall will focus the loading at those intervals and will allow the use of lighter non-loadbearing walls for the subdivision of areas.

There is no guarantee that existing structures will be able to deal with additional loadings, and it can often be difficult to prove the capacity of existing structures to cope. There are always options, but these will inevitably increase costs and affect the viability of a project.

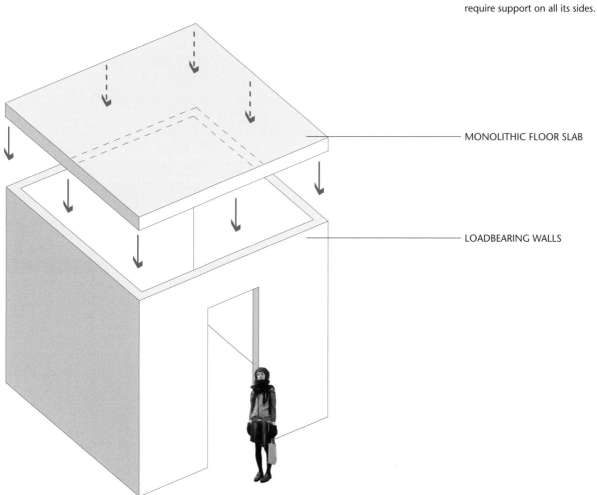

LOADBEARING WALLS: CONCRETE FLOORS
A concrete floor, cast in situ, will act as a monolithic slab and require support on all its sides.

MONOLITHIC FLOOR SLAB

LOADBEARING WALLS

Loadbearing walls

It is comparatively simple to identify a loadbearing wall. If it aligns directly with a wall or walls on an upper floor then it is likely to be transferring their weight to the foundations. If it is removed, these upper floors will collapse. Loadbearing walls will also support floors. All walls surrounding a monolithic concrete floor slab, particularly if the concrete has been cast in situ, are liable to be loadbearing, but where support for the floor depends on concrete or metal beams or timber joists, then only the walls that support the ends of these will be supporting the floor. The location of such beams may be indicated by the presence of 'piers', or attached columns, which increase the loadbearing capacity of a wall at the points where the beams meet it.

LOADBEARING WALLS: BEAMS
When beams are used to reduce the specification and size of floor members, the load will be concentrated where beams meet wall. Often 'piers' (embedded columns or projecting masonry sections increased in size to take the extra load) indicate the location of beams and the points where support must be retained.

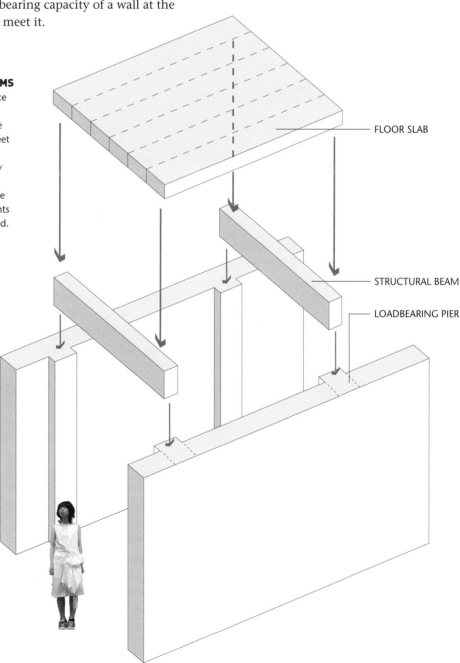

FLOOR SLAB

STRUCTURAL BEAM

LOADBEARING PIER

FLUSH MORTAR JOINT

WEATHERED MORTAR JOINT

KEYED MORTAR JOINT

RECESSED MORTAR JOINT

Masonry

Bricks are probably the most common material used in the construction of internal and external loadbearing walls. They are modular components, manufactured in standard sizes – the most common is nominally 215mm long, 102.5mm wide and 65mm high. The mortar joints that bind them are nominally 10mm, so that in calculating the dimensions of an area of brick wall the length of brick plus joint (225mm) and the height plus joint (75mm) are used. Unless they are necessary to provide structural support it is unusual to build new brick walls within an interior. They are heavy, often require new concrete foundation strips, and wet mortar joints have to be allowed time to dry, holding up progress on site.

Bonds

Brick walls are usually constructed so that vertical mortar joints do not line through. This increases the structural cohesion of the wall – the decorative pattern caused by this overlapping and interlocking is known as the 'bond'. In its simplest form, a 102.5mm-thick wall, bricks will overlap by half their length, essentially a two-dimensional lapping. A brick with its long side exposed in this way is described as a 'stretcher'. An exposed short side is called a 'header' and is used to tie the stretchers above and below together. Variations on this basic principle create different patterns. A horizontal line of brickwork is known as a 'course'.

Joints

There are various different ways of finishing mortar joints. The most common internal, and external, method is to finish the mortar flush with the face of the brickwork. 'Weathered' and 'keyed' joints are used externally to shed rainwater from the face of the wall while creating a shadow that emphasizes the joint. If water collects on an exposed horizontal brick surface it facilitates penetration of the porous core, which will be fractured when the water freezes. A squared-off or 'recessed' joint, which would collect rainwater if used externally, may be used to emphasize the joint in new internal walls. It is essentially a decorative device.

Pointing

The careful finishing of mortar joints is referred to as 'pointing' and is normally carried out using a 'pointing' trowel. In older construction, mortar joints are frequently weak – particularly when traditional lime-based mortars are affected by damp, which can cause mortar to soften significantly. It is normal to 'rake out' defective mortar and 're-point' the joints. Usually modern cement-based mortars will be used for this, but in restoration work, or when new and existing joints must be matched visually, lime-based mortars must be used.

Brick slips

When it is not feasible to use a solid brick wall, the visual effect may be achieved with brick 'slips' – 20mm-thick fired clay tiles of the same length and height as normal bricks that may be fixed to plywood sheets on wooden framing. The joints can be filled with mortar to complete the illusion. When bricks or brick slips are used purely as decoration it is possible to eliminate the interlocking and overlapping of the bond, lining through all mortar joints as an expression of the non-structural nature of the wall. It is important to provide enough edge support to ensure structural stability, often utilizing a perimeter steel frame.

Plaster

Often, bricks used for internal and external walls of a building shell will be concealed behind 10–12mm of plaster. While this finish may be retained and repaired, it is not unusual for plaster to be removed to expose brickwork patterns and texture as a decorative finish. Removing plaster, usually by chipping it from the brickwork using a hammer and chisel, can be time-consuming. Fragments stick to the brick, but can be removed by wire-brushing or pressure-washing, which also embellishes the brick's surface. The exposed face of brickwork will normally be finished with a clear sealant to eliminate dust and darken its colour.

TIP CLUES IN THE BOND

It is often possible, by looking at the bonding pattern of a brick wall, to determine not only its likely thickness but also whether or not it is loadbearing.

This is particularly useful with walls, such as those dividing adjacent properties, that have no windows or doors to reveal their thicknesses.

In modern construction, external brick walls are almost invariably of cavity construction and therefore the face of each skin will read as lines of stretchers (known as 'stretcher bond'). However, windows and doors will still reveal overall thicknesses. Traditional cavity walls are generally 250mm or 275mm thick.

When stretchers and headers alternate, whether vertically (English) or in horizontal courses (Flemish), it is safe to assume that the wall is at least 215mm thick and therefore likely to be loadbearing. This is also of interest with a party wall (one shared by two abutting buildings) where it indicates that it is feasible to build structural elements into the shared wall up to half its width.

A loadbearing wall, particularly on the lower floors of a high building, may be thicker than 215mm, but that will not be clear from the bonding pattern.

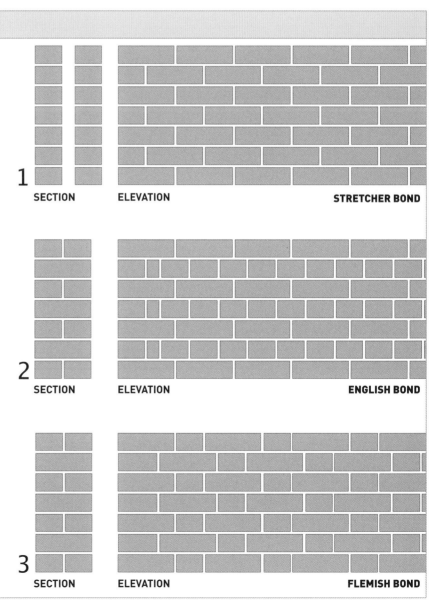

1
SECTION   ELEVATION   STRETCHER BOND

2
SECTION   ELEVATION   ENGLISH BOND

3
SECTION   ELEVATION   FLEMISH BOND

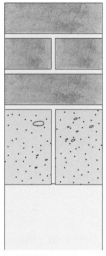

SINGLE LINTEL

DOUBLE LINTEL

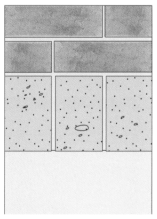

TRIPLE LINTEL

LINTEL WIDTHS

Standard prestressed concrete lintels will support a 102.5mm-thick brick wall. For wider walls, lintels of this standard width may be aggregated to match the standard widths of brick and blockwork walls.

Creating openings in loadbearing walls

There will seldom be any need for an interior designer to contemplate making door or window openings in external walls, particularly as the most interesting interior projects are often generated by the need to overcome the awkward locations of such existing elements. However, it is possible to remove sections of loadbearing walls, replacing them with a beam resting on stable support points, but it is prudent to take specialist advice from a building surveyor or structural engineer on anything other than the simplest interventions. An interior designer is not expected to have, and has no need to have, expertise in this area, just as the surveyor and engineer will have no capacity for the creation of successful interiors.

Door lintels

It is generally a simple matter to make door openings – they are unlikely to be wider than 900mm. Normal practice is to remove the section of brick- or blockwork and insert a reinforced-concrete precast lintel across the gap. Two pockets on either side of the head, probably no greater than the length of a brick, will provide support for the lintel. The lintel will probably be two brick courses deep and one brick tall to make re-plastering of the area simple. For walls more than a brick-width thick, it is normal to insert as many lintels as it takes to match the width of the wall.

Large lintels

When a bigger opening is required, the principle of making the opening and inserting the lintel will be the same but, because the loading is greater, it will be necessary to spread the load over a greater area of supporting masonry. The elements of loadbearing masonry construction – brickwork, blockwork and stonework – all have a recognized loadbearing capacity, and the greater the load the greater the length of pocket required. Precast concrete lintels can be laid directly on to a bed of mortar on the exposed masonry.

Steel lintels

These offer an alternative to concrete, but their comparatively smooth and impervious surfaces do not provide as satisfactory a key for the mortar that will bond them to the brickwork. Steel lintels are more normally used within steel-framed construction, when they can be bolted to steel-supporting elements through pre-drilled holes in both components.

Calculating lintel lengths

All structural building materials have a designated 'bearing strength', which is the weight they can support before crumbling, cracking and collapsing. This figure is recognized for the purposes of structural calculations by the statutory bodies responsible for approving new construction.

The calculation is a simple one. The 'dead' and superimposed weights are divided by the bearing strength of the supporting material – this will give the area necessary to support the combined loads. The length of lintel is calculated by dividing the area by the width of the supporting wall. While designated bearing strengths are precise for newly manufactured products, there is a high factor of safety for those relating to existing materials, which can make justifying proposals difficult.

SUPPORTING AN OPENING
The overlapping of bricks created by standard bonds provides structural support by directing the loading of the wall area above to the flanking walls. Only the triangular area over the opening requires direct support.

Moisture ingress

In solid-wall construction, it is difficult to identify the source of damp since moisture, unhindered by a cavity, can transfer to the inner surface at any point. It is prudent to understand the principles underpinning the construction of openings in external walls so that damage resulting from new internal work can be avoided, and existing defects may be diagnosed and made good.

Problems are almost always the result of moisture ingress, which results in areas of dampness and the deterioration of internal finishes, or poor insulation properties, which affect occupants' comfort and waste heating fuels.

In cavity-wall construction, water ingress is most likely around door and window openings, with deterioration of frames and the compounds that seal gaps

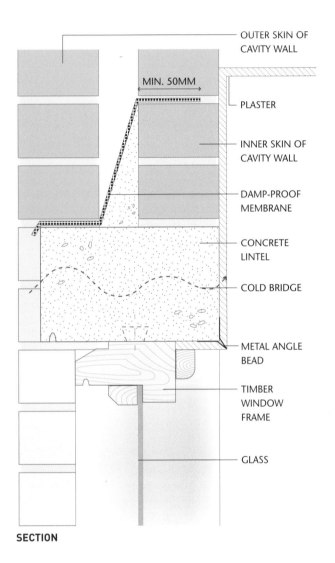

OUTER SKIN OF CAVITY WALL

MIN. 50MM

PLASTER

INNER SKIN OF CAVITY WALL

DAMP-PROOF MEMBRANE

CONCRETE LINTEL

COLD BRIDGE

METAL ANGLE BEAD

TIMBER WINDOW FRAME

GLASS

SECTION

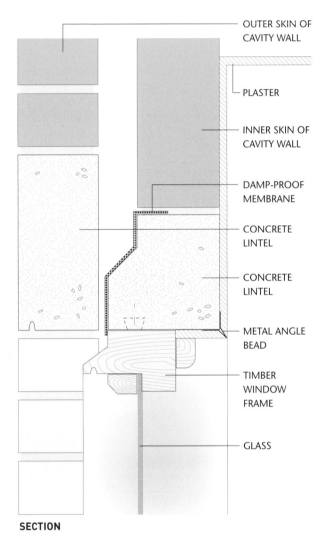

OUTER SKIN OF CAVITY WALL

PLASTER

INNER SKIN OF CAVITY WALL

DAMP-PROOF MEMBRANE

CONCRETE LINTEL

CONCRETE LINTEL

METAL ANGLE BEAD

TIMBER WINDOW FRAME

GLASS

SECTION

SINGLE LINTEL
Window-head detail. The single lintel creates a 'cold bridge' effect, so that the inner face of the lintel is significantly colder than the outer, and results in condensation and localized deterioration of the plaster finish.

DOUBLE LINTEL
Window-head detail. Separation between two lintels prevents cold bridging. The impervious damp-proof membrane conducts moisture to the exterior and seals the gap between lintel and window frame.

between them and the masonry. In this instance, sealants can be replaced. Where bricks 'close' the cavity at openings, a vertical impervious damp-proof membrane prevents moisture passing to the inner skin. Impervious thermal insulation compounds may be pumped into the cavity, preventing the passage of moisture to the inner skin.

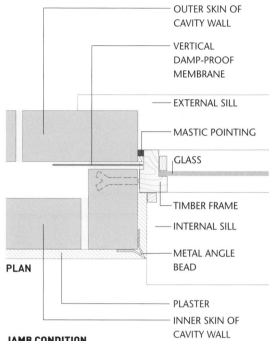

JAMB CONDITION
A recess in the outer face of the frame houses a mastic seal between the frame and brickwork.

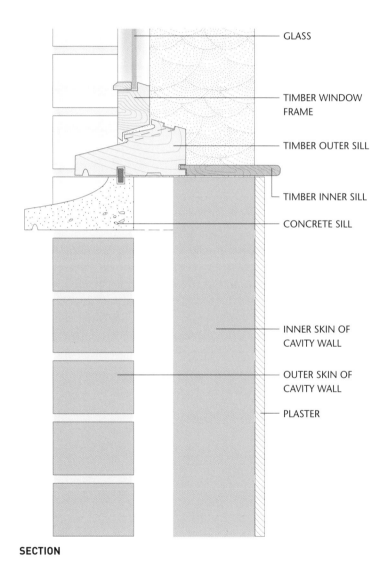

SILL IN CAVITY WALL
Angled surfaces conduct water away from the vulnerable junctions of frame and brick openings. Grooves in the underside of sills prevent water running back into the fabric.

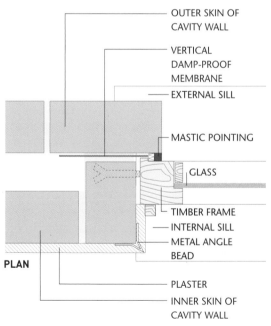

RECESSED JAMB CONDITION
Setting back the inner skin of the cavity creates a slot for a mastic seal between frame and brickwork.

Lining external walls

Until the advent of cavity construction, external walls were solid and, with brickwork construction in particular, this usually meant an external wall with a thickness of no more than 215mm. There was little to prevent moisture saturating the brick fabric and damaging the plaster on the inner face. The single skin also meant that there was no insulating barrier between the outer and inner faces of the wall. Saturation of the wall meant that the lime mortar used in construction was damaged, becoming soft and losing its adhesive qualities. Wooden door and window frames were also vulnerable because solid construction allowed water to penetrate around the sides of the frame without the opportunity for air circulation offered by the cavity construction. Such timber elements were thus more prone to rot, accelerating the deterioration of the structure.

Damp-proof membranes

The solution is to create a degree of separation within the existing perimeter of the interior – in effect to form an inner skin and to treat the existing solid external wall as the outer skin. The problem with this tactic is that it reduces internal room dimensions, so it must use as little space as possible.

Attached inner walls One option is to fix an impervious waterproof membrane to the inner face of the existing wall. This is usually a plastic sheet fixed against the wall in vertical strips with sealed joints. There is no true

cavity, and some danger that if the existing wall is subject to heavy water penetration moisture will condense on the outer face of the membrane. It is therefore considered better practice to use a bitumen-impregnated corrugated sheet, which allows circulation of air against the existing inner surface. It is possible to plaster directly on to the inner surface of this sheet, although this does little to increase the heat-insulating properties of the wall.

Freestanding inner walls It is more effective to build a second, freestanding inner wall using a wooden or aluminium framing system clad with plasterboard on its inner face. The skeletal nature of the supporting framework leaves spaces that may be packed with fibreglass or polystyrene insulation. The incursion of the new wall on to the existing plan can be reduced by screwing or nailing timber battens directly to the existing wall. The battens hold the waterproof membrane in position and form a framework to which the plasterboard sheets may be fixed. The battens are unlikely to be more than 44mm thick, reducing by about half the thickness of insulation possible compared to an attached inner wall.

It is not necessary to remove existing plaster, and the new plasterboard linings will give a smoother and truer surface than the old. This may, however, appear odd in an older property where internal walls that do not require lining may appear more characterful. The only solution, to line the inner walls as well, is expensive and will eradicate further vestiges of character.

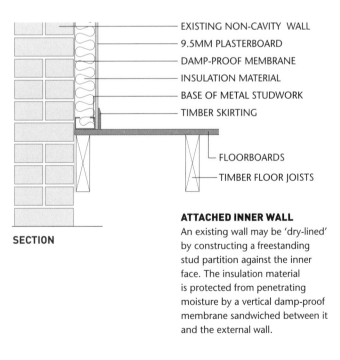

EXISTING NON-CAVITY WALL
9.5MM PLASTERBOARD
DAMP-PROOF MEMBRANE
INSULATION MATERIAL
BASE OF METAL STUDWORK
TIMBER SKIRTING

FLOORBOARDS
TIMBER FLOOR JOISTS

SECTION

ATTACHED INNER WALL
An existing wall may be 'dry-lined' by constructing a freestanding stud partition against the inner face. The insulation material is protected from penetrating moisture by a vertical damp-proof membrane sandwiched between it and the external wall.

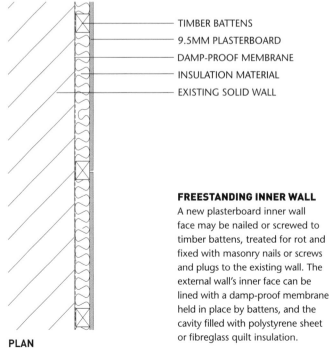

TIMBER BATTENS
9.5MM PLASTERBOARD
DAMP-PROOF MEMBRANE
INSULATION MATERIAL
EXISTING SOLID WALL

PLAN

FREESTANDING INNER WALL
A new plasterboard inner wall face may be nailed or screwed to timber battens, treated for rot and fixed with masonry nails or screws and plugs to the existing wall. The external wall's inner face can be lined with a damp-proof membrane held in place by battens, and the cavity filled with polystyrene sheet or fibreglass quilt insulation.

Non-loadbearing walls

The practice of using framed construction to provide the basic structure for non-loadbearing walls is well established – thin timber laths, about 6mm thick, 50mm wide and 1200mm long would be nailed to vertical timber posts, which provided the necessary structure and which were approximately 100 x 50mm and spaced at around 400mm centres.

This structure was finished with three coats of plaster to a thickness of approximately 12mm. Quantities of plaster oozed between the battens and, when hardened, provided a key to support the flat, finished plaster skim. This method reduced the weight of new walls but was time-consuming, and the economics of the modern building industry have rendered it obsolete except in high-quality conservation projects. When a historical interior is protected by law, it is of course necessary to get approval for all projected changes.

Repairing existing walls

Where small areas of traditional lath-and-plaster wall must be repaired, it is possible to do this by removing the damaged material and replacing it with 9.5mm plasterboard, and finishing this with a thin skim coat that will bring the level up to match that of the existing wall.

It can be difficult to make a completely imperceptible join between the old and the new in existing walls, and the junction is prone to cracking because of the different response to temperature and moisture of the various materials involved. When making any alterations, it is important to consider the compatibility of new and existing materials.

There are always likely to be problems associated with joining new elements, which increasingly have a machine-produced precision, to old ones, which frequently have the imprecision of the handmade and the idiosyncrasies that result from age. It is often a more satisfactory practical – and aesthetic – solution to design a visible gap between the two. It is, for example, physically difficult to butt a new plastered partition up to a fairfaced masonry wall. It is difficult to achieve a pristine plaster finish against the irregularity of masonry, and the visual crispness of the new element will be compromised. The mechanical precision of a metal plaster stop can help achieve a satisfactory solution.

Openings in non-loadbearing walls

Openings in non-loadbearing walls present fewer problems. It may, however, be necessary with wider openings to calculate the depth and length of lintel required to support the wall area above the opening – particularly with irregular stonework, where there will be limited cohesive interlocking of individual pieces.

With framed partitions, it is much simpler to make new openings by cutting through the framing posts and the less substantial wall material that they support. It is generally sufficient to trim the opening with new timber and to insert a new timber lintel. Dimensions for this may have to be calculated for wider openings.

TIP THE ROUGH AND THE SMOOTH: ALTERATIONS TO EXISTING WALLS

The nature of the construction of new walls or partitions means that they tend to be very perfect objects, particularly when compared to the more handmade and worn elements of the original structure with which they may come into contact. It is never a good idea to try to emulate the idiosyncrasies of old construction. The result always fails to convince and a better solution is to create a small gap between old and new and, if the new wall is plastered, to use an expanded metal plastering bead to ensure a completely straight and robust edge.

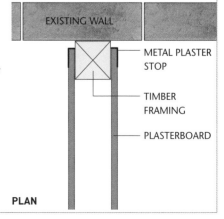

EXISTING WALL

METAL PLASTER STOP

TIMBER FRAMING

PLASTERBOARD

PLAN

CHAPTER 2 NEW WALLS

Basic principles

In interior design projects, new walls are often referred to as 'partitions', particularly when they are non-loadbearing. Partitions can be designed to carry loads if existing foundations are capable of supporting the additional weight, or if new foundations are provided – however, this is likely to cause significant disruption and extra work.

Bricks and blocks

Bricks or blocks, and certainly stone, are avoided in the construction of partitions because they are heavy, and this can be a particular problem with the sub-division of an upper floor, which may often be incapable of taking additional concentrated loading. The time taken for the wet sand-and-cement mortar used in masonry construction to dry also imposes time delays that can be critical in the viability of some projects. Unless such partitions are to be left 'fairfaced' – that is, with the decorative texture of their surface materials and joints left exposed – it is normal to finish them with 12mm of plaster applied in three coats, each of which needs to dry before the next may be applied and this causes additional delay. A different variety of plaster is used for each of the three coats.

Sizes Bricks have a standard size, 215mm (length) x 102.5mm (width) x 65mm (height), and are laid with a 10mm mortar joint. Blocks vary in size, but the most common size is 440mm long x 215mm high. Their width varies from 50mm to 200mm in 50mm increments. There are various 'bonds', which are the patterns created by the mortar joints, but by far the most common is when the bricks or blocks overlap by half their length. This interlocking improves the strength of the wall.

Plastering Both bricks and concrete blocks come in a range of qualities. When it is intended that they will be given a plaster finish, then the quality of their exposed faces is not important. When plastering, concrete blockwork – which is faster to lay because of its greater unit size – will usually be favoured. Where there is no significant structural obligation, lightweight blocks, which are easier to handle, may be specified.

The finishing coats of plaster may be omitted in favour of a 'fairfaced' appearance. This exposes not only the pattern of the chosen bond but the colour and texture of the brick or block. With brickwork, variations are usually the result of the different clays and firing times used during manufacture.

Concrete

A concrete wall will exacerbate all the problems of weight and construction time. It will be particularly heavy and should really only be used where this weight is useful – for example, as a means of reducing sound transference between areas. Concrete is poured, when wet, into a mould, known as a 'shuttering' or 'formwork', which is normally a timber or steel frame clad in plywood or metal sheeting that creates a container for the concrete mix while it dries. The shuttering must be constructed on site, the concrete poured in, vibrated to eliminate air pockets and left to 'cure', or dry. It can take three weeks to gain 90 per cent of its final strength, and the more slowly it cures the stronger it will be. Such times are unlikely to be acceptable in an interior project unless justified by very particular practical requirements.

When the concrete has hardened, the shuttering is removed. If the intention is to use the raw material as the finished wall surface, it must be sealed to stabilize the unavoidable surface dust. Pouring concrete in an existing building shell creates practical problems that may eliminate it as a viable option. If the proposed wall is required to span between an existing floor and ceiling, then the wet mix cannot be poured into the formwork. It must be pumped through holes at as high a level as is practical to ensure that it fills the void. It is difficult to pack concrete densely at the top, and some patching is likely to be necessary when the shuttering is removed.

Alternatives to concrete It is possible to use lightweight concrete, in which the larger aggregate (normally stone) is replaced by vermiculite, perlite or other less dense solids. The time-consuming problem of pouring wet concrete into temporary shuttering remains. Lightweight precast concrete panels may also be used but the dimensions of these are likely to be restricted by access to the site, making visible jointing of panels necessary. This needs to be anticipated during the detailed design stages.

However, given that concrete in an interior is likely to be chosen for its visual qualities rather than its structural or sound-reduction capacities, there are alternatives that will satisfy aesthetic ambitions. It is possible to achieve the appearance, if not the weight and solidity, of a concrete wall by applying a 12mm sand-and-cement render to a lightweight 'stud' frame. A 3mm skim coat of grey plaster will provide an equally convincing facsimile. With both methods, the finished face must be given a clear seal – producing a darker, slightly glossy, appearance.

Stud partitions

The stud partition offers a much quicker construction method than brickwork, blockwork or concrete, or the traditional lath and plaster, but with no reduction in quality. The first two coats of wet plaster are replaced by plasterboard sheets that may either be finished with a 3mm skim of plaster, which is quick to apply and dry, or be painted directly, after some simple filling of joints.

Plasterboard

Plasterboard sheets consist of a core of gypsum plaster between two sheets of paper. One side, the lighter coloured, can be painted directly for a finished surface while the darker, more porous, side provides an absorbent key for a skim coat of plaster. Sheets come in a number of standard sizes. The most common is 2400 x 1200mm, and either 9.5mm or 12.5mm thick. The 2400mm dimension determines the height of rooms in most new buildings. This standard height is less frequently encountered in older buildings, but it is worth considering the feasibility of lowering a ceiling to 2400mm when constructing new enclosed areas within a taller space. Elimination of joints speeds the building process and reduces labour costs.

Plasterboard and skim technique

The basic framework of a stud partition remains the same as for traditional lath-and-plaster construction, although framing members are smaller in cross-section and more smoothly finished. The skeleton framework is clad in sheets of plasterboard to create a base wall surface, which is then finished with a 3mm coat of plaster that visually eliminates joints and fixings. This thin coat dries quickly and provides a smooth, comparatively non-absorbent surface that is particularly suitable for painting.

Drywall technique

It is increasingly common to use the 'drywall' technique, eliminating a wet skim phase. This was originally evolved to increase the mechanization of large-scale, repetitive construction, reducing building time and labour costs. It remains most effective in large-scale projects with repetitive subdivisions, ideally consisting of multiples of standard board sizes, but can also be effective in some simpler jobs because it eliminates the need to employ a specialist plasterer. While the erection and finishing of drywalling requires specialist tools and techniques, speed of construction makes it cost-effective and, as long as the joints and the arrises (sharp, straight edges) involved are not too many or too complex, it will provide a satisfactory finish.

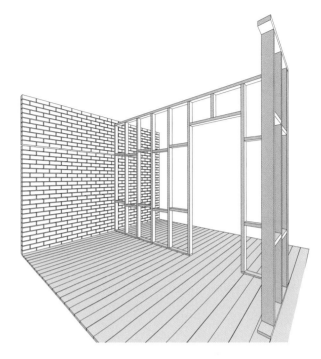

STUD PARTITIONS
Wood or metal stud framing can provide the structure for lightweight internal walls. Framing should be fixed to secure elements – walls, floors, ceiling slabs or joists – to ensure stability.

HEAD SUPPORT BETWEEN JOISTS
When running at right angles to ceiling joists, head plates should be nailed or screwed at each crossing. When parallel to joists, they should be positioned directly under one of them. When this is not possible, bridging joists at 400mm centres should be inserted to provide secure fixing points.

Constructing stud partitions

Fixing plasterboard cladding

Plasterboard sheets are fixed to vertical and horizontal framing, which may be lengths of either planed softwood or very thin aluminium. The dimensions of framing members can be calculated to make a structural wall capable of supporting an upper floor level. A structural engineer can calculate sizes and specify grades of timber and fixing methods to meet statutory requirements.

The skeleton frames that result are seldom wholly rigid; it is not until the plasterboard cladding has been fixed in position that the frame becomes firm. Although plasterboard is brittle, the frequency of fixing, with nails and screws at 150mm centres, spreads stress sufficiently to ensure that there is no damage, while the framing members are stabilized by the rigidity of the sheet.

Standard sizing

While any size of timber may be used, standard practice is to use specialist softwood framing. This comes in a number of sizes: the most common are 38 x 63mm and 38 x 88mm, usually in 2400mm lengths. These are specified as CLS ('Canadian Lumber Sizes'). The rectangular sections are planed on all four faces, have slightly rounded corners and are pressure treated for resistance to wet and dry rots. Pressure treatment ensures that the preservative liquid effectively penetrates the whole section.

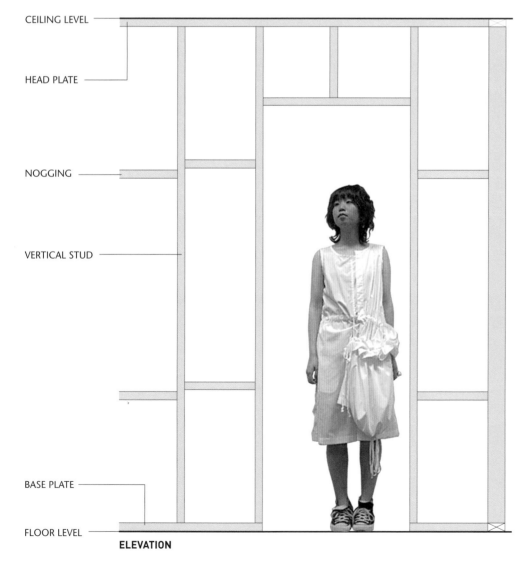

CEILING LEVEL

HEAD PLATE

NOGGING

VERTICAL STUD

BASE PLATE

FLOOR LEVEL

ELEVATION

STANDARD STUD FRAME
Top, or 'head', plates and bottom, or 'sole', plates are screwed or nailed to a structurally stable component (e.g. timber joists or concrete floor slab). Vertical studs are centred (400mm for 9.5mm plasterboard and/or 600mm for 12.5mm) along the length of a wall. Noggings (horizontal bracing timbers) provide lateral support at 800–900mm vertical centres. A staggered position makes fixing through the vertical stud into the end of the nogging simple. The centre of the final two studs will vary in response to site dimensions, but should not exceed standard spacing for the wall.

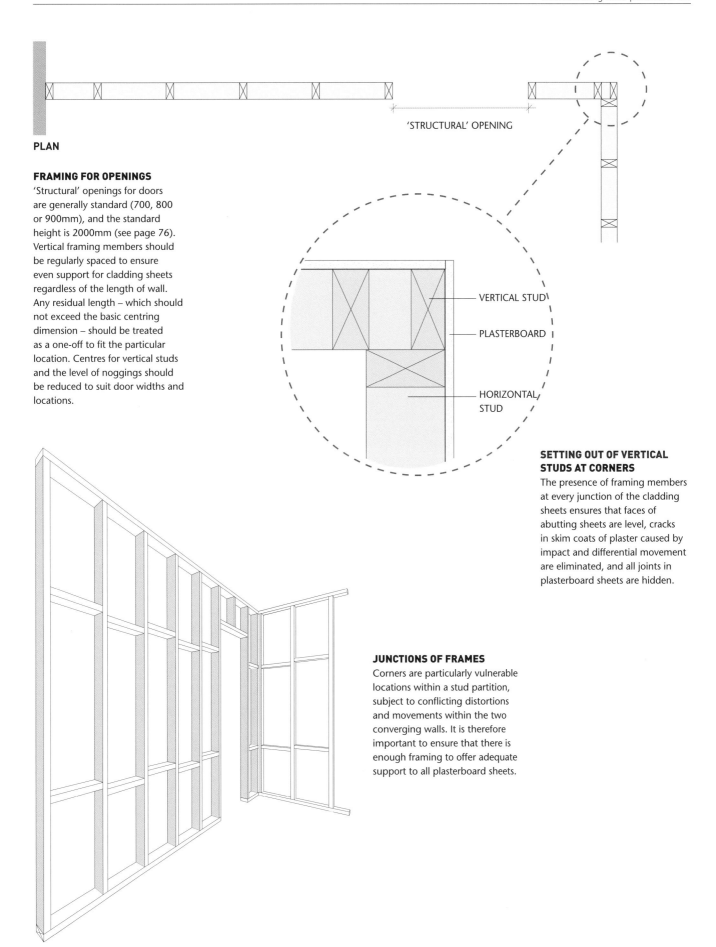

PLAN

FRAMING FOR OPENINGS

'Structural' openings for doors are generally standard (700, 800 or 900mm), and the standard height is 2000mm (see page 76). Vertical framing members should be regularly spaced to ensure even support for cladding sheets regardless of the length of wall. Any residual length – which should not exceed the basic centring dimension – should be treated as a one-off to fit the particular location. Centres for vertical studs and the level of noggings should be reduced to suit door widths and locations.

'STRUCTURAL' OPENING

VERTICAL STUD

PLASTERBOARD

HORIZONTAL STUD

SETTING OUT OF VERTICAL STUDS AT CORNERS

The presence of framing members at every junction of the cladding sheets ensures that faces of abutting sheets are level, cracks in skim coats of plaster caused by impact and differential movement are eliminated, and all joints in plasterboard sheets are hidden.

JUNCTIONS OF FRAMES

Corners are particularly vulnerable locations within a stud partition, subject to conflicting distortions and movements within the two converging walls. It is therefore important to ensure that there is enough framing to offer adequate support to all plasterboard sheets.

Clout nails

Fixing to the softwood framing, when the surface is to be finished with a skim coat, is traditionally by galvanized 'clout' nails. The galvanizing process, a protective zinc alloy coating on mild steel, ensures that the nails do not rust, which is important because the expansion and deterioration of rusted metal will cause the plaster covering it to be shed. The large diameter of the head of a 'clout' nail spreads its grip across a greater area of the comparatively fragile plasterboard surface.

Drywall screws

Self-tapping 'drywall screws', which are also rust resistant, are used to fix sheets to aluminium and softwood studs when the latter are used in drywall construction. The screws are tightened until their heads are slightly below the surface of the plasterboard, which creates a shallow recess that is then filled with a proprietary compound. This is then sanded smooth until it is level with the face of the plasterboard.

Screws are beginning to replace nails, as electrically powered screwdrivers are now making them as quick to use as nails, while the elimination of the impact of hammering reduces damage to the studwork. This is particularly beneficial when plasterboard needs to be applied to both sides of a stud frame, as hammering on the second side of the frame to be fixed can cause nails to loosen on the first.

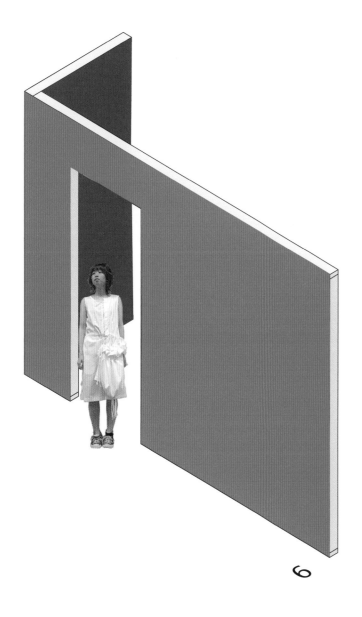

6

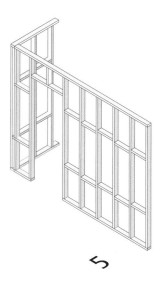

5

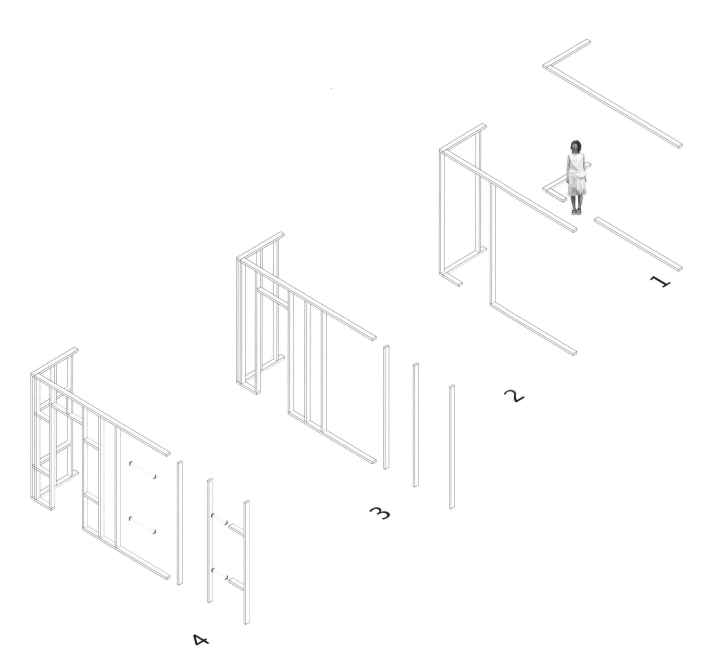

CONSTRUCTION SEQUENCE FOR STUD PARTITION

Standard construction is simple.
1 The head and sole plates are attached to the floor and ceiling. The sole plate is cut to accommodate the door opening.
2 Vertical members are inserted on a module (400 or 600mm) to suit the width dimension of a standard plasterboard sheet.
3 They are nailed in position with timber framing or fixed with self-tapping screws for aluminium.
4 Additional horizontal bracing is added at approximately 800mm centres, subject to the height of the wall.

5 The complete assembled frame is comparatively rigid but, because of the simple nature of the butt joints and fixings, is not wholly stable.
6 The addition of cladding sheets and filling of the joints between them makes a rigid monolith.

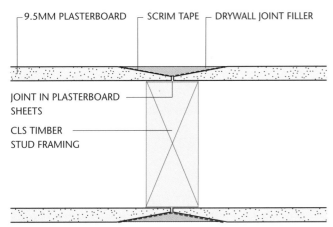

┌ 3MM PLASTER SKIM COAT   ┌ SCRIM TAPE   ┌ 9.5MM PLASTERBOARD

JOINT

CLS TIMBER
STUD FRAMING

PLAN

SKIMMING A JOINT

When the plasterboard sheets are skimmed with a 3mm finishing coat of plaster and the joint reinforced with scrim tape, all evidence of the fixing clout nails disappears. The joints can be butted and, as long as the gap at the joint is bridged by scrim tape to eliminate cracking, there will be no evidence of the join.

┌ 9.5MM PLASTERBOARD   ┌ SCRIM TAPE   ┌ DRYWALL JOINT FILLER

JOINT IN PLASTERBOARD
SHEETS

CLS TIMBER
STUD FRAMING

PLAN

DRYWALL JOINTS

In drywall construction the tapered edges of plasterboard sheets meet to form a shallow recess, into which joint filler can be dressed over a scrim-tape 'bridge'. When dry, it is sanded level with the face of the boards before painting.

Joints in plasterboard sheets

Whether plasterboard cladding is painted directly, as in drywall construction, or given a skim coat before painting, all junctions of plasterboard sheets must have studwork, whether timber or metal, behind them. Vertical and horizontal framing pieces provide a common plane, to which both the abutting sheets are nailed or screwed. This ensures that the faces of both will be precisely aligned, making the elimination of visible evidence of the junction easier.

In either system there are two vulnerable areas: the joints between panels and the external corners. Joints are vulnerable because the thin coat of plaster or filler that bridges them is the weakest spot on the wall surface and will crack with any movement that results from impact or from thermal expansion and contraction.

Bridging joints

The solution is to insert a bridging strip that runs the entire length of the joint, which provides a continuous reinforcement that gives physical coherence to the whole plastered surface.

Skimming For a skim coat the bridge is provided by a 48mm-wide strip of 'scrim' tape, a loosely woven fine mesh. This now normally has a self-adhesive backing, but may also be fixed by bedding in a thin smear of plaster that runs the length of the joint or internal corner before the skim coat proper is applied.

Drywall construction The butting edges of boards are slightly tapered. The joint is bridged with a strip of self-adhesive, heavy-duty paper, and the recess formed by the tapering edges is filled with a proprietary paste, which, when dry, is smoothed off and sanded to give a finished face flush with the surfaces of the boards.

External corners

External corners are particularly vulnerable to impact damage. In traditional construction the practice was to reinforce corners with a timber strip, usually a quadrant moulding, that was better able than the plaster to withstand impact and which also gave a ready-made straight edge against which the final coat of plaster could be finished.

Skimming The same principle holds for making corners with a skim coat, except that a metal, usually aluminium, corner strip, or 'bead', replaces the timber quadrant. A slightly rounded continuous edge forms the angle of the corner and provides the straight line against which the plaster coat may be finished. A perforated or expanded metal mesh inner edge provides a reinforcing key for the plaster. The bead is nailed or screwed to the framing members, and those for skimmed surfaces are described as 'shallow coat'. Similar profiles are used for three-coat finishes, when they are described as 'deep coat'. Beads for both types come in a variety of profiles designed to offer options in locations, such as at skirtings and architraves, where edges of plaster would be both vulnerable and difficult to form accurately.

Drywall construction In drywall construction, corners are reinforced by means of a strip of heavy-duty paper to which are glued two 10mm-wide metal strips. When wrapped around a corner, with a metal strip on each of the faces, the slightly raised strip again provides a straight edge against which the finishing compound may be dressed and sanded.

Finishing When both versions of the corner, or angle, bead are finished they should be just visible on the apex of the corner, because the finishing coat or joint filler should not be deeper than their projection from the surface. After painting, they will be indistinguishable from the rest of the wall surface. Both can adapt to fit corners that are not exactly right angles. The paper-based drywall component is particularly flexible.

CORNER JOINTING IN DRYWALL CONSTRUCTION

Left
Corners in drywall construction are reinforced by two metal strips, glued to a robust paper tape.

Right
The tape is folded with metal strips on each side of the corner and fixed with these strips against the plasterboard. The uneven junction is evened out with filler and, after painting, disappears.

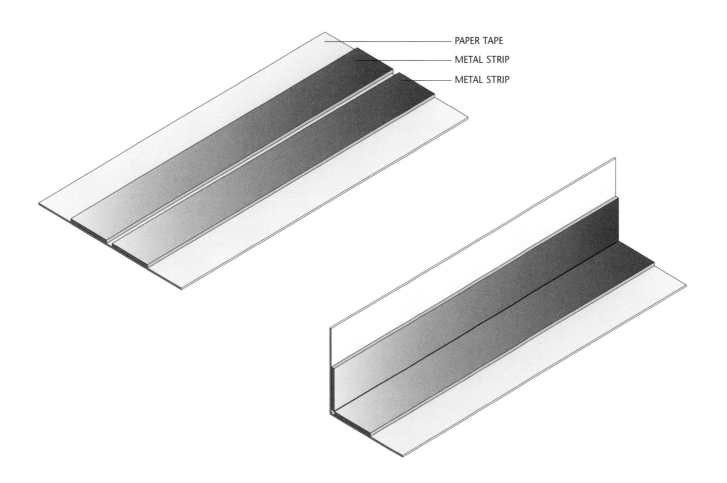

PAPER TAPE

METAL STRIP

METAL STRIP

STEP BY STEP FINISHING DRYWALL STUD PARTITIONS

The final stage in drywall construction is a refinement of the familiar building practice of filling holes and cracks. Holes are the heads of screws, driven just below the surface of plasterboard sheets, and cracks are the gaps, no more than a few millimetres wide, between sheets. When joints and corners have been bridged and reinforced with specialist tapes, the filler paste is spread over them and sanded smooth and dry, flush with the face of the plasterboard. After painting, all evidence of fillings disappears.

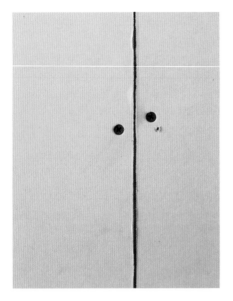

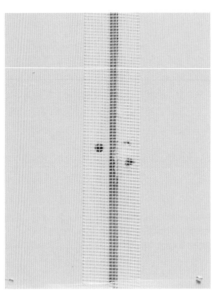

1 Plasterboard sheets are fixed, with rust-resistant screws, at 150mm centres to the stud frame. The joints need not be tight or precise. Screw heads will be driven slightly below the level of the plasterboard.

2 The self-adhesive scrim tape is then placed to bridge the joint.

3 The first filling compound is applied to fix the tape in position.

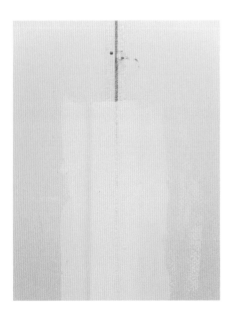

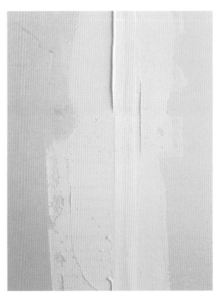

4 This first application flattens the tape and also provides a level base for the subsequent layers of filler.

5 Filler is applied generously to allow for an even distribution along the length of the joint.

6 The filler is worked along the joint so that it finishes as flat to the surface of the plasterboard as is possible.

7 The filler is sanded to eliminate the slight pitting that follows the hand-levelling process, and to further reduce any filler that remains above the level of the plasterboard.

8 Heads of screws, sunken below the face of the plasterboard sheet, are covered with dabs of filler that are then roughly levelled by hand.

9 Sanding smooths and evens off the filler and reduces it to the level of the plasterboard. When painted, variation in level and texture will be invisible.

VERTICAL STUD FRAME
(CLS TIMBER OR METAL)

PLASTERBOARD

3MM PLASTER SKIM COAT

GALVANISED 'CLOUT' NAIL OR
PLASTERBOARD SCREW

METAL EXTERNAL CORNER BEAD

INTERNAL ANGLE SCRIM TAPE

PLAN

Reinforcement of junctions in stud partitions

Junctions of sheets tend to be vulnerable and therefore comparatively complex – they have to deal with the meeting of different stud partitions, and there is potential for considerable impact damage. It is crucial that every junction of sheets, whether vertical or horizontal, has a piece of framing behind it. This ensures that there can be no local movement or distortion of an unsupported edge, and that the faces of sheets are perfectly aligned because they are each fixed to the same framing piece.

Reinforcement of corners

The solution for corners is to use three vertical framing members that are themselves nailed or screwed together to ensure that they do not move unilaterally. They provide what is, in effect, a monolithic structural element to which the four plasterboard sheets meeting in the corner can be securely fixed.

Internal corners The joints themselves also require reinforcement. The internal corner is comparatively safe from impact damage, only vulnerable to differential movement of the converging walls – a length of scrim tape will be sufficient to deal with the limited movement.

External corners The external corner is significantly more vulnerable to impact damage and needs more robust angle protection. A 'thin coat' expanded metal angle will provide a resilient and straight line to define the corner and will also provide a guide against which the plasterer can judge the depth of the skim coat. With drywall construction a reinforced paper strip is less obviously robust but will be able to deal with reasonable day-to-day impacts. The bulge that it creates above the face of the plasterboard can be visually eased out by the addition and smoothing of the joint-filling compound.

STUD PARTITION CORNER WITH REINFORCEMENTS
Metal corner beads establish straight arrises and protect against impact damage on external corners, while scrim tape reinforces plaster against movement damage in internal corners and at the joints in plasterboard sheets.

Metal framing for stud partitions

Advantages

Lightweight aluminium framing has been evolved to minimize the amount of material used, and is a very quick, and more fire-proof, method of building stud partitions if the plan and section are kept simple.

The standard framing components slot together quickly and if, at the design stage, consideration is given to the use of standard components, labour costs can be minimized.

Disadvantages

The specialized evolution of the system makes variations from the standard more complex than with timber stud. Since the framing is lightweight, with folded profiles to increase rigidity, it does not offer flat surfaces to make butting it together as simple as for wooden structures.

Used primarily for drywall partitions, the limited filling of joints does not create the same monolithic structure that would follow the addition of a skim coat. As a result it has no structural capacity beyond that of providing support for plasterboard cladding, shelving and cupboards, though is still capable of dealing with most reasonable impacts.

SELF-TAPPING PLASTERBOARD SCREW

METAL STUD FRAME

PLASTERBOARD

EXTERNAL ANGLE SCRIM TAPE

INTERNAL ANGLE SCRIM TAPE

PLAN

METAL STUD PARTITION CORNER

A standard plan layout for metal stud framing.

STANDARD METAL COMPONENTS

Metal framing members at a corner and on a straight run.

PLASTERBOARD

METAL STUD FRAME

Conventional skirtings

Traditional skirting

Skirtings evolved to cover the junction of floor and wall in traditional construction. It was impossible to achieve a satisfactorily robust junction between the wooden floor and plaster wall finish, and there was almost invariably a gap between the ends and edges of floorboards and the wall finish. The wooden skirting provided a resilient masking for this weak spot, and its potential as a vehicle for pre-fabricated decorative moulding was exploited. It developed into something complex that could be tall in response to the generous proportions of grander rooms, and inflate the status of less spectacular spaces. High skirtings were usually made from at least two components fixed together on site. The line of the join was lost in the complexity of the moulding, and a deliberate recess could disguise the modest movement of joints that occured with expansion and contraction of natural materials.

MDF skirting

Modern aesthetics have dispensed with the idea of the monumental skirting, and have examined the possibility of eliminating the element altogether. The traditional material for skirtings was timber but this is often replaced by MDF (medium density fibreboard) sections, which may be moulded to reproduce simpler, traditional forms. MDF has the advantage of consistency of section and performance, something which has become difficult to achieve with cheap softwood mouldings. MDF versions often come ready primed for the paint finish that the material requires. The sharp edges expose the softer core material and are vulnerable to impact.

Plastic and metal skirting sections

Moulded plastic or pressed metal (usually aluminium) skirting sections are frequently used with proprietary partitioning systems and their hollow sections provide a useful zone for wiring circulation. They tend to come with a paint finish, and while this restricted palette may be welcomed in expedient space-planning exercises it is unlikely to appeal to committed interior designers. Recently developed aluminium sections incorporate hot-water circulation pipes and provide a space-saving alternative to radiators and a more energy-efficient alternative to underfloor heating for the even distribution of heat throughout a room.

Skirtings are fixed after floor and wall finishes (other than paint and wallpaper) have been installed, and the abutting edges of these can be left comparatively rough. The gap between them allows for movement.

Installing skirting

Nails Fixing a skirting with nails is fast, but the impact of driving them in can damage both the surface of the skirting and the wall plaster. It is good practice to have a timber 'ground', which is flush with the face of the plaster, to absorb the impact and provide a more substantial intermediary fixing between the skirting and the stud frame. The head of the nail should be driven a little below the surface of the wood using a nail 'punch', the indentation filled and the area sanded before painting.

Screws These do not cause the same impact problem as nails but are more time-consuming to use, requiring pre-drilling of the fixing hole and more extensive filling and sanding. It is possible to drive the head of the screw below the surface of softwood skirting, but this tends to break the fibre of the wood and force jagged shards above the surface that also require filling and sanding.

Adhesive It is increasingly common to use a specialist adhesive to fix skirtings directly to the plastered wall surface. This eliminates the need to make good the local damage caused by nails and screws, but is unsuitable for walls that are not perfectly straight. Almost all existing surfaces, even those in recently constructed buildings, will have some irregularities.

Visible gaps

Since existing floors are seldom perfectly level, particularly where the ends of exposed floorboards meet a wall, there is sometimes a discernible gap between floor and skirting. If not too severe this may be accepted as an inevitable symptom of age in an older building, but where unacceptable for aesthetic or practical reasons it may be filled, preferably with a proprietary flexible filler. This, if applied carefully and painted, should be visually unobtrusive.

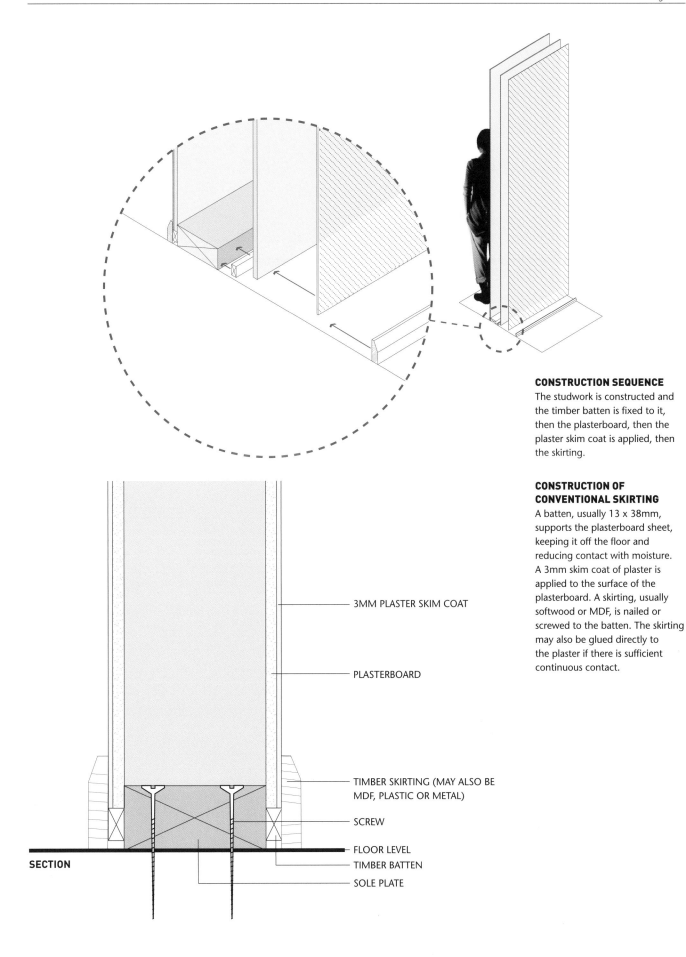

CONSTRUCTION SEQUENCE
The studwork is constructed and the timber batten is fixed to it, then the plasterboard, then the plaster skim coat is applied, then the skirting.

CONSTRUCTION OF CONVENTIONAL SKIRTING
A batten, usually 13 x 38mm, supports the plasterboard sheet, keeping it off the floor and reducing contact with moisture. A 3mm skim coat of plaster is applied to the surface of the plasterboard. A skirting, usually softwood or MDF, is nailed or screwed to the batten. The skirting may also be glued directly to the plaster if there is sufficient continuous contact.

3MM PLASTER SKIM COAT

PLASTERBOARD

TIMBER SKIRTING (MAY ALSO BE MDF, PLASTIC OR METAL)

SCREW

FLOOR LEVEL

TIMBER BATTEN

SOLE PLATE

SECTION

Alternative skirtings

Shadow-gap skirting

It is feasible to dispense with the skirting strip and to resort to the 'shadow gap' option, but this does not so easily overcome problems at the junction of uneven floors and walls. The narrow gap, which is best constructed using a proprietary metal plastering bead, can be difficult to clean and plaster at the base and, because it remains close to floor level, can be vulnerable to impact damage. The construction sequence also becomes more complicated since floor finishes need to be laid before the walls can be plastered. The junction will be neater if the edge of the floor finish is overlapped by the wall.

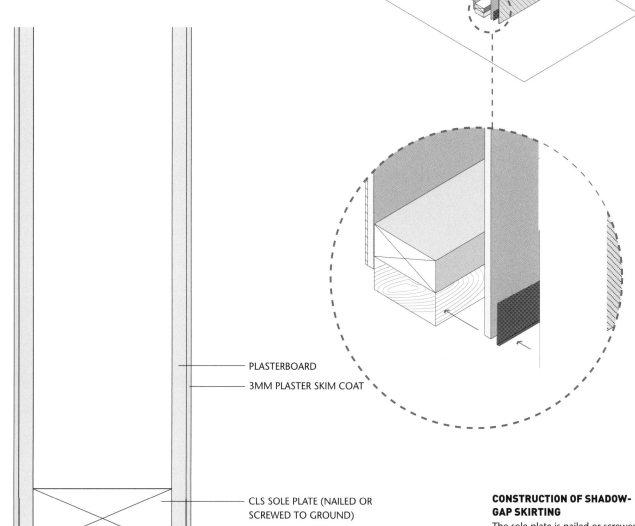

PLASTERBOARD

3MM PLASTER SKIM COAT

CLS SOLE PLATE (NAILED OR SCREWED TO GROUND)

PROPRIETARY METAL PLASTER STOP BEAD

PAR SOFTWOOD GROUND (NAILED OR SCREWED TO EXISTING FLOOR)

FLOOR LEVEL

SECTION

CONSTRUCTION OF SHADOW-GAP SKIRTING

The sole plate is nailed or screwed to a planed softwood ground. The plasterboard sheet is nailed or screwed to the sole plate and covers the junction between it and the ground. The lower edge of the 3mm skim coat of plaster is protected by an expanded metal stop.

Timber skirting with shadow gap

A more practical solution is to retain the gap but separate it from the floor with a simple timber skirting section, the face of which is flush with that of the plaster. The plaster bead provides a clean, straight bottom edge for the plastered surface and the timber skirting deals more effectively with impact at floor level. If the skirting is painted, it will be read as part of the wall. If it uses the same wood as the floor finish and is left unpainted, it will relate visually to the floor.

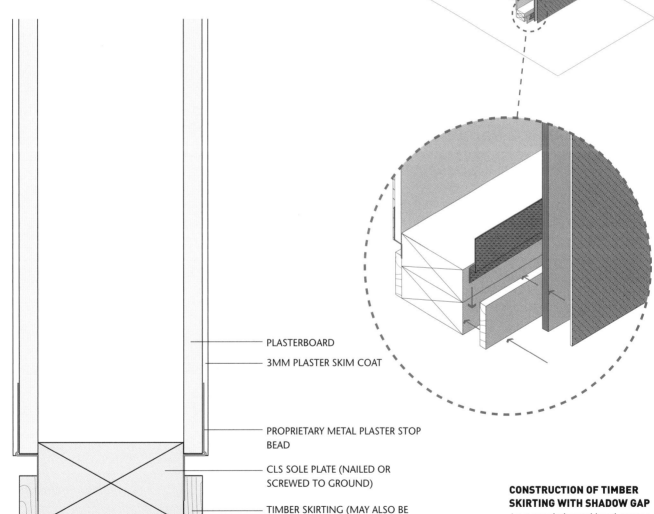

PLASTERBOARD

3MM PLASTER SKIM COAT

PROPRIETARY METAL PLASTER STOP BEAD

CLS SOLE PLATE (NAILED OR SCREWED TO GROUND)

TIMBER SKIRTING (MAY ALSO BE MDF, PLASTIC OR METAL)

CLS SOLE PLATE (NAILED OR SCREWED TO EXISTING FLOOR)

FLOOR LEVEL

SECTION

CONSTRUCTION OF TIMBER SKIRTING WITH SHADOW GAP
An expanded metal bead creates the gap above the softwood skirting. It also defines and protects the finished edge of the plasterboard and skim coat to the bottom edge of the plaster.

Conventional cornices

Cornices essentially serve the same purpose as skirtings. They mask the potentially unsightly junction of wall and ceiling. In traditional lath-and-plaster construction it was difficult to get a satisfactory right angle, and when floor joists also served as ceiling joists the junction of wall and ceiling was vulnerable to movement caused by loadings on the floor above. Long joist spans were particularly liable to deflection and vibration.

Traditional cornice construction

Like skirtings, cornices were pre-fabricated, normally made of plaster and cast in moulds that could be used many times. They became a medium for elaborate decoration. Moulded sections were made and fixed in lengths. Junctions were comparatively easy to make good in situ with fresh plaster, and imperfections tended to be lost in the intricacies of the decorative detail.

Fixing methods Lighter lengths could be fixed in place with plaster 'dabs' but for most installations – and all those with deep sections – nail or screw fixings provided initial support that would be reinforced with plaster dabs. Standard straight runs, which could be cut to fit specific locations, were augmented by a corner piece. The centre mouldings, usually at hanging points for light fittings, masked areas of ceiling plaster that were necessarily difficult to finish with precision.

Retaining existing mouldings Extant traditional mouldings offer ready-made decorative detail and tend to be prized by most clients. Good examples may also be listed for preservation, and their retention and restoration made a condition of planning permission. It is, however, not unusual for sections of cornice to be damaged as a result of deterioration of the building fabric or the installation of modern services. It is not difficult, in terms of detailing, to repair such damage but it is expensive, invariably carried out by specialists who make moulds from surviving areas and recast and refit replacement sections.

Installing new cornices

It is easy to buy modern pre-fabricated sections of varying degrees of elaboration. The best-quality examples continue to be plaster cast in moulds, although plastic versions offer a cheaper alternative and, because they are lighter, are easier to fix with proprietary adhesives.

If cornices are used at all in modern construction they tend to be simple, typically a concave quadrant moulding, but continue to serve the traditional function of covering what is likely to be a crude alignment of wall and ceiling. Because they are planted on, and therefore projecting beyond the face of the wall, they offer a distinct change of plane at which to make changes in paint colour.

Right-angle junctions

If it is decided to settle for the unadorned right-angle junction, the corner must be reinforced by scrim tape, embedded in the skim coat on both wall and ceiling. This will be enough to eliminate cracking but does not make the formation of a clean angle easier. With an imperfect junction, the expedient solution is to paint the wall and ceiling the same colour so that unevenness is not further delineated. When colour differentiation is desired, then one solution is to take the colour of the wall up to form a border with the main ceiling colour or to take the ceiling colour on to the wall to create what is, in effect, a two-dimensional cornice.

WALL AND CEILING JUNCTIONS
Traditionally, moulded plaster cornices (**1**) covered the junction of walls and ceilings because the right angle caused construction difficulties. Omitting a cornice (**2**) conforms to Modernist principles rejecting applied ornament.

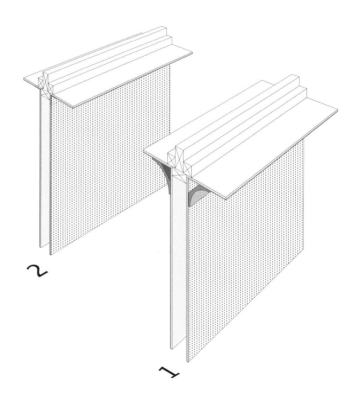

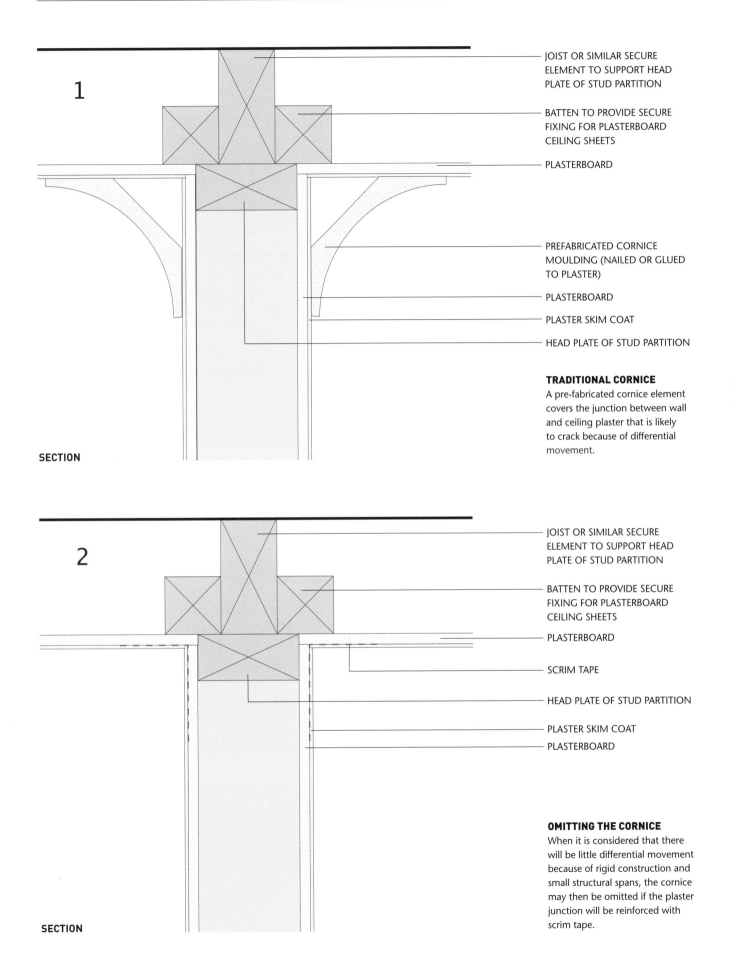

1

JOIST OR SIMILAR SECURE ELEMENT TO SUPPORT HEAD PLATE OF STUD PARTITION

BATTEN TO PROVIDE SECURE FIXING FOR PLASTERBOARD CEILING SHEETS

PLASTERBOARD

PREFABRICATED CORNICE MOULDING (NAILED OR GLUED TO PLASTER)

PLASTERBOARD

PLASTER SKIM COAT

HEAD PLATE OF STUD PARTITION

SECTION

TRADITIONAL CORNICE
A pre-fabricated cornice element covers the junction between wall and ceiling plaster that is likely to crack because of differential movement.

2

JOIST OR SIMILAR SECURE ELEMENT TO SUPPORT HEAD PLATE OF STUD PARTITION

BATTEN TO PROVIDE SECURE FIXING FOR PLASTERBOARD CEILING SHEETS

PLASTERBOARD

SCRIM TAPE

HEAD PLATE OF STUD PARTITION

PLASTER SKIM COAT

PLASTERBOARD

SECTION

OMITTING THE CORNICE
When it is considered that there will be little differential movement because of rigid construction and small structural spans, the cornice may then be omitted if the plaster junction will be reinforced with scrim tape.

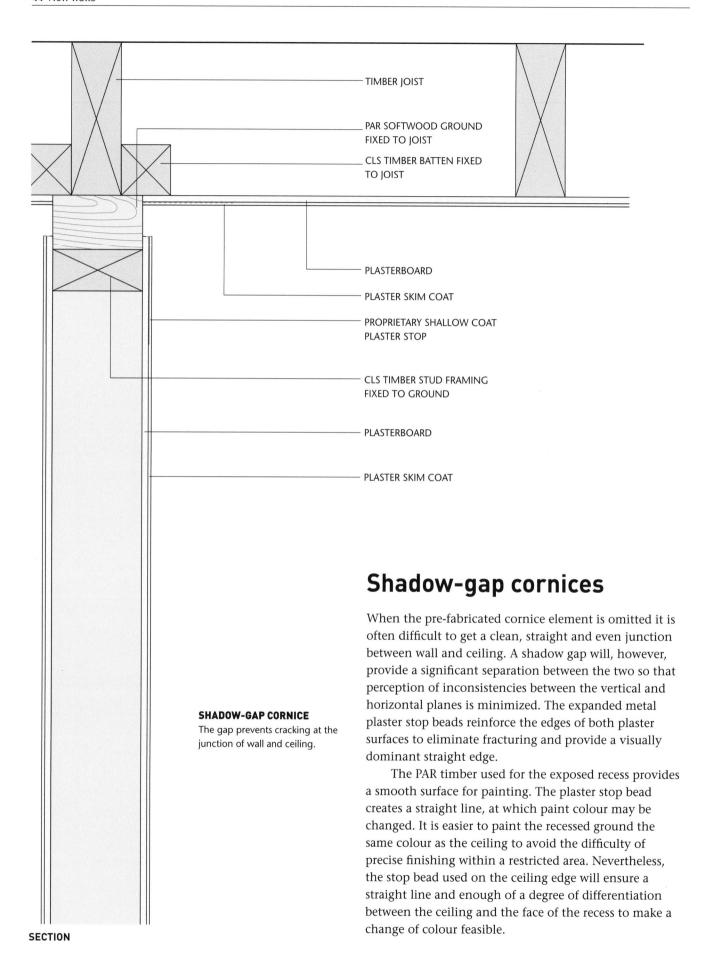

TIMBER JOIST

PAR SOFTWOOD GROUND
FIXED TO JOIST

CLS TIMBER BATTEN FIXED
TO JOIST

PLASTERBOARD

PLASTER SKIM COAT

PROPRIETARY SHALLOW COAT
PLASTER STOP

CLS TIMBER STUD FRAMING
FIXED TO GROUND

PLASTERBOARD

PLASTER SKIM COAT

SHADOW-GAP CORNICE
The gap prevents cracking at the
junction of wall and ceiling.

SECTION

Shadow-gap cornices

When the pre-fabricated cornice element is omitted it is often difficult to get a clean, straight and even junction between wall and ceiling. A shadow gap will, however, provide a significant separation between the two so that perception of inconsistencies between the vertical and horizontal planes is minimized. The expanded metal plaster stop beads reinforce the edges of both plaster surfaces to eliminate fracturing and provide a visually dominant straight edge.

The PAR timber used for the exposed recess provides a smooth surface for painting. The plaster stop bead creates a straight line, at which paint colour may be changed. It is easier to paint the recessed ground the same colour as the ceiling to avoid the difficulty of precise finishing within a restricted area. Nevertheless, the stop bead used on the ceiling edge will ensure a straight line and enough of a degree of differentiation between the ceiling and the face of the recess to make a change of colour feasible.

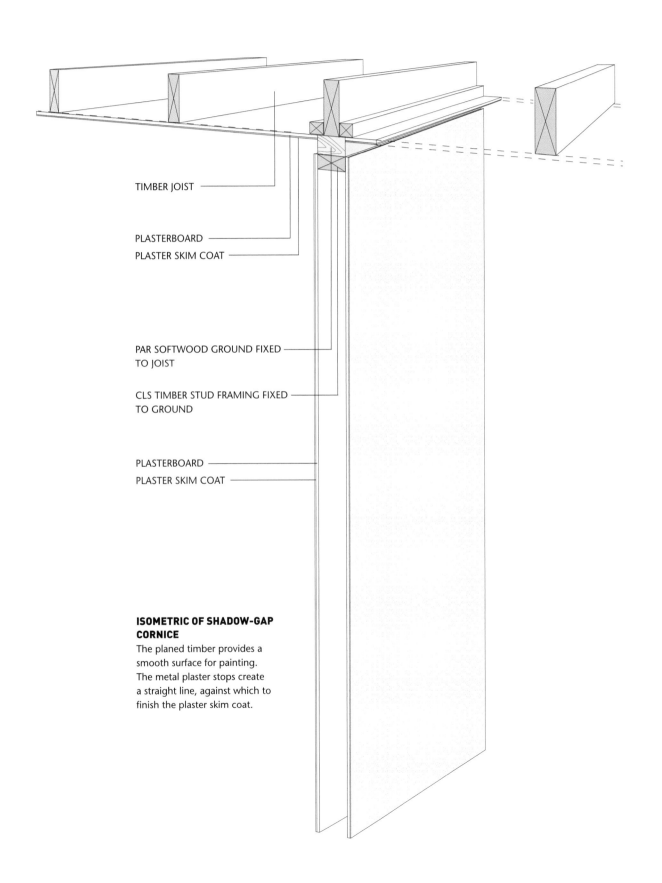

TIMBER JOIST

PLASTERBOARD
PLASTER SKIM COAT

PAR SOFTWOOD GROUND FIXED
TO JOIST

CLS TIMBER STUD FRAMING FIXED
TO GROUND

PLASTERBOARD
PLASTER SKIM COAT

**ISOMETRIC OF SHADOW-GAP
CORNICE**
The planed timber provides a
smooth surface for painting.
The metal plaster stops create
a straight line, against which to
finish the plaster skim coat.

Soundproofing walls

Weight of materials and rigid construction are the most effective means of reducing the passage of sound within a building. Concrete walls and floors, cast monolithically, provide the optimum solution but are usually impractical and only justified for specialist projects. Bricks and mortar are second best, slightly superior to concrete blocks, which are lighter. However, in new interiors it is usually impossible to use any of these, other than the most lightweight blocks, because existing floor structures will be incapable of taking additional concentrated loadings. The 12mm finishing plaster needed adds more weight.

Solutions for stud partitions

Stud frame with plasterboard cladding solves structural problems but is not good for serious sound reduction. The hollow construction exacerbates the problem, as sound may be transferred comparatively easily across the void and through the studwork that directly connects both faces. The plasterboard cladding vibrates and becomes a 'sounding box' for sound transmission.

Increasing cladding weight A skim-coat finish is better than drywall construction, and two layers of plasterboard on each face will increase the overall mass while also reducing reverberation.

Specialist materials It is also possible to utilize a specialist plasterboard, identified by a blue paper face, that can improve sound reduction. In addition, transmission of airborne sound across the voids in stud partitions can be reduced if an absorbent quilt material is inserted between the framing.

Additional stud frame The studs themselves, in contact with both faces, form an acoustic bridge. A solution is to build two independent stud frames to break continuity. This is comparatively complicated and takes up space.

Sound-masking It can be simpler to incorporate 'sound-masking', the introduction of unobtrusive background sound in an environment, to reduce the clarity and thus the capacity of overheard sounds to distract and irritate.

Planning In effect, all construction solutions other than sheer mass and monolithic construction have limited soundproofing success. It is better to deal with the problem by clever planning, grouping and isolating areas that need quiet – using, for example, storage rooms as buffer zones. Where a significant problem is anticipated, it is appropriate to take advice from an acoustic specialist.

REDUCTION OF SOUND TRANSFERENCE THROUGH VOIDS

Sound can travel easily through voids under floors or above suspended ceilings, where spaces have been created for the distribution of wiring, pipes and ducts. Where transference is likely to be criticial, partitions should be built off the original floor level and carried above the new ceiling level to the soffit of the existing floor to create a continuous barrier. In this example, the width of framing at the upper level of the wall is reduced in response to the change of ceiling level: a demonstration of how a practical necessity may be aesthetically refined.

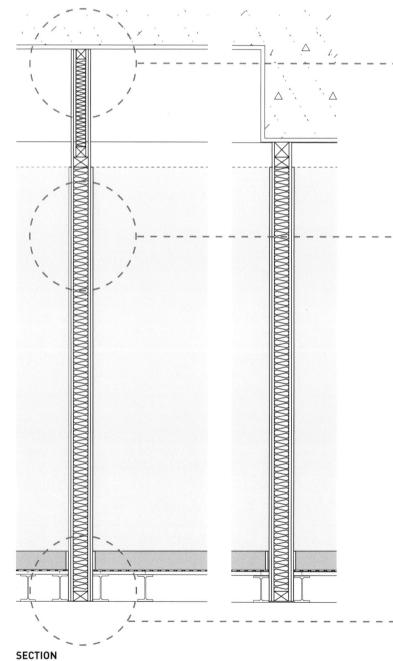

SECTION

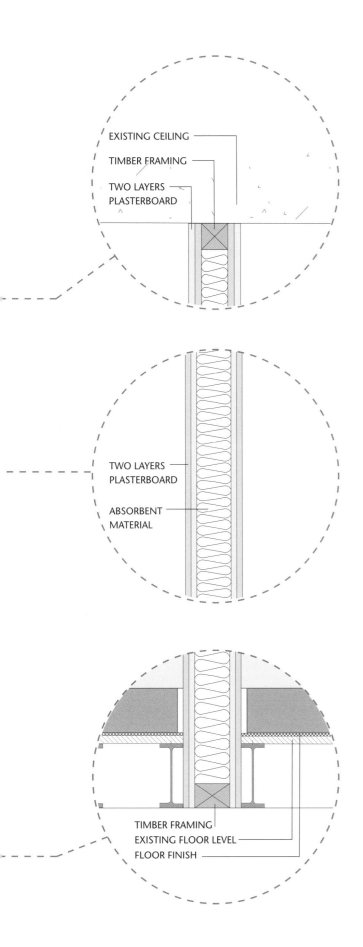

EXISTING CEILING

TIMBER FRAMING

TWO LAYERS
PLASTERBOARD

TWO LAYERS
PLASTERBOARD

ABSORBENT
MATERIAL

TIMBER FRAMING
EXISTING FLOOR LEVEL
FLOOR FINISH

Fireproofing walls

The basic requirements for fireproofing are, in many respects, similar to those for soundproofing. Non-combustible materials – concrete, brick and blockwork – obviously provide effective barriers. The materials and comparatively fragile construction of stud partitions present problems.

Design criteria

The basic principle of fire prevention and control is that an outbreak of fire should be contained within the area where it started. Basic construction is adequate for the lowest level – usually half an hour – of containment.

Escape routes, corridors and stairs are required to provide a longer period of protection, usually an hour. Precise requirements, however, depend on the building's function, its configuration and the number of occupants. It is sensible to check at an early stage in the design process with the appropriate local authorities that any proposals meet their criteria.

Improving ratings The greatest problems are caused by door and window openings, but when necessary the fire rating of stud partitions can be improved by a number of stratagems (these are described in the published regulation documents), which are accepted as meeting the required standards.

A skim coat improves the rating, as does – with more extreme requirements – the use of two sheets of plasterboard on the face of a partition. Some plasterboard sheets, faced with pink-coloured paper, have improved fire ratings.

Ducting Used for electrical cables, plumbing pipes and air-conditioning equipment, ducting can cause problems when it passes between separated areas. This can occur horizontally in walls and vertically between floors. Usually these will be enclosed, for cosmetic reasons, within ductwork, and the means of isolation is achieved without concern for its visual impact.

It is important, however, that the requirements are precisely described in drawing and word to ensure that they are exactly met.

Fireproofing metal columns

Steel columns, particularly I-sections, provide structural components for most interior projects. They can be cut to size and curved with great accuracy off site. They may be pre-drilled for bolting together on site, and their erection is quick and comparatively clean. They are strong in tension and acceptably capable of dealing with compression loadings.

Their only weakness when compared to concrete structural members is that they behave poorly in fire. One solution is to give them a protective coating of concrete but this requires the building of a mould, or formwork, into which the concrete may be poured and allowed to set. This is difficult and disruptive to carry out within the confines of an interior site.

It is also possible to treat steelwork with a paint that will protect it sufficiently against fire to meet regulations – this is an appropriate treatment where exposed steelwork is an acceptable aesthetic solution.

Encasing beams in plasterboard cladding

Usually it is more important to conceal the steelwork by casing it in a plasterboard skin, which will normally provide an acceptable level of fire protection. The job is simple but, because of the amount of comparatively complicated framing construction necessary, it is most common to use softwood framing for the plasterboard cladding. The latter will be finished with a skim coat to provide an appropriate level of fire protection and also to ensure the straight and strong arrises that an expanded metal corner bead can provide.

Enhancing spaces This casing may be built tight to a structural column, but it is worth considering if the plan form should be modified to make a contribution to the project as a whole. The casing may shift the perceived structural axis to refine alignments within the interior, or the aesthetically random proportions of the structural member may be reconfigured.

There is no need to attach the new framing structure to the steelwork, as it can be satisfactorily fixed to floor or ceiling. When there is a suspended ceiling, it will be necessary to encase the steelwork above it to ensure complete protection over the whole length of a column, although its visual impact need not be considered.

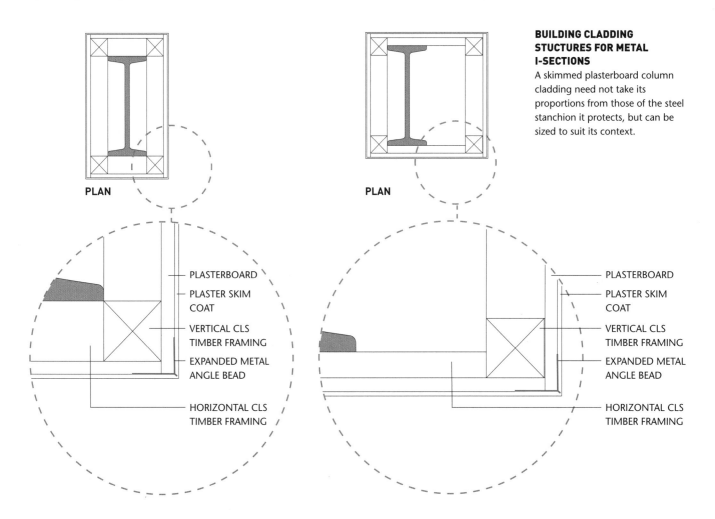

PLAN

PLAN

PLASTERBOARD

PLASTER SKIM COAT

VERTICAL CLS TIMBER FRAMING

EXPANDED METAL ANGLE BEAD

HORIZONTAL CLS TIMBER FRAMING

PLASTERBOARD

PLASTER SKIM COAT

VERTICAL CLS TIMBER FRAMING

EXPANDED METAL ANGLE BEAD

HORIZONTAL CLS TIMBER FRAMING

BUILDING CLADDING STUCTURES FOR METAL I-SECTIONS

A skimmed plasterboard column cladding need not take its proportions from those of the steel stanchion it protects, but can be sized to suit its context.

Installing services

Order of installation

First fix The installation of basic service elements for electricity and plumbing must take place before finishes are applied. This is known as the 'first fix' and involves completion of the whole distribution network, including the location of wires without power and pipes without water at the points where they connect to fittings.

Second fix This final connection of services, the 'second fix', takes place after wall finishes, with the possible exception of paint, have been applied.

Approaches to installation

Partition walls Essential service wires and pipes are frequently circulated within the hollow core of partition walls. They are passed through holes bored in the centre of timber studs or cut out of metal studs at manufacture.

Masonry In brick or block walls, grooves, or 'chases', can be cut mechanically or by hand into the face of the wall, but this is time-consuming and messy.

Concrete Chases may be cut in concrete walls, but if the concrete is particularly dense then the process will be difficult. When new concrete walls, floors and ceilings are being poured, it is normal practice to incorporate within them a metal or plastic 'conduit', which is a hollow-cored strip, circular or rectangular in section, through which wiring may be passed. Pipes for circulating water are laid directly in the concrete.

Conduits An alternative is to mount pipes and cables, in metal or plastic conduit, on the surface, but this is obviously not acceptable in most circumstances. Wiring lies loosely in conduits and thus may be pushed through when the conduit is in place. Replacement of wiring is simple, as new lengths may be attached to redundant wires and pulled through as the old are removed.

METAL STUDWORK
In metal studwork, pipes and wires are threaded through holes cut out during manufacture (top).

METAL CONDUITS
Surface-mounted metal conduits (middle).

PLASTIC CONDUIT
Surface-mounted plastic conduit (bottom).

CHAPTER 3 ALTERNATIVE PARTITIONS

Curving walls

It is generally good practice to use straight lines in all aspects of construction. Curved walls may be spectacular but they are more difficult to build and therefore more difficult to do well.

Curved materials

Materials are generally manufactured in straight lengths, and flat planes and rectangular spaces tend to cope more efficiently with furniture and equipment. However, plasterboard, thin plywood and MDF may be bent comparatively easily on site and all are also available in forms specifically designed for curved surfaces. Sheets with grooves on the face can be fixed to a supporting frame. These grooves reduce resistance to bending and eliminate both tearing of the convex face and compression of the concave.

It is comparatively simple to cut two-dimensional curves out of sheet materials. Plywood and MDF may be cut with great precision. Other strand boards will give less exact edges, while plasterboard will give a broken and fragile edge.

Generally, the more elaborate the form the more important it is that it should be pre-fabricated off site. Three-dimensional curved walls are more difficult to construct, although just as the computer makes them easier to draw so it can also translate drawn forms into the data necessary for efficient production.

Plans and layouts

It is also important, and sometimes difficult, to make a satisfactory transition between a curved and a straight line, and between two curves, even when the work is carried out on site. The transition will work best if the line from the centre of a curve to the point where it joins a straight wall makes a right angle with it. Two curves should intersect on the line that joins their centres.

Existing elements

The junction of new curved walls and existing straight ones demands particular consideration. Here, it is not merely a matter of the conjunction of different materials but recognition that formal three-dimensional gestures

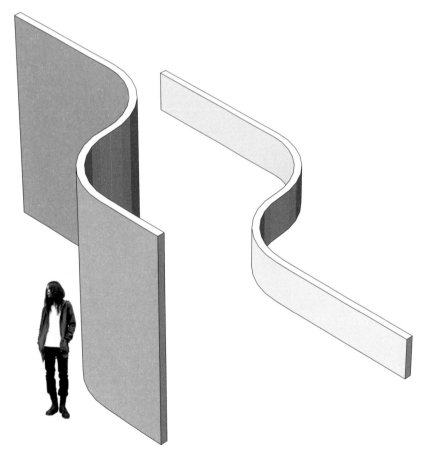

JOINING CURVES

The components of any complex curved form should flow freely, without any abrupt or awkwardly angled changes in direction. The transition will often work best if the centre of the curve is at a right angle to the straight elements.

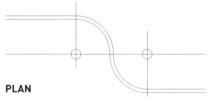

PLAN

TIP DON'T DILUTE

Curved walls are used to create visual impact, but if too many are employed in one interior their effect will be diluted. They will usually be more dramatic if they are counterpointed by straight or angled walls.

should be expressed positively. This is most effectively achieved if there is visual separation between the curve and the wall it joins, allowing their distinctive forms to be clearly perceived. Where the construction and finishing of the junction is difficult, particularly when the space between the two walls reduces, a separation helps builders operate effectively.

Devices for solving the problem are simple. The first requires that the curve stops short of the wall it is meeting and the second that it finishes parallel with it. In both cases a recess is formed which may be used to house a concealed light source or, if larger, to provide storage.

Angled walls

Similar problems exist when an angled wall meets a straight wall. In fact, when the angle between the two is particularly acute the problem of accessibility for construction and use of the space created is exacerbated.

It remains good practice to visually separate the two and to close the gap between them by setting back the connecting length of wall – again creating a recess, again suitable for concealing a light source or storage. In the acute angle, it may make sense to sacrifice unusable floor area by moving the enclosing wall face until its dimension makes a negotiable space.

SHADOW GAPS

When angled and curved walls meet straight walls it is a good idea to leave a shadow gap or recess. This avoids the problems of achieving a well-made junction and, as importantly, visually separates elements, making them and the junction between them more significant. Three options are: the curved wall stops short (**1**); the curve runs parallel to the straight wall (**2**); if an angled wall is stopped short of a straight wall, a difficult physical and visual junction is avoided – if the resulting internal angle is too acute the space between the walls can be difficult to finish or clean. This may be solved if the short connecting wall is located to allow room for both operations to be carried out (**3**).

TIP SEE BOTH SIDES

Since curves and angles are often used to create significant visual gestures, their effect on the area to their rear must not be overlooked. It is easy to create residual space that does not benefit from the flamboyant curve, and it is therefore worth considering whether the plan should be squared off and a perimeter created that is more sympathetic to the straight lines and right angles of furniture and utilitarian activities.

Building curves

Brickwork and blockwork

When making curves with bricks or blocks, the required radius should be set out on the floor either as a drawn line or with a physical template, which is usually cut out from cheap sheet material. While it is possible to obtain 'special' curved bricks, these are produced for a limited range of radii and are not readily available.

It is standard practice to use conventional straight-sided bricks or blocks so that the built wall emerges as a series of facets, each the length of an individual brick or block. For tighter curves it is better to use a smaller brick module to minimize the depth of plaster needed for a smooth curve. The success of the end result will depend on the plasterer's skill and eye.

Stud partitions

To make curves in stud partitions, the basic construction principles for a straight wall apply but it is impractical to bend a length of sole plate or head plate. The timber will resist bending, particularly along the greater of its two sectional dimensions. Curves should therefore be constructed in short, straight lengths spanning between the vertical framing. A continuous, true curve can be cut from sheets of 19, 21 or 24mm plywood to provide an accurate line against which the sheet material may be fixed on the top and bottom edges, where discrepancies in the geometry would be more apparent against the planes of floor and ceiling.

Metal lath sheeting There are two options for the base to which plaster may be applied. The first, expanded metal lath sheeting, is designed to receive three coats of plaster, like a brick or blockwork wall. The three-dimensional perforations of the lath, fixed with galvanized clout nails or screws to the stud framing, provide a key for the first coat of plaster, some of which will ooze through the apertures. When the plaster sets, the lath becomes rigid and forms the first slightly rough and uneven version of the curve, which is refined with the final two coats.

Plasterboard The second option is to use plasterboard and to finish it with a conventional skim coat. Specially manufactured plasterboard sheets can be bent to radii as tight as 250mm. These can be difficult to obtain and

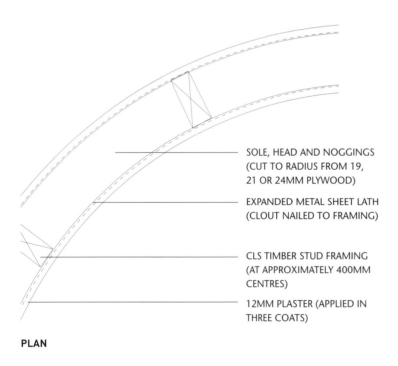

SOLE, HEAD AND NOGGINGS
(CUT TO RADIUS FROM 19,
21 OR 24MM PLYWOOD)

EXPANDED METAL SHEET LATH
(CLOUT NAILED TO FRAMING)

CLS TIMBER STUD FRAMING
(AT APPROXIMATELY 400MM
CENTRES)

12MM PLASTER (APPLIED IN
THREE COATS)

PLAN

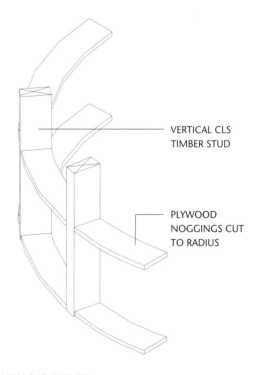

VERTICAL CLS
TIMBER STUD

PLYWOOD
NOGGINGS CUT
TO RADIUS

TYPICAL CURVED PARTITION
Components and fixing methods are the same as those used in the making of straight lengths of wall.

FRAMING FOR CURVED PARTITIONS
Vertical framing is made of studs in Canadian Lumber Sizes. Horizontal noggings may be short lengths of straight stud of 19, 21 or 24mm plywood cut to the correct radius.

for a small job, or one with only a few curved sections, it is probably more expedient to modify standard sheets. The convex face of a curve can be scored with lines at approximately 50mm centres and cut vertical to the direction of the curve. The skim coat will fill the V-shaped grooves on the convex face.

Achieving curves While plasterboard is essentially a rigid and brittle sheet material, it can be given a degree of pliability if wetted until the gypsum core has been moistened. This can be done effectively with a paint roller and takes 15 minutes for adequate penetration. It is then possible to shape it around the armature of the stud framework. The tendency of the board to bend may be initiated if the sheets are raised off the continuous flat supporting surface recommended for storage and leant against a wall or laid to bridge between end supports. The sheets' natural tendency to bend under their own weight will be enhanced if they are stored in a damp atmosphere where the core of the board will absorb moisture.

It is better practice to fix sheets with clout nails as their bigger head offers an improved grip on the curved surface, which can be under some pressure. It is also better to lay sheets so that the bend is over the longer dimension. This will require a slight reconfiguration of the horizontal framing members to ensure continuous support behind joints in the boards. If done well this establishes a consistent curve, on which a minimum variation in the thickness of skim coat will be necessary.

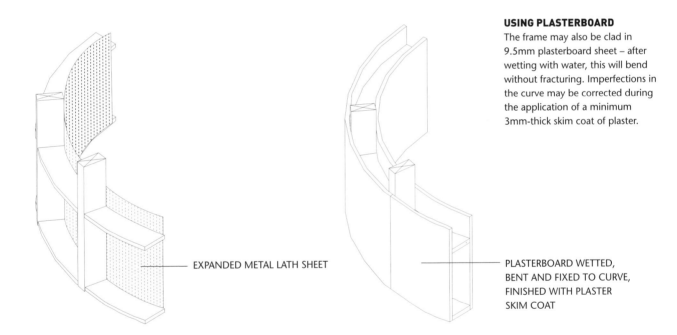

USING PLASTERBOARD
The frame may also be clad in 9.5mm plasterboard sheet – after wetting with water, this will bend without fracturing. Imperfections in the curve may be corrected during the application of a minimum 3mm-thick skim coat of plaster.

EXPANDED METAL LATH SHEET

PLASTERBOARD WETTED, BENT AND FIXED TO CURVE, FINISHED WITH PLASTER SKIM COAT

USING EXPANDED METAL MESH
Expanded metal lath may be nailed or screwed to the frame to provide a key for plaster. If noggings are curved accurately the lath can be fixed to them at more frequent centres, so that less correction is needed during the plastering process to create a smooth curve.

TIP DISGUISING IMPERFECTIONS

If the plaster on a curve is not convincingly smooth, then it is expedient to eliminate any light source that washes across its surface. The same principle applies to uneven straight planes. Irregularities in both are exaggerated by elongated transverse shadows.

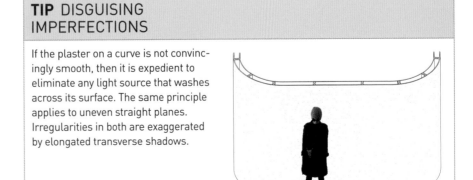

Freestanding walls

It is not unusual for a wall, particularly a stud partition, unconnected to any other, to be used to subdivide an area. This will cause no problems if it is fixed at both floor and ceiling levels, because it can take lateral stability from both elements. If, however, the intention is that the new wall should not reach the ceiling, it will, even if securely fixed to the floor, lack the stability to support additional loadings or to withstand impact, and it will be necessary to employ one of a number of strategies illustrated here.

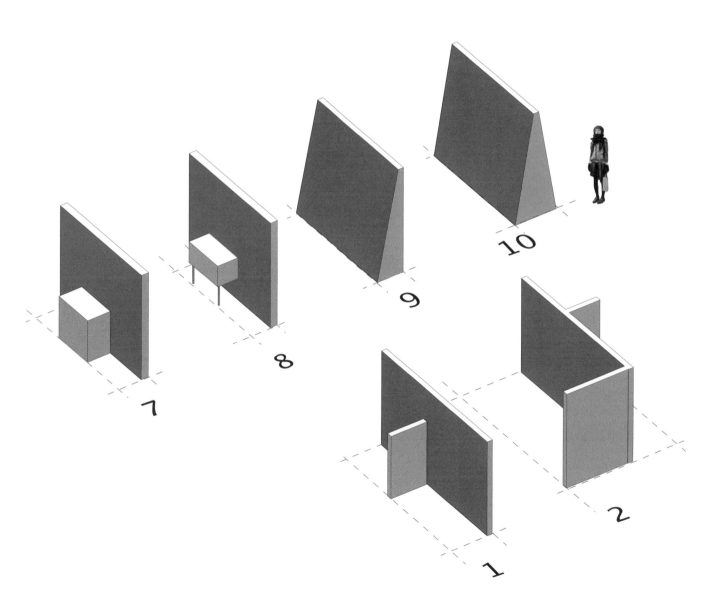

FREESTANDING KIOSK

The rear wall of a freestanding kiosk (left) gains stability from its broad base, and from the L-shaped counter. These elements do not touch, so the form of each is very clear.

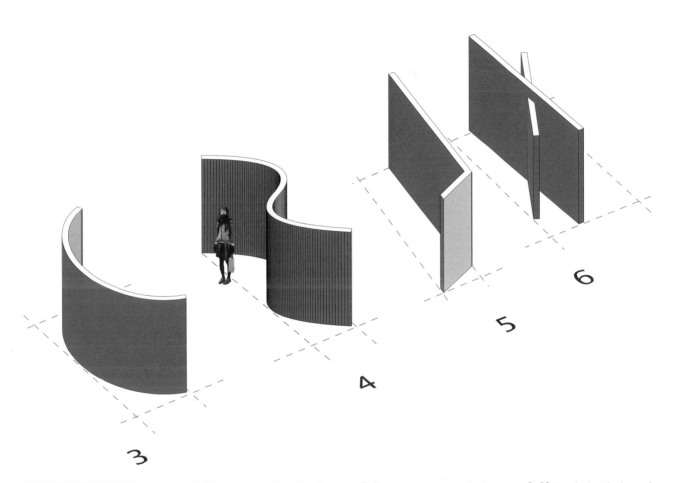

ENSURING STABILITY IN FREESTANDING WALLS

1–2 Extensions of a structure at right angles to the run of the wall will provide lateral bracing. Their location and length may be varied depending on intuitive assessment of particular conditions or advice from an engineer. They may be shorter and lower than the main wall, but the longer the points of contact and connection, the stronger the structure. If it is important that the visual integrity of a main wall is not compromised, then the bracing walls may be finished differently and the detail of the junction treated to suggest physical separation.

3–4 Curves notionally widen the base of the structure and adjust its centre of gravity.
5–6 Angled additions also widen the effective base.

7–8 Lateral support can also be derived from low-level furniture units along all, or a significant proportion of, the wall length. These offer opportunities for a wider, more substantial fixing to the floor and a counterweight against the tendency of the wall to pivot around a narrow base fixing. Detailing can make the furniture components visually distinct, and if they stop short of the ends of the wall they will read as separate elements.

9–10 Broadening the base of a wall will lower its centre of gravity, and allow more opportunities for floor fixings. One or both vertical sides can be angled.

'Floating' walls

Walls designed to demarcate areas may hang from the ceiling and stop short of the floor. However, it is never sensible to attempt this if they are to descend to a height where people come into contact with them, because any pressure will cause them to pivot around the fixing point and put excessive stress on that joint.

The solution is to incorporate 'columns' that run between ceiling and floor or between the lower structural member of the suspended wall and the floor, with adequate anchorage to both. The elements of such structures can be detailed so that the cladding sits in front ('proud') of the framing, in order that the wall plane is visually dominant. It is, however, always worth considering the value of visual separation if, once the area is inhabited by people and furniture, the impact is lost.

Ceiling fixings

It is possible to provide isolated fixings to a ceiling element capable of providing adequate structural support. However, these will be most effective if they behave as columns contained within the thickness of the wall and spanning from the floor to stable elements in or above the ceiling. If they are attached only to the top of the new wall their junction will be less substantial. Exposed lengths of column can be made visually distinct from the wall surface. They may be finished differently, and if the face of the wall sits in front of them its top line will remain unbroken. If they are set back from the ends of the wall their visual impact will be further reduced.

Alternative fixings

It is often difficult to make a secure structural connection at ceiling level. Sometimes the ceiling height may make it impossible and sometimes the damage caused in the construction may be unacceptable.

Fixings can usually be made discreetly at floor level, and most structures are sufficiently heavy to preclude their moving. The danger is that they will fall because their base is too narrow. Without access to ceiling support the solution is, where possible, to connect the top of the structure to an existing wall or column, or to design the whole in a way that allows components of the whole to be joined at high level. This strategy is particularly useful for exhibition structures that are generally short-lived.

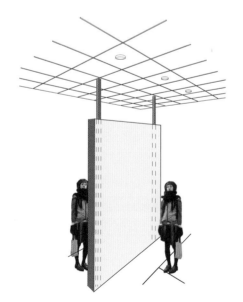

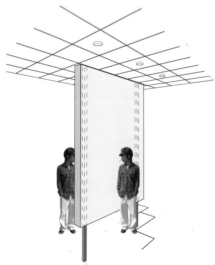

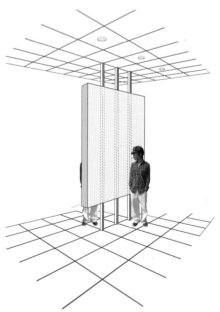

EXPOSED CEILING FIXINGS
While the partition can be securely fixed to the floor, its height will make it unstable and liable to oscillate. Minimal connections at ceiling height prevent its overturning.

EXPOSED FLOOR FIXINGS
While the partition suggests that it is 'floating' above floor level, the discreet fixing at floor level prevents it oscillating and weakening its ceiling connection.

EXPOSED FLOOR AND CEILING FIXINGS
A wall element can be held clear of floor and ceiling. The fixing at ceiling level must be to a very secure, rigid structural element – it cannot be supported adequately by plasterboard, which will fracture under impact pressure.

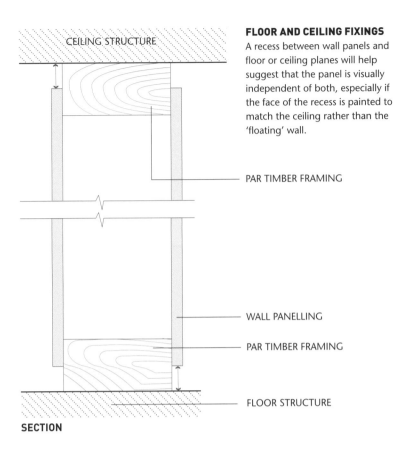

CEILING STRUCTURE

PAR TIMBER FRAMING

WALL PANELLING

PAR TIMBER FRAMING

FLOOR STRUCTURE

SECTION

FLOOR AND CEILING FIXINGS

A recess between wall panels and floor or ceiling planes will help suggest that the panel is visually independent of both, especially if the face of the recess is painted to match the ceiling rather than the 'floating' wall.

EXAMPLE OF STABILIZED STRUCTURE

Freestanding elements joined overhead to avoid any risk of overturning.

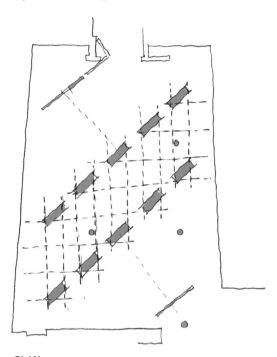

PLAN

CROSS-BRACING

High-level connections and cross-bracing give a wide stable base to two 10mm-thick freestanding partitions (above).

OVERHEAD STRUCTURES

The stabilizing structure overhead accommodates existing columns while also creating a sense of enclosure in the space below (top right).

'OUTRIGGERS'

The principle of overhead bracing applies to more permanent structures where walls are connected to and take support from 'outrigger' columns (above). The circular element gives extra rigidity to the comparatively fragile blue cross-supports.

Base fixings for partitions

It is important to provide a secure fixing for the base of exposed supports. One useful method for timber posts is a pre-fabricated metal sleeve, welded to a base plate that is drilled to facilitate a screw fixing to the subfloor.

The plate can be covered by the floor finish, which can be cut precisely around the sleeve. The timber post can be machined to fit the sleeve precisely, with its visible faces aligned with those of the sleeve. When it is not practical to lose the base plate in the depth of the floor finish, or when the existing floor finish is to be retained, one solution is to separate the sleeve from the base plate by a thin metal rod, strong enough to support the imposed load. The post may be secured in the sleeve with a bolt or screws. The post may project beyond the confines of the sleeve. Separation dramatizes the junction of post and floor, and the plate may be visually upgraded.

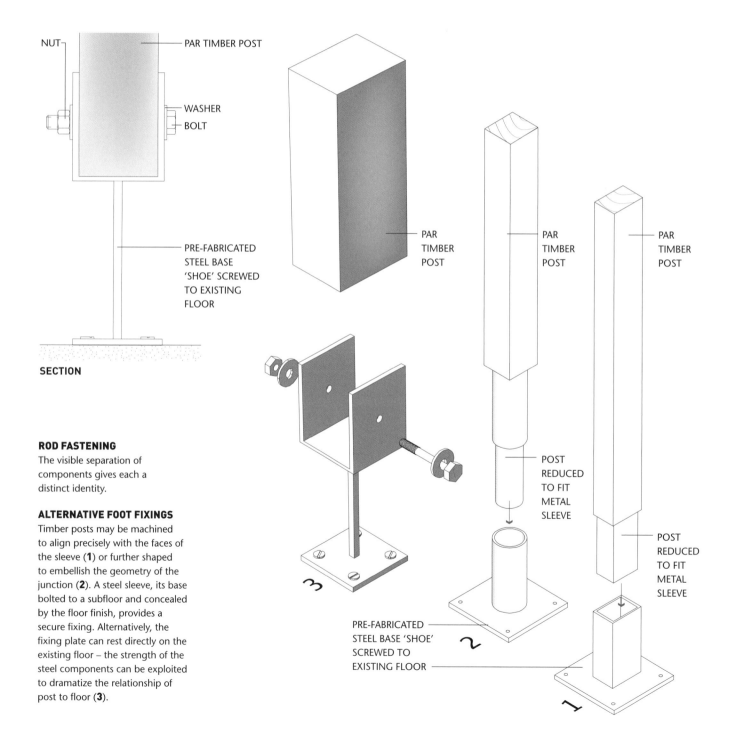

NUT

PAR TIMBER POST

WASHER

BOLT

PRE-FABRICATED STEEL BASE 'SHOE' SCREWED TO EXISTING FLOOR

SECTION

PAR TIMBER POST

PAR TIMBER POST

PAR TIMBER POST

POST REDUCED TO FIT METAL SLEEVE

POST REDUCED TO FIT METAL SLEEVE

PRE-FABRICATED STEEL BASE 'SHOE' SCREWED TO EXISTING FLOOR

ROD FASTENING
The visible separation of components gives each a distinct identity.

ALTERNATIVE FOOT FIXINGS
Timber posts may be machined to align precisely with the faces of the sleeve (**1**) or further shaped to embellish the geometry of the junction (**2**). A steel sleeve, its base bolted to a subfloor and concealed by the floor finish, provides a secure fixing. Alternatively, the fixing plate can rest directly on the existing floor – the strength of the steel components can be exploited to dramatize the relationship of post to floor (**3**).

Cladding isolated partitions

It would be possible to clad isolated partitions with plasterboard sheets, but the number and vulnerability of edges suggests that it is appropriate to use a more resilient sheet such as 6mm plywood, MDF or even opaque, translucent or transparent plastic. While the rigidity of these materials will contribute to the stability and durability of the structure, they do present problems for the filling of joints. The inevitable movement will cause joint filler, unless it has a degree of flexibility, to crack.

A solution is to accept visible joint lines and arrange them to make a pattern. The most critical and vulnerable joints are those on vertical edges, and one possibility is to make a robust, mitred joint – the ends are cut at 45 degrees where they meet to avoid exposing the core of the panel materials and to suggest a thicker, solid element. These can be difficult to fabricate in the busy environment of the worksite, thus shadow gaps and recessed planes offer more expedient solutions.

CLADDING OPTIONS FOR ISOLATED PARTITIONS

1 Planed timber framing is set back 6–10mm from the edge of the cladding panel. Panel and frame may be painted to read as one unit.

2 With a sheet material such as MDF, which can be cut to give a robust edge, a recess can be made that avoids the need to make a precise joint between butting panels.

3 Mitred joints suggest a solid panel, but require precise fabrication and are probably best constructed in a workshop.

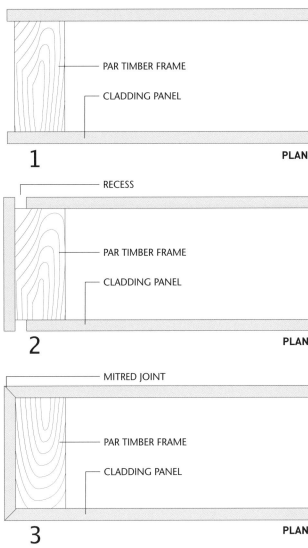

PAR TIMBER FRAME

CLADDING PANEL

1 PLAN

RECESS

PAR TIMBER FRAME

CLADDING PANEL

2 PLAN

MITRED JOINT

PAR TIMBER FRAME

CLADDING PANEL

3 PLAN

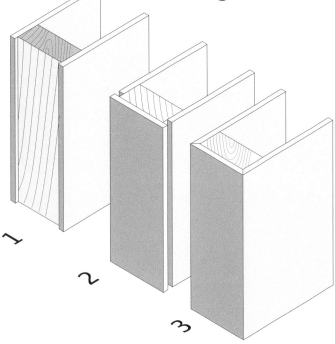

Fixing methods

All sheet materials for partitions will need to be attached to a supporting frame. Some will require a fixing that may remain visible as a feature of the wall; others will require a fixing that is better concealed.

A vertical or horizontal framing member should be located behind every joint to ensure that the faces of adjacent panels line through and that the hollow core is not exposed. There are two basic principles for dealing with what are likely to be visible joints.

Cover strips

The traditional method is for joints to be finished with a cover strip, which has the virtue of masking imperfections in the construction. The strips may be used to clamp the panels in position, in which case the method of fixing them to the frame will be visible. Alternatively, the primary method of fixing the panels themselves may be hidden by the cover strips. With this second option the fixing of the cover strip, either by gluing or with 'panel pins', may be more discreet since it only supports its own weight. Evidence of visible fixings is most easily eliminated if the strip is to be painted.

Shadow-gap solutions

A more 'modern' solution, intended to eliminate cover strips, exposes the joint, expressing it as a recess between cladding materials. This 'shadow gap' is typically about 10–12mm wide and disguises slight discrepancies between adjoining elements but requires greater precision in its assembly than a cover strip, particularly to ensure that the width of joint recess does not vary along its length.

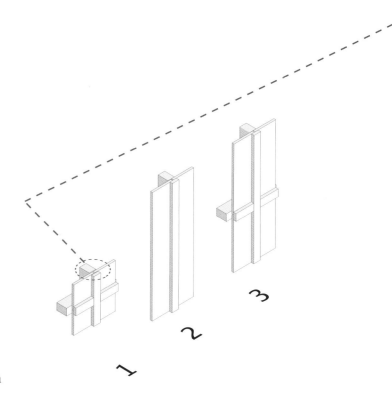

1
2
3

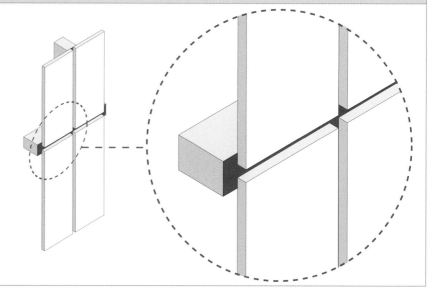

TIP FINISHES FOR SHADOW-GAP PARTITIONS

Framing, when exposed by a shadow gap, needs to have an acceptable quality of finish and is often painted or stained a darker hue to emphasize the shadow and disguise any imperfections.

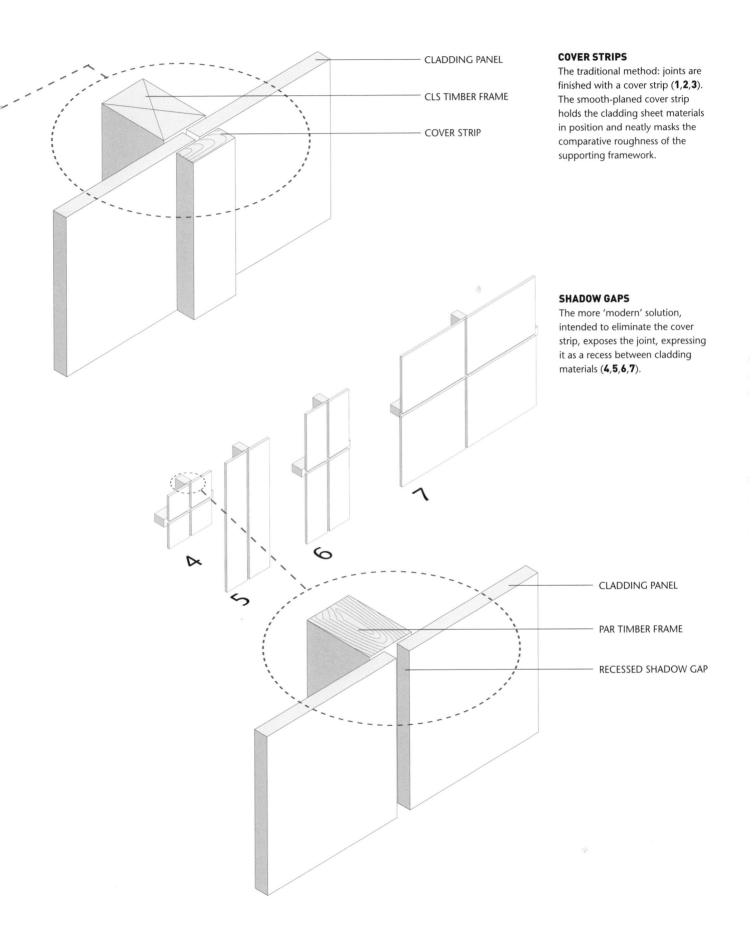

CLADDING PANEL

CLS TIMBER FRAME

COVER STRIP

COVER STRIPS

The traditional method: joints are finished with a cover strip (**1**,**2**,**3**). The smooth-planed cover strip holds the cladding sheet materials in position and neatly masks the comparative roughness of the supporting framework.

SHADOW GAPS

The more 'modern' solution, intended to eliminate the cover strip, exposes the joint, expressing it as a recess between cladding materials (**4**,**5**,**6**,**7**).

CLADDING PANEL

PAR TIMBER FRAME

RECESSED SHADOW GAP

Invisible fixings

It is possible to make completely invisible fixings. Cladding elements can be fixed to studwork from behind if this is anticipated and an appropriate construction sequence established. It is usual to use screws, as panels will require only modest bracing during assembly. It is possible to reduce the length of screw required for rear fixing – a recess can be made in the framing timber using a drill bit with a diameter big enough to accommodate the head of the screw and the screwdriver. It is, however, more usual to use a metal angle pre-drilled to take screws, which may therefore be shorter, easier to fix and able to offer a more direct and robust fixing.

Demountable partitions

An alternative method, which is particularly useful when it is desirable to have demountable partitions to allow access to service ducts, is to hook panels on to wall brackets or battens. It is usually enough to hang only from the top edge and allow gravity to hold them in position. A gap at least 5mm greater than the overlap of the brackets or battens must be left between the top of the hung panel and the ceiling or horizontal surface above it. This ensures it can be manoeuvred over the bracket or batten before being dropped into position.

Timber split battens In its traditional form the hanging mechanism, described as 'split batten', involved fixing one section of a timber batten, cut at an angle, to the supporting structure and the other to the back of the panel. It was simple to hook the batten fixed to the back of the panel behind that on the wall, and also possible to slide it sideways to even out joint widths.

Metal split brackets Timber is being replaced by a metal 'split bracket' alternative that offers greater precision and projects less from the supporting structure. Where a more rigid or permanent fixing is required, a number of hangers may be distributed over the height of the panel, at approximately 800mm centres, to increase contact with the support.

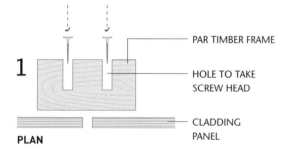

1

PAR TIMBER FRAME

HOLE TO TAKE SCREW HEAD

CLADDING PANEL

PLAN

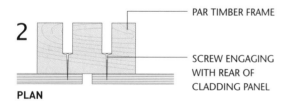

2

PAR TIMBER FRAME

SCREW ENGAGING WITH REAR OF CLADDING PANEL

PLAN

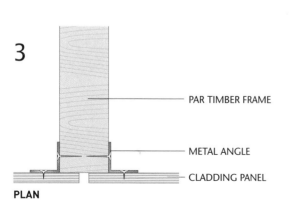

3

PAR TIMBER FRAME

METAL ANGLE

CLADDING PANEL

PLAN

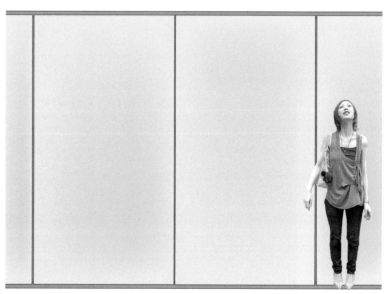

REAR-FIXING WALL PANELS
1–2 It can be difficult to make a secure connection when a long screw is inserted into a thin panel, and it is often more effective to drill a hole to allow the use of a shorter thinner screw.
3 Mild steel or aluminium angles allow fixings to framing and panels with short screws.

WALL PANELS WITH CONCEALED FIXINGS
For screw fixings, rear access will be required for installation and subsequent access will be impossible unless planned for. 'Split bracket' methods allow front installation and easy removal, which is particularly useful for cladding duct spaces within walls.

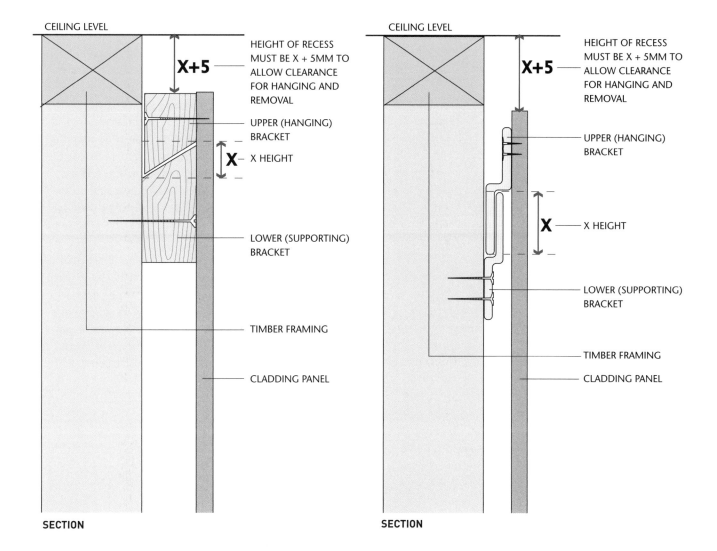

CEILING LEVEL

X+5

HEIGHT OF RECESS MUST BE X + 5MM TO ALLOW CLEARANCE FOR HANGING AND REMOVAL

UPPER (HANGING) BRACKET

X X HEIGHT

LOWER (SUPPORTING) BRACKET

TIMBER FRAMING

CLADDING PANEL

SECTION

CEILING LEVEL

X+5

HEIGHT OF RECESS MUST BE X + 5MM TO ALLOW CLEARANCE FOR HANGING AND REMOVAL

UPPER (HANGING) BRACKET

X X HEIGHT

LOWER (SUPPORTING) BRACKET

TIMBER FRAMING

CLADDING PANEL

SECTION

TIMBER SPLIT BATTEN

The batten on the back of the cladding panel is dropped behind that attached to the wall. Since there is no rigid fixing, horizontal adjustment is possible.

METAL SPLIT BRACKET

Timber split battens are increasingly being replaced by metal brackets that use the same principle. They project less beyond the face of the supporting wall, and are easier to fix.

VERTICAL BATTENS

It is good practice to leave a gap of at least 10mm between adjacent panels, since there will be some slight variation in hanging angle which will become obvious if they are too close. This gap, however, needs to be blocked with a vertical batten to hide unfinished surfaces behind it. The batten will also keep the panel at a constant distance from the supporting structure.

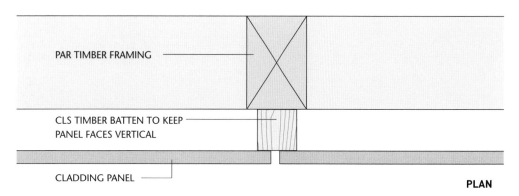

PAR TIMBER FRAMING

CLS TIMBER BATTEN TO KEEP PANEL FACES VERTICAL

CLADDING PANEL

PLAN

Glazed partitions

Glass is a popular option for partitions. It conducts light to those interior spaces without access to windows and opens up long views across subdivided spaces. Its shortcomings are that it must be toughened or laminated to give it the necessary strength to resist inevitable impacts, and it has poor fire resistance and poor sound-reductive properties. These problems may be solved with various specialist glasses and details. Manufacturers are continually developing new products, but these tend to be significantly more expensive than standard products.

Ensuring visibility

The paradox is that clear glass partitions are used where, ideally, a designer would have no division. They provide the means to make a wall that effectively disappears, but this can cause difficulties. It does not register on people's peripheral vision so they may collide with it, painfully and embarrassingly. The usual solution is to use translucent or opaque dots or stripes at eye level. Known as

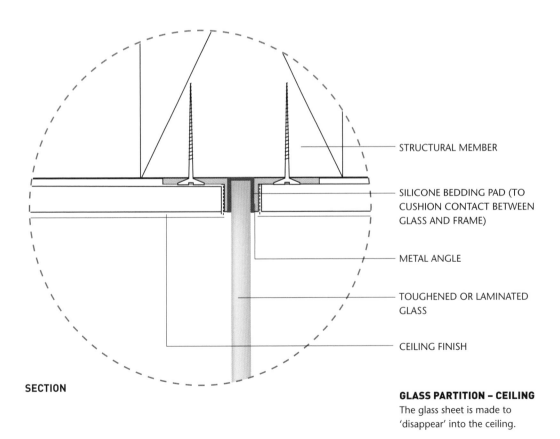

STRUCTURAL MEMBER

SILICONE BEDDING PAD (TO CUSHION CONTACT BETWEEN GLASS AND FRAME)

METAL ANGLE

TOUGHENED OR LAMINATED GLASS

CEILING FINISH

SECTION

GLASS PARTITION – CEILING
The glass sheet is made to 'disappear' into the ceiling.

'manifestation', these can be sand-blasted or acid-etched into the clear glass at production stage or applied later as adhesive film. They offer some opportunity for decorative pattern but may underline the element of compromise.

Invisible framing

When glass is used to minimize the presence of a partition, it will also be desirable to minimize the visual impact of the necessary framing. This may be achieved successfully if the glass sheet is made to 'disappear' into the floor, walls and ceiling.

This is not particularly difficult to achieve, but the glass must be installed early in the construction process – normally out of the usual operational sequence – and it is liable to complicate other work. While the toughened glass necessary to meet safety requirements is unlikely to be damaged by normal abuse, if replacement is necessary this is liable to be difficult as it will have a significant impact on finishing work carried out after its installation.

TIP SIGNALLING ON GLAZED PARTITIONS

The conventional mechanisms for preventing people colliding with fully glazed partitions, such as a row of red dots at eye level, are familiar and represent a compromise to achieving the original concept of a wholly transparent plane. It is sensible to accept and exploit the need for a warning device and to add a more considered pattern, whether sand-blasted or laser-cut adhesive plastic sheets. Occupants of rooms behind glass walls may also welcome the increased privacy that results.

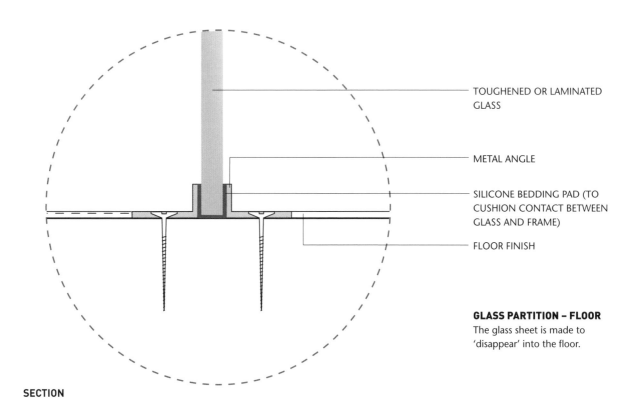

TOUGHENED OR LAMINATED GLASS

METAL ANGLE

SILICONE BEDDING PAD (TO CUSHION CONTACT BETWEEN GLASS AND FRAME)

FLOOR FINISH

GLASS PARTITION – FLOOR
The glass sheet is made to 'disappear' into the floor.

SECTION

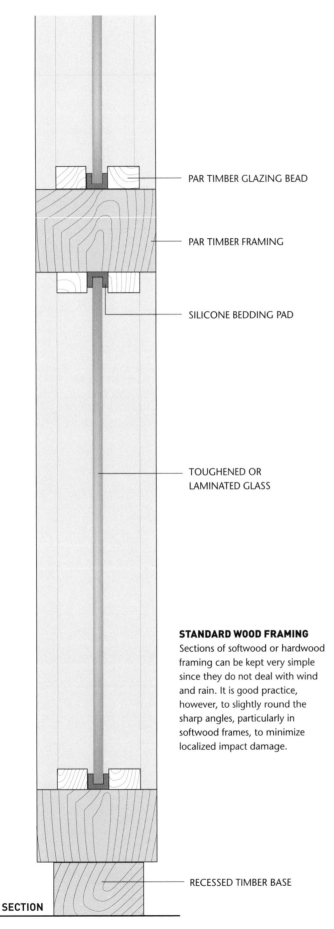

PAR TIMBER GLAZING BEAD

PAR TIMBER FRAMING

SILICONE BEDDING PAD

TOUGHENED OR
LAMINATED GLASS

STANDARD WOOD FRAMING
Sections of softwood or hardwood
framing can be kept very simple
since they do not deal with wind
and rain. It is good practice,
however, to slightly round the
sharp angles, particularly in
softwood frames, to minimize
localized impact damage.

RECESSED TIMBER BASE

SECTION

Frames for glazed partitions

If the designer is not committed to making a partition
that is near-invisible, an opportunity arises to make
creative use of the framing pattern. Such a frame is
generally easy to construct as it is not required to keep
out the weather. The (usually wooden) cross-section can
be as simple or as complex as desired, and does not have
to be moulded and chamfered.

In addition, the reduction of glass panel size offered
by framing can improve the fire-resistance qualities of the
partition, reducing the specification and cost of the glass
used. It is conventional, and therefore economical, to
run framing members horizontally and vertically. Where
appropriate, however, it is comparatively simple to make
an irregular or angled pattern.

Framing materials

The most frequently used framing materials are
hardwood, usually stained to exploit colour and grain,
or softwood, stained or painted. Metal framing is equally
effective, allows a smaller section and may better match
the aesthetic intention of the interior as a whole.

Whether using wood or metal it is good practice to
use a soft, resilient strip between glass and frame, to allow
a slight degree of flexibility that will reduce the chances
of the glass cracking when any movement occurs. It was
traditional to use thin lengths of leather but now rubber
or silicone strips, often with adhesive edges, are standard.
They have very little visual impact.

'Off-the-shelf' systems

There are metal framing systems, usually aluminium,
that may be bought off the shelf and, like all proprietary
products, impose some restrictions. However, if these
are understood early in the design process they may be
used positively. Such systems tend to provide a framing
member with a comparatively large but very simple
cross-section.

Fixing mechanisms The methods for fixing such
frames to supporting elements and holding the glass in
position are complicated and comparatively crude, but
are concealed by cleaner clip-on casings. More robust
and rigid standard sections can reduce bulk. These
usually have visible screw or nut-and-bolt fixings, and
consequently a more industrial appearance.

Curved glass

It is difficult, and therefore expensive, to curve glass, so
it is more normal to translate the curve into a series of
facets. The idea of the curve can be reasserted by curving
horizontal framing members.

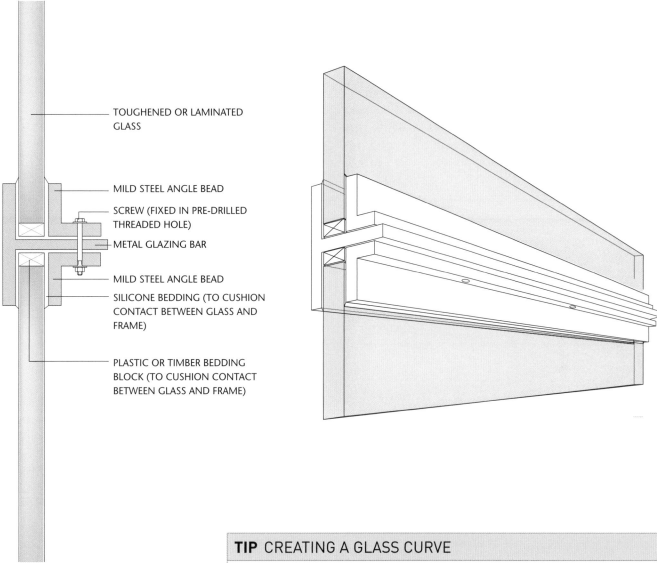

TOUGHENED OR LAMINATED GLASS

MILD STEEL ANGLE BEAD

SCREW (FIXED IN PRE-DRILLED THREADED HOLE)

METAL GLAZING BAR

MILD STEEL ANGLE BEAD

SILICONE BEDDING (TO CUSHION CONTACT BETWEEN GLASS AND FRAME)

PLASTIC OR TIMBER BEDDING BLOCK (TO CUSHION CONTACT BETWEEN GLASS AND FRAME)

SECTION

STANDARD METAL FRAMING
Simple metal sections can be aggregated to form a suitable framing system.

TIP CREATING A GLASS CURVE

Emphasizing horizontal elements in a glass curved wall expresses the implied geometry more clearly. Vertical members interrupt the flow of the curve.

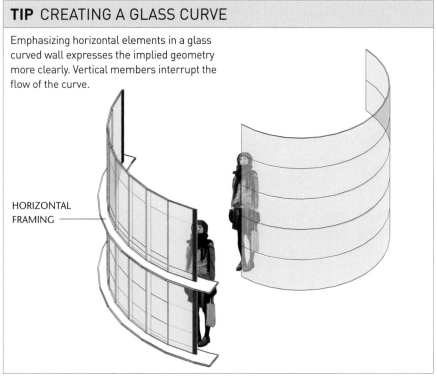

HORIZONTAL FRAMING

Framing and beading

The relative configurations of the frame and the bead that hold the glass in place are crucial in determining how the pattern of a window or glazed screen is perceived. It is, as in any joinery, unwise to line the faces of frame and bead through as there will inevitably be some minor misalignment apparent to the observer, especially one in regular intimate contact with the element.

The solution is to set the face of one of the elements back from the other, or to introduce a shadow gap between two nominally aligned faces. In timber construction, corners are usually mitred and beads are fixed with panel pins, screws or glues.

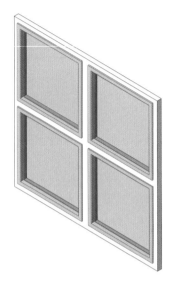

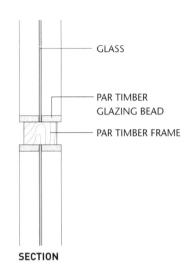

GLASS

PAR TIMBER GLAZING BEAD

PAR TIMBER FRAME

SECTION

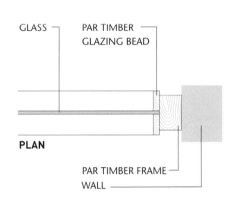

GLASS

PAR TIMBER GLAZING BEAD

PAR TIMBER FRAME

WALL

PLAN

FRAME WITH PROJECTING BEADS
The beads project and the frame recedes visually.

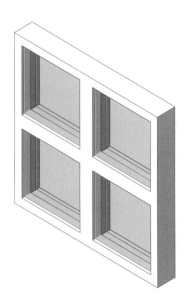

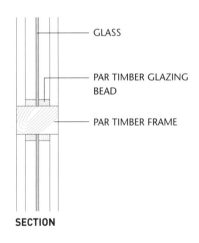

GLASS

PAR TIMBER GLAZING BEAD

PAR TIMBER FRAME

SECTION

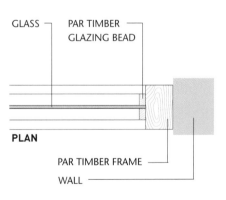

GLASS

PAR TIMBER GLAZING BEAD

PAR TIMBER FRAME

WALL

PLAN

FRAME WITH BEADS SET BACK
The frame dominates because the glazing beads are set back.

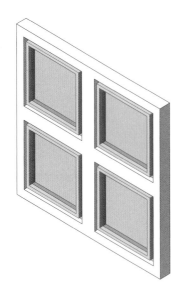

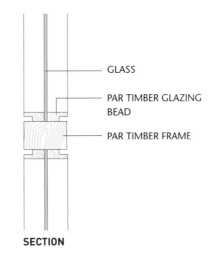

GLASS

PAR TIMBER GLAZING BEAD

PAR TIMBER FRAME

SECTION

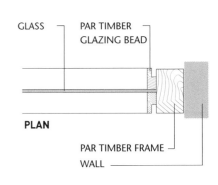

GLASS

PAR TIMBER GLAZING BEAD

PLAN

PAR TIMBER FRAME

WALL

FRAME WITH RECESS

Frame and beads appear to be in the same plane. The recess visually separates them, masking minor misalignments on their faces.

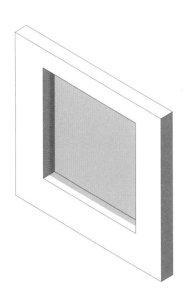

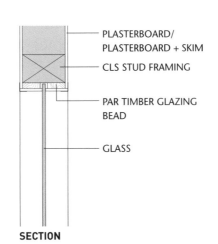

PLASTERBOARD/ PLASTERBOARD + SKIM

CLS STUD FRAMING

PAR TIMBER GLAZING BEAD

GLASS

SECTION

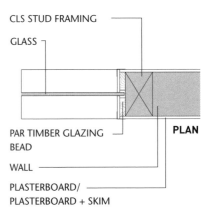

CLS STUD FRAMING

GLASS

PAR TIMBER GLAZING BEAD

WALL

PLASTERBOARD/ PLASTERBOARD + SKIM

PLAN

HIDDEN FRAME

The glass disappears into the wall. This option requires that the glass is inserted before the finishing of wall surfaces is completed, which may cause some complications during construction and more extensive work if replacement is necessary. Skim plaster should be finished against an expanded metal bead.

Joining glass sheets

The overall size of glass sheet that may be used in a project depends on the dimensions of the doors, and sometimes stairs, that give access to a site. It is usually possible, except with tight stair or corridor access, to use a single sheet of glass that can span the conventional, modern floor-to-ceiling height of 2400mm.

It is possible to make fairly innocuous joints to seal the junctions of glass sheets using a clear silicone strip, but these will be visible and are a compromise in the creation of an 'invisible' partition. Large glass panels have significant inherent strength, and while it is possible to join them with modern specialist adhesives it remains more usual to use metal connectors.

Metal joints

In tall spaces in particular it is often necessary to make both horizontal and vertical joints, and these must be structurally stable as they are unconnected to floors, walls or ceilings. Stainless steel is most often used because of its strength and appearance. There are a number of manufactured jointing elements that will provide the necessary structural integrity.

Glass sheets need to be pre-drilled to accommodate the screws and bolts. Holes should be larger than the diameter of the screw or bolt, to allow for adjustment on site and to absorb movement. Washers (metal or rubber, or both) should be an integral part of the element in order to cover the larger hole.

Flat clamps Jointing elements can be flat clamps, which may be standard, mass-produced items or can be designed to meet project-specific aesthetic criteria. All need to conform to basic principles of pre-drilled holes, for on-site adjustment, and resilient washers, to allow joints to be tightened without cracking the glass.

Metal 'finger' joints and glass fins Three-dimensional 'finger' joints give a degree of depth that helps brace the glass against impact along its length. This bracing can be increased if the projecting fingers are connected vertically to create a single bracing element. An alternative to using a metal connecting piece for this is the glass fin, fixed to the wall sheets by metal clamps or by the specialist adhesives that are increasingly used in glass structures.

FLAT CLAMPS
1–2 A flat plate, to which the corners of four sheets of glass are bolted, provides structural continuity. Joints may be sealed with translucent silicone filler.

METAL FINGER JOINTS
3–4 Steel or aluminium 'finger' units provide rigid connection between sheets of glass. The projection of the unit at right angles to the glass also gives lateral bracing.

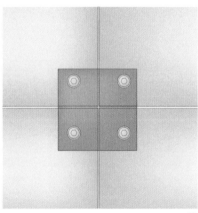

ELEVATION 1

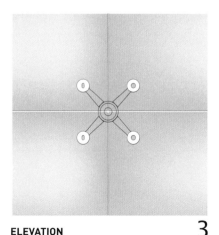

ELEVATION 3

GLASS WALL PANEL

FLAT METAL PLATE

PLAN 2

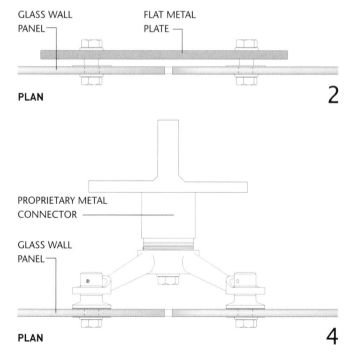

PROPRIETARY METAL CONNECTOR

GLASS WALL PANEL

PLAN 4

Lateral bracing

When a number of glass panels are connected in both their vertical and horizontal planes, the wall created will require lateral bracing to stiffen the joints against pressures exerted on its face. Vertical or horizontal fins, or both, fixed at right angles will provide a continuous connecting member between glazed panels, and a rigid skeleton that increases the effective structural depth of the wall plane and its resistance to lateral forces.

The fin can be a solid strip of metal, although this may be deemed visually obtrusive. The mass of metal may be reduced by cutting out areas that have no structural role, but the more common alternative is to substitute a fin of toughened glass, which can easily meet structural obligations with a minimal visual presence.

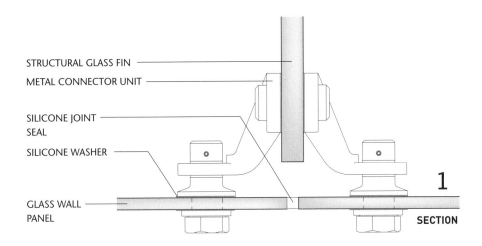

STRUCTURAL GLASS FIN

METAL CONNECTOR UNIT

SILICONE JOINT SEAL

SILICONE WASHER

GLASS WALL PANEL

1 **SECTION**

FIN FIXINGS
1 An adaptation of the finger joint connects a glass fin to the wall panels.
2–3 Flat plates connect two fins both vertically and horizontally to the wall panels.

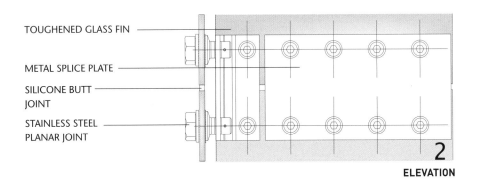

TOUGHENED GLASS FIN

METAL SPLICE PLATE

SILICONE BUTT JOINT

STAINLESS STEEL PLANAR JOINT

2 **ELEVATION**

LATERAL BRACING
4–5 Toughened glass can have significant structural strength and when used as a vertical or horizontal fin can provide lateral bracing.

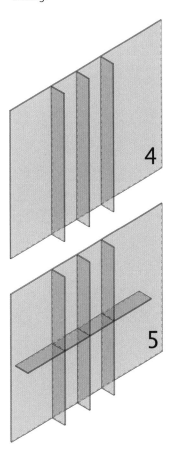

TOUGHENED GLASS PANEL

SILICONE WASHER

SILICONE BUTT JOINT

STAINLESS STEEL PLANAR BOLT

TOUGHENED FIN

3 **PLAN**

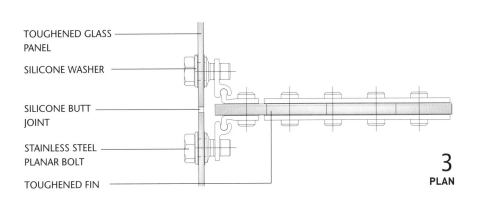

CHAPTER 4 DOORS

Basic principles

Doors manufactured for interiors are not required to cope with weather. Consequently, there is considerable freedom in the construction of the opening panels (or leaves) and the frames that trim wall openings and carry the hinges on which the leaves pivot. Essential principles of installation are important as the opening and shutting of door leaves subjects adjacent finishes to continuous impacts. If these principles are understood, there is scope for creative variations on standard solutions.

Standard materials and sizing

While leaves and frames may be manufactured from metals and plastics, it is normal to use timber. Hardwoods are favoured for the decorative qualities of their grains, while softwoods are usually painted. Leaves are seldom manufactured specifically for a project unless a significant aesthetic gesture is sought; they are almost invariably specified from the wide range of options offered by specialist manufacturers. They may be heavy, with solid panelled and framed timber, or extremely light, with a hollow core of honey-comb cardboard in between two skins of 3mm plywood or hardboard, glued to a perimeter 27 x 19mm softwood. Standard frame sections are also manufactured, and save construction time.

The core construction of leaves is often determined by their role as fire-resistant elements. Any upgrading can significantly increase their weight and thus influence decisions about frames and the type and number of hinges, and perhaps about the construction of supporting walls. The core construction of a wall, whether masonry or stud framed, is comparatively crude, and openings for doors reflect this. Widths of 700, 800 and 900mm wide and a height of 2000mm are easiest to achieve in the confusion of site construction. The more precise, factory-made dimensions of standard frames and door leaves are designed to fine-tune these raw openings. Leaves are typically 526, 626, 726 and 926mm wide and 2040mm high, and, with frame widths of 32mm, fill basic openings with a clearance of 2mm to allow opening and shutting. Internal leaves are 35 and 40mm thick (the former is more common). Internal fire doors are 44mm thick.

Door construction

Jambs and heads The word 'jamb' refers to vertical framing on each side of a door and 'head' to the horizontal framing on its upper edge. Both have the same section. Normally they are timber, which is easily adapted on site, but since dimensions for door frames are standardized, metal and plastic are viable – particularly in large, repetitive installations. The jamb's role is to make a

robust junction between the wall and the door opening, and to support the leaf.

Both the jambs and head are nailed or (particularly for metal studwork) screwed (often through wooden packing pieces that fill gaps between components) into the faces of the raw door opening. When a concrete lintel is used in masonry construction, it is sufficient to nail or screw the head to the vertical jambs. The frame should project far enough beyond the faces of the unfinished wall to align with the finishing material – for example, it should project 12.5mm for plasterboard and skim.

Architraves The junction between frame and wall finish is most vulnerable to cracking; the traditional solution is to mask it with a cover strip: the 'architrave'. This is the most common and reliable solution and, while elaborate carved examples have largely disappeared, modestly sized and moulded strips deal with the problem effectively.

It is possible to fix the architrave to the frame directly, though it is better practice to insert a 13mm treated softwood 'ground' as a buffer to absorb hammer impact and to nail through or into. Fixing with screws or glue will not cause impact damage but the recesses of screw heads will require more filling before painting.

Junctions of vertical jamb and horizontal head architraves should be cut with 45 degree mitres so that the lines of mouldings, no matter how simple, continue unbroken and no end grain is exposed. They are normally carried to the floor and provide a face against which the sawn end of the skirting may be finished. Skirting should not be wider than the architrave, so that it may be finished against it without exposing the end grain.

Fixing architraves Given advances in adhesive quality, mouldings are often glued in position. However, given the unevenness of existing surfaces, it is sensible to use a nail or screw fixing. With these, the heads should be sunk below the surface of the moulding and the shallow indentation filled, sanded and lost in the painting process.

Stops The 'stop' is the element of frame against which a door closes. It need not be continuous around the opening, but usually is, for visual coherence and reduction of draughts or noise. It may be nailed, screwed or glued to the main frame element – this may be governed by fire regulations. For a high performance, the frame and stop need to be cut from a single piece of wood – an expensive option. The stop should be set back by the width of the door leaf from the face of the frame, so that frame and door face line through on the side that the door opens.

Hinges

Hinges are also standard components, but it is important to specify type and number. Heavy doors, with extensive glazing or a high fire resistance, will require more than the normal pair of hinges. Some doors, again often for reasons of fire resistance, will need to be self-closing and some hinges can meet this requirement, either operating by gravity or springs. They may not have the strength of a conventional wall-mounted door closer but, if regulations permit their use, they are more discreet.

TRADITIONAL DOOR-FRAME CONSTRUCTION

The architrave covers the joint between plaster and frame, which is liable to crack and fracture, and provides a vertical face against which the skirting is finished. The batten provides a solid connection between architrave and stud frame, and protects the plaster during nailing.

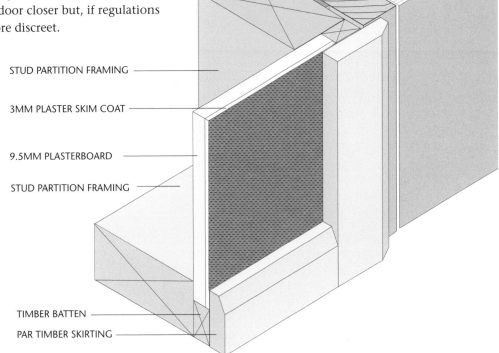

STUD PARTITION FRAMING

3MM PLASTER SKIM COAT

9.5MM PLASTERBOARD

STUD PARTITION FRAMING

TIMBER BATTEN

PAR TIMBER SKIRTING

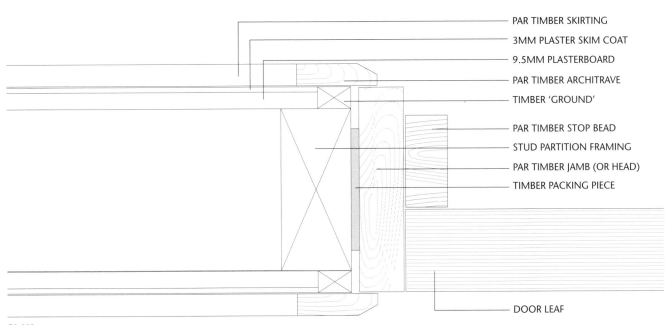

PAR TIMBER SKIRTING

3MM PLASTER SKIM COAT

9.5MM PLASTERBOARD

PAR TIMBER ARCHITRAVE

TIMBER 'GROUND'

PAR TIMBER STOP BEAD

STUD PARTITION FRAMING

PAR TIMBER JAMB (OR HEAD)

TIMBER PACKING PIECE

DOOR LEAF

PLAN

Modern detailing for doors

While the timber members of a door frame are comparatively robust, wall surfaces, typically finished in plaster or plasterboard, are more vulnerable. It is standard practice, therefore, to use proprietary metal plaster stops and beads to provide a protective edge to plaster surfaces or to create a shadow gap.

The shadow-gap option omits architraves, creating a separation between frame and wall that eliminates the possibility of cracks or minor misalignments. It enhances the perception of the wall as the dominant visual element and the door as a secondary insertion. There are two basic configurations: the front edges of the frame may align, or appear to do so, with the faces of the finished walls; or the frame may sit back within the thickness of the wall, further emphasizing the latter's visual dominance.

Preventing problems

The shadow gap poses problems with exposed edges of plaster or plasterboard surfaces and junctions of skirtings and frames. They may be strengthened with expanded metal beads for plaster finishes, or metal reinforcement strips for drywall construction. When the dimensions of proprietary beads are considered at the start of the process, neat alignments are simple to achieve and, if a strategy is evolved for finishing skirting boards against frames, exposed timber end grains can be avoided.

A range of expanded metal plaster stops offers detailing options, and may be used with 13mm three-coat or 3mm skim-coat finishes. They are a dull grey in their natural state, but can be painted to match adjacent surfaces and to be perceived as integral to them.

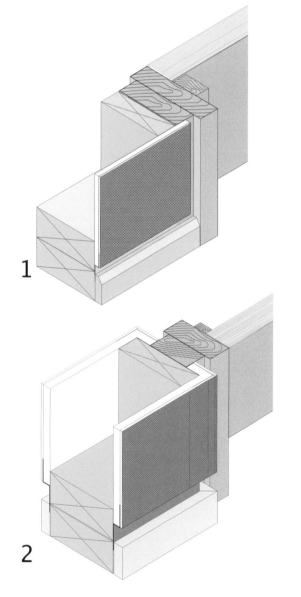

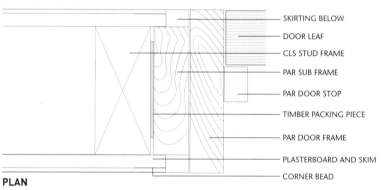

PLAN

- SKIRTING BELOW
- DOOR LEAF
- CLS STUD FRAME
- PAR SUB FRAME
- PAR DOOR STOP
- TIMBER PACKING PIECE
- PAR DOOR FRAME
- PLASTERBOARD AND SKIM
- CORNER BEAD

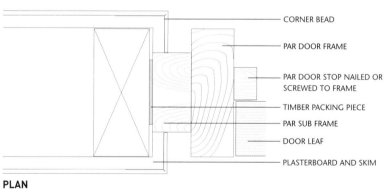

PLAN

- CORNER BEAD
- PAR DOOR FRAME
- PAR DOOR STOP NAILED OR SCREWED TO FRAME
- TIMBER PACKING PIECE
- PAR SUB FRAME
- DOOR LEAF
- PLASTERBOARD AND SKIM

SHADOW-GAP FRAME

1 A frame with a width that corresponds to that of the wall can be given visual independence with a timber ground that makes a shadow gap between the frame and wall.

2 A door with no fire-resistance obligations can sit back within the width of a standard wall thickness. The frame can be fixed directly to the structure of the wall, but the ground creates a shadow gap that visually separates wall and frame.

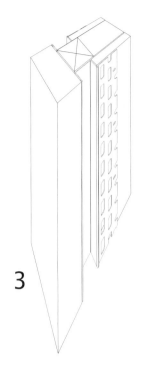

3

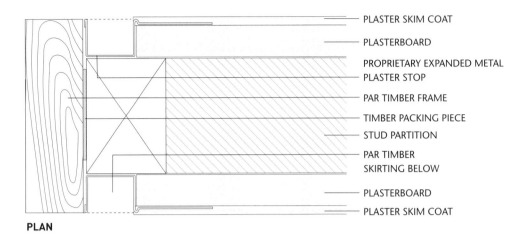

PLASTER SKIM COAT

PLASTERBOARD

PROPRIETARY EXPANDED METAL
PLASTER STOP

PAR TIMBER FRAME

TIMBER PACKING PIECE

STUD PARTITION

PAR TIMBER
SKIRTING BELOW

PLASTERBOARD

PLASTER SKIM COAT

PLAN

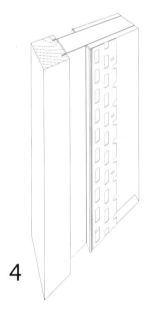

4

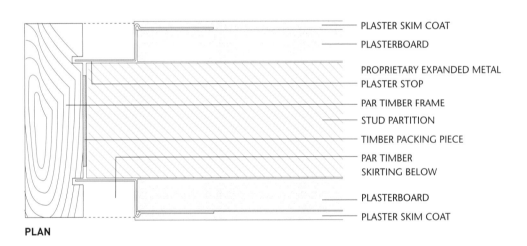

PLASTER SKIM COAT

PLASTERBOARD

PROPRIETARY EXPANDED METAL
PLASTER STOP

PAR TIMBER FRAME

STUD PARTITION

TIMBER PACKING PIECE

PAR TIMBER
SKIRTING BELOW

PLASTERBOARD

PLASTER SKIM COAT

PLAN

EXPANDED METAL PLASTER STOPS

3 The expanded metal plaster stop provides a straight line against which a plaster skim coat can be precisely finished and a ready-made shadow gap that, when painted, is visually indistinguishable from the painted plaster and frame. The point where it touches the frame will, however, be likely to show as a light line. It will also be difficult to line through the edge of the stop and the frame exactly.

4 If grooves are made in the frame to accommodate the expanded metal plaster stop, the resulting detail will better avoid misalignment and make it easier to leave the frame unpainted while painting the stop and wall.

TIP ARCHITRAVES

Plaster stops and beads offer accurate edges, but their very precision means that they may not sit satisfactorily with the imprecision of existing construction. In the typically unsympathetic conditions on site, there are difficulties in making satisfactory junctions using what are comparatively inflexible metal strips. The traditional architrave, which evolved to deal with areas of construction that are vulnerable and difficult to finish to a high standard, is worth considering for all such locations.

Sliding doors

These are useful to open up or combine spaces, but should look equally good open or closed and probably, in either case, be perceived as an integral part of the adjacent walls.

Sliding mechanisms

There is no need to design these, as a wide range is offered by specialist manufacturers. The priority is to integrate generic versions into the fabric of an interior. Some are designed to be visible but it is usual to incorporate them, when open, in the depth of the supporting wall, increasing its width if necessary. The structure and fixing of the sliding mechanism should be robust enough to support the weight of the door – glazed ones are particularly heavy.

Recesses

When thickening a wall to accommodate the mechanism, a recess for the door can be made by adding additional stud framing. Alternatively, a slot to house the open door leaf may be created. Again, this simply needs logical reinterpretation of the principles of stud-wall construction. It could involve two parallel sets of stud framing, but there are manufactured solutions that confine the overall wall width to standard dimensions and even facilitate the use of curved doors in curved partitions.

Floor channels

Sliding doors must be stabilized at floor level to avoid swinging at right angles to the opening. This can be achieved by a floor channel in which a guide peg or wheel may run. Channels create practical problems by collecting dirt, and aesthetic ones when the metal channel is incompatible with a floor finish. It is possible to minimize this by using a metal channel in the base of the door and a floor 'pin' with which the channel will engage. The door overlaps and conceals the pin in open and closed positions. If doors are heavy, it may be sensible to provide wheels in the lower edge to transfer loading directly to the floor. These act as guides within a floor recess, which need not be more than a few millimetres deep as the door's weight will reduce the tendency to swing.

Sound insulation

Sliding doors need clearance on all sides to run easily, creating problems if higher levels of performance are required, particularly in soundproofing. Required standards will probably not be met by conventional components, so the containing shell may need to be adapted to accommodate a proprietary option. Sound transference can be reduced by pneumatic buffers. Once a door is locked in position, these can be inflated to seal gaps.

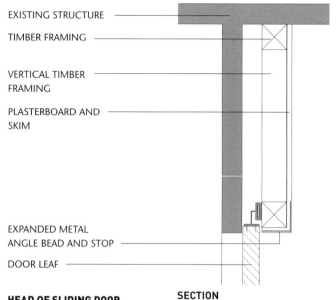

EXISTING STRUCTURE

TIMBER FRAMING

VERTICAL TIMBER FRAMING

PLASTERBOARD AND SKIM

EXPANDED METAL ANGLE BEAD AND STOP

DOOR LEAF

SECTION

HEAD OF SLIDING DOOR
Some proprietary sliding-door mechanisms are designed to remain visible, but more utilitarian models may be specified when the intention is to build a structure out from the existing wall to form a recess to house the door head.

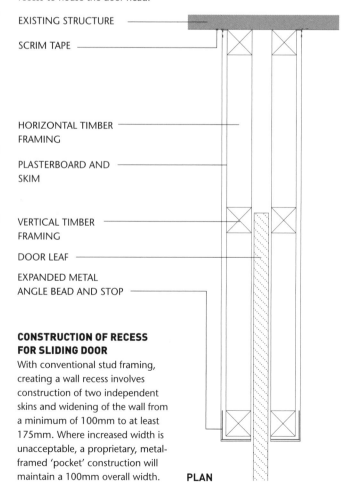

EXISTING STRUCTURE

SCRIM TAPE

HORIZONTAL TIMBER FRAMING

PLASTERBOARD AND SKIM

VERTICAL TIMBER FRAMING

DOOR LEAF

EXPANDED METAL ANGLE BEAD AND STOP

CONSTRUCTION OF RECESS FOR SLIDING DOOR
With conventional stud framing, creating a wall recess involves construction of two independent skins and widening of the wall from a minimum of 100mm to at least 175mm. Where increased width is unacceptable, a proprietary, metal-framed 'pocket' construction will maintain a 100mm overall width.

PLAN

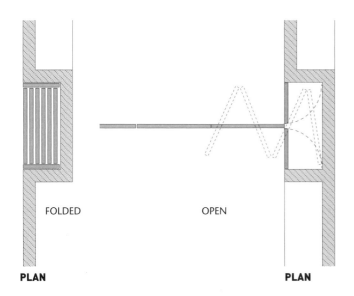

FOLDED   OPEN

PLAN   **PLAN**

Folding sliding doors

It is not unusual to have multiple sliding doors, usually relying on sliding/folding mechanisms, to subdivide large spaces. It is sensible to research proprietary solutions and to accommodate their practical requirements at the beginning of the design process. The basic principles are the same as for single panels but, because of their size, their subdivision and detailing will inevitably have a significant influence on the detailing of other surfaces.

It is important to consider how the opened door panels may be integrated into the fabric of the space. This normally involves the thickening of walls or the introduction of storage recesses, and requires planning rather than detailing ingenuity since the principles of the wall construction will be conventional.

FOLDING SLIDING DOORS
A wall widened to house sliding door panels creates opportunities for storage (left). Hinged panels close the recess when the doors are extended (right).

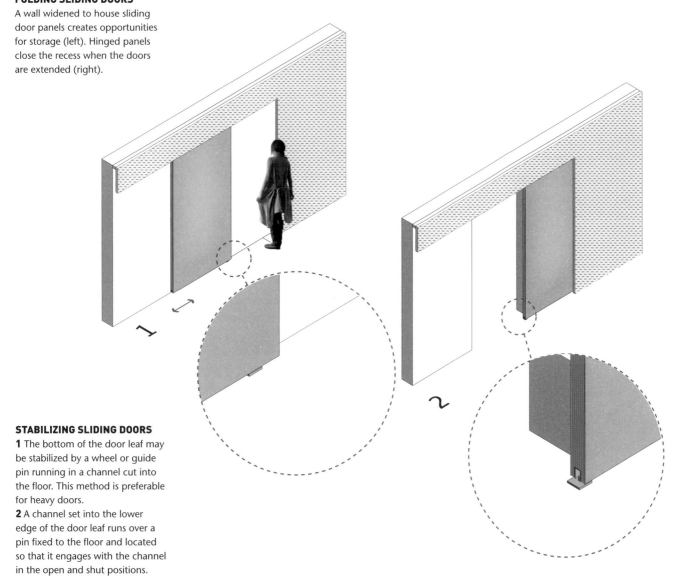

STABILIZING SLIDING DOORS
1 The bottom of the door leaf may be stabilized by a wheel or guide pin running in a channel cut into the floor. This method is preferable for heavy doors.
2 A channel set into the lower edge of the door leaf runs over a pin fixed to the floor and located so that it engages with the channel in the open and shut positions.

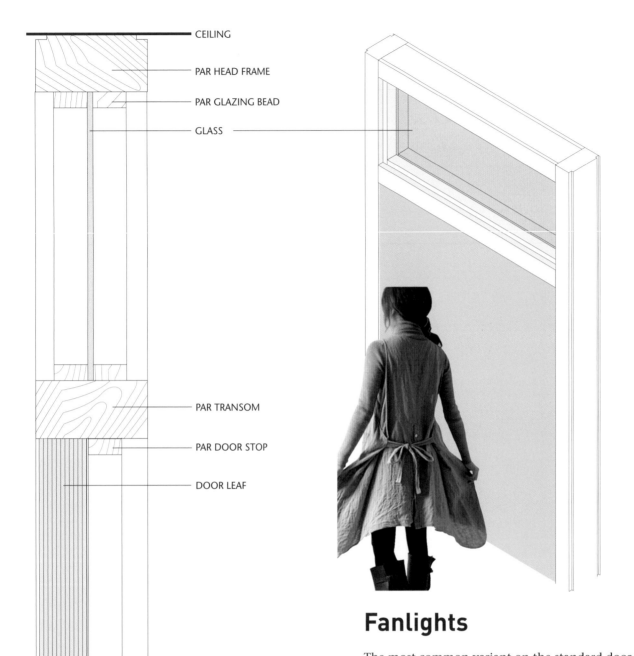

CEILING

PAR HEAD FRAME

PAR GLAZING BEAD

GLASS

PAR TRANSOM

PAR DOOR STOP

DOOR LEAF

SECTION

DOOR WITH FANLIGHT
The frame continues to ceiling
height, with a recess all round to
disguise uneven wall and ceiling
finishes. The intermediate frame is
inserted to respond to a standard
door-leaf height. The area above
the door is glazed conventionally.
However, if the door is fire-rated
then the glass will have to achieve
the required rating. In most
projects this will involve the use of
'wired' glass.

Fanlights

The most common variant on the standard door is that
with a window, or 'fanlight', above it. This is such a
commonly used option that it has become a standard
item in most door manufacturers' catalogues, to fit the
most common floor-to-ceiling heights of 2300mm and
2400mm found in most newly built interiors. It may well
be necessary to produce one-off specials to fit the non-
standard dimensions of existing buildings.

The fanlight offers a way of carrying a limited
amount of borrowed light to corridors as well as visually
extending the door element from floor to ceiling. The
principle is simple. The side frame extends to the full
height of the room with an intermediate 'head' frame to
receive the top of the door and support the glass. Stops
and glazing beads are applied using standard techniques
and fixings.

Glass in doors

The area of glass in a door can vary from small vision panels to an entire single sheet of glass. All glass used must be strong enough to withstand not only fire but the impact caused by vigorous use. In all but the very smallest panels it will be necessary to use reinforced glass.

Wired glass

The most common and economical reinforcement is wired glass, clear or translucent, with a – usually square – mesh embedded in its core. The fine mesh holds the glass together if it cracks as the result of impact or fire, meeting approved standards. A common aesthetic problem with wired glass is that the core mesh does not necessarily conform to the geometry of the glass panel, so lines on the edge will not necessarily be parallel to the framing.

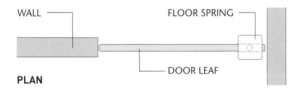

WALL — FLOOR SPRING —

DOOR LEAF

PLAN

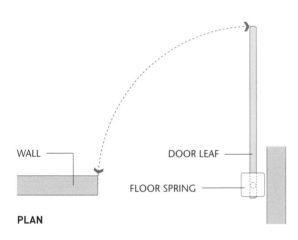

WALL — DOOR LEAF —

FLOOR SPRING —

PLAN

UNFRAMED GLASS DOOR WITH PIVOT HINGES RECESSED INTO FLOOR AND CEILING PLANES
A door with pivot hinges on its top and bottom edges does not need frames, and when open allows walls to read as unbroken planes.

VISION PANELS
An approved window to an escape stair in a public building, using wired glass.

Vision panels

These are often a practical requirement (preventing collisions in busy areas) or a safety requirement (allowing the inhabitants of rooms to be aware of events beyond their walls – an integral element in fire-escape provision). Clear or translucent, toughened, fire-resistant glass meets practical demands but is more expensive than wired glass.

Unframed glass doors

It is possible to use an unframed glass panel as a door leaf and to exploit the aesthetic impact of this, avoiding supporting framing and stops by hinging the panel on its top and bottom edges. This solution cannot meet fire-resistance requirements and the glass panel will be expensive, but the principal problem is likely to be housing the floor- and ceiling-level hinges. Timber structures are unlikely to provide robust fixing points, and it may be impossible to cut sufficiently into concrete floors and ceilings to make a satisfactory connection. Appropriate hinges are standard products from specialist manufacturers, often with springs to hold panels in the closed and open positions. The designer's responsibility is to detail the work necessary for their installation. It is also prudent to consult the supplier for advice on specific installations.

Doors in glazed screens

When a wall or a substantial floor-to-ceiling wall section is glazed, it is generally referred to as a 'glazed screen'. It will often include a door, probably glazed but sometimes solid. It is normal practice for such large screens to be manufactured in sections off site, in a joinery workshop with specialist machinery, to ensure a more accurate and soundly constructed product. The complete element will then be assembled on site.

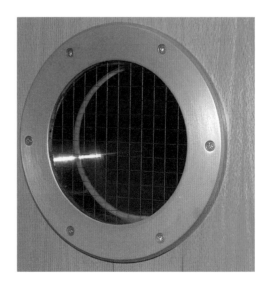

Non-standard doors

Non-standard-sized doors need to be made in specialist workshops. All doors experience significant internal tensions: being asymmetrically hung, comparatively thin and effectively two-dimensional, they have a tendency to warp along their length. To counter this, which becomes more critical as doors get bigger, timber must be well seasoned and joints precisely made and glued.

Tall doors

With tall doors, which can stretch from floor to ceiling, the door leaf is often kept narrow to accentuate its relative height. Since larger doors are liable to be heavier and more likely to warp, it is normal practice to use three hinges instead of two.

Since a floor-to-ceiling door is used to minimize the separation implied by a conventional door opening, it is often considered desirable to eliminate the door frame. This can be achieved by floor- and ceiling-level hinges connected to the top and bottom edges of the door leaf. When fully opened, these will set a leaf further out from the edge of the wall. Stops can be built discreetly into the ceiling or wall so that they appear to be integral to those elements rather than part of the door installation.

Fixed panels

Where the primary concern is for a visual floor-to-ceiling element, the section of wall above the door head may be omitted and a thinner fixed panel, typically a composite timber board or glazed panel, inserted to extend the door recess to the ceiling. The framing of the door can be extended to incorporate the upper panels.

Wide doors

If a door is particularly wide it is often expedient to add a small wheel at right angles to its length, or a ball castor, near the unsupported end. Either may be discreetly housed in the width of the bottom rail of the leaf. The continuous action of these can wear a visible trail in the floor and, with heavy doors, it is not uncommon to insert a metal track, usually brass, in or on the floor surface.

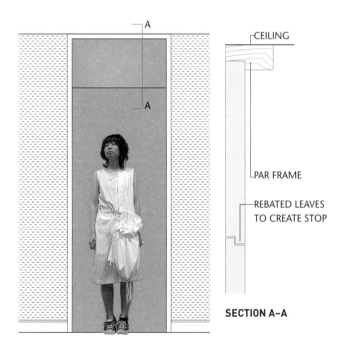

SECTION A–A

PLAN B–B

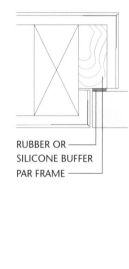

RUBBER OR
SILICONE BUFFER
PAR FRAME

FRAMED DOOR WITH PANEL
The jambs stretch from floor to ceiling. The door leaf can be split with a rebated stop at conventional door-head height.

TALL FRAMELESS DOORS
The door leaf sits within a wall recess. Additional framing supports a rubber or silicone buffer that protects plasterwork. Conventional side hinges may be replaced by floor- and ceiling-mounted pivots to leave plaster surfaces unbroken.

Fire regulations for doors

One of the most important considerations in designing or specifying doors is meeting the requirements of relevant fire regulations. These lay down minimum periods for which door leaves, and their frames, should be able to withstand fire and contain flames and smoke within the area of an outbreak. The period of resistance varies according to the activities contained within the room and its relationship to the recognized escape route – a designated path protected by walls and door construction from fire and smoke within the area of an outbreak.

Door leaves The most common periods of resistance specified are half an hour and an hour. Door leaves are produced to meet these and more, often by variations in the composition of the core. For a designer, it is normally a matter of specifying levels of resistance, as most door leaves are mass-produced. Regulations also require that some doors leading to escape routes have vision panels. While it is possible to design a one-off fire-rated door, the process is complex – it may be difficult to justify the cost of time in design and manufacture. If attempted, then close liaison with the fire officer responsible for final approval is vital throughout production.

Door frames These may be bought to meet minimum requirements, but since the requirements are less complex than for leaves it is possible to experiment more freely with form. The most significant criterion is that frames should meet minimum dimensional standards, relating primarily to the thickness of door leaves. While frames may be cut out of solid timber, there is a concession that the stop on a frame providing half an hour's fire resistance can be a separate piece fixed with screws.

Frameless doors Where frameless doors have to meet a fire-resistance standard, this can be achieved by the insertion of 'intumescent strips' into the edges of the leaf. Heat from a fire will cause these to expand and fill gaps between leaf and frame to prevent the passage of smoke and flames.

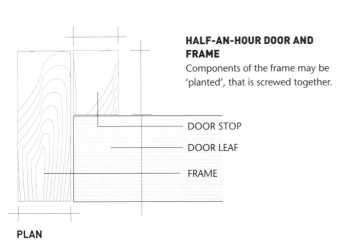

HALF-AN-HOUR DOOR AND FRAME
Components of the frame may be 'planted', that is screwed together.

DOOR STOP

DOOR LEAF

FRAME

PLAN

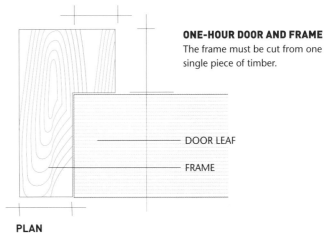

ONE-HOUR DOOR AND FRAME
The frame must be cut from one single piece of timber.

DOOR LEAF

FRAME

PLAN

TIP BEING DISCREET: FRAMELESS DOORS

Rebated meeting edges allow one half of a frameless double door, when locked shut, to act as a stop for the half in use. An intumescent strip, which expands when exposed to heat, incorporated into a groove in the edge of the door leaf will ensure that necessary fire regulations are met.

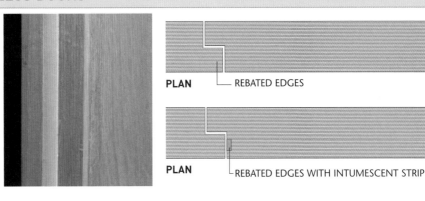

PLAN REBATED EDGES

PLAN REBATED EDGES WITH INTUMESCENT STRIP

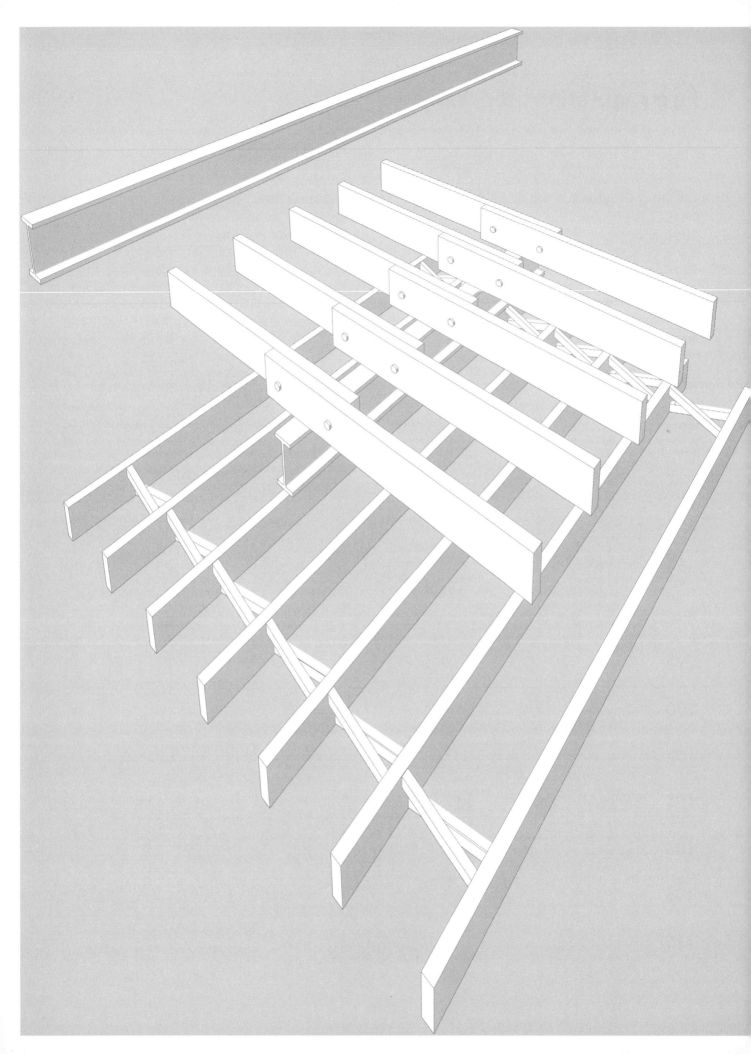

CHAPTER 5 FLOORS

Solid ground floors

Solid ground floors are laid directly on to the earth. The earliest and simplest version of these merely involved compacting of the earth, with excavation or filling to create a solid, level surface. This was very vulnerable to wear, which persistently created dust. Its durability was improved by the addition of a more processed finishing layer – often of brick, tile or wood – although the last of these was vulnerable to moisture that penetrated the earthern subfloor.

More recent solid ground floors have used poured concrete, which is easy to level, to create a durable surface. Standard construction involves the removal of topsoil (because it contains organic matter), to reach the inert subsoil stratum. The site level is made up with loose stones, known as 'hardcore', over which is poured approximately 100–150mm of 'oversite' concrete.

Damp-proof membranes

The gradual penetration of damp through the porous concrete is the greatest problem with any solid ground floor. The intention must be to create a waterproof barrier to hold back the moisture that will damage most interior finishes.

It is now accepted practice to incorporate within the poured concrete a damp-proof membrane (or DPM), an impervious layer that prevents rising moisture penetrating the fabric of the building. This is either laid as a plastic sheet over the subfloor, alongside insulation material, or painted onto it. A 50mm-deep fine concrete screed is poured on to the damp-proof membrane and vibrated mechanically to produce a smooth surface to receive a range of flooring materials.

Repairs to poured concrete It is important when making any changes to an interior not to damage the damp-proof membrane. While it is possible to make an impervious repair to a damaged membrane, the process is messy, involving significant cutting back and making good of both the membrane and the concrete floor. Sometimes damage is unavoidable, as when new columns are inserted to support additional upper levels.

The particular problem with such remedial work is that shortcomings in the difficult repair work often do not become apparent until enough time has elapsed for moisture to penetrate the joints of old and new membrane sections. Given the speed with which most interior work is carried out, new finishes may have been installed, and damaged, before evidence of faults appears.

Installing new damp-proof membranes When an older floor does not have a damp-proof membrane it is worth trying, and sometimes possible, to lay a membrane directly on top of the existing top surface and underneath the new finish. This strategy may determine the choice of floor finish. A thin, interlocking engineered board, which can be laid loose, is particularly suitable. It is important to turn the new membrane as far up the wall as possible, behind a skirting or wall finish, and it should be bonded to the damp-proof course within the wall to create an unbroken barrier against all moisture penetration.

Damp-proof courses

The damp-proof membrane is generally joined to a damp-proof course (or DPC), another impervious membrane built horizontally into one course of brickwork or blockwork of the external and internal walls to prevent moisture rising vertically through them.

Without an efficient damp-proof course, damp can rise through the fabric of the walls and degrade wall finishes. The connection between this and the floor membrane is critical in maintaining a complete seal. If a damp-proof membrane has not been installed, then it is unlikely that a damp-proof course will have been.

Injecting into masonry Where no damp-proof course exists it is possible to inject a fluid into all masonry walls that will make them impervious. Such work, which involves the boring of small holes about 5mm in diameter into the wall to ensure penetration of fluid to its core, is normally carried out by specialists. It is worth seeking advice from a number of specialist companies before undertaking any damp-proofing work.

AVOIDING DAMP IN FLOORS AND WALLS

The creation of a cavity within the width of an external wall has become common practice, and ensures that any moisture that penetrates the external skin runs down its inside face and is expelled through apertures near ground level. In the case of brickwork these are vertical joints left free of mortar. It is important that this ejection route is maintained – if the level of exterior finish is allowed to rise above the internal floor level, water will be retained in the cavity and breach the damp-proof membrane. A level 50mm concrete screed will normally be laid on top of 100mm of 'oversite' concrete, with the membrane between them. It is essential that moisture from below the floor slab should not be allowed to rise through the inner wall skin. This is prevented by a sealed connection between floor and wall membrances.

OUTER BRICK SKIN

CAVITY

DAMP-PROOF COURSE (MINIMUM 150MM ABOVE GROUND LEVEL)

INNER BRICK SKIN

CONCRETE BACKFILL (TO PREVENT WATER COLLECTING IN CAVITY)

DAMP-PROOF MEMBRANE

FLOOR FINISH

50MM CONCRETE SCREED

150MM 'OVERSITE' CONCRETE

HARDCORE (MINIMUM 150MM OF RUBBLE TO EVEN OUT GROUND LEVELS)

SECTION

Suspended ground floors

'Suspended' ground floors offer a means of avoiding rising damp and of dealing with significant changes of site level without having to carry in and compact a large volume of hardcore.

Construction

Essentially the same methods of construction are used as for upper floors, with timber joists at 400mm centres supporting timber floorboards. The size of timbers may be reduced by constructing 'dwarf' walls below the floor, which will reduce spans. Timbers are liable to come into contact with moisture wherever they meet supporting elements. While isolation with impervious materials, such as strips of felt or even slate, is simple to achieve where joists meet dwarf walls, it is more difficult where joists are built into external walls.

Ventilation

It is important that spaces under suspended floors are well ventilated as localized rotting can occur at points where timbers meet external walls; this will result in subsidence of floors. Care should be taken that any ventilation grilles built into external walls remain clear after work is completed to ensure continued air circulation.

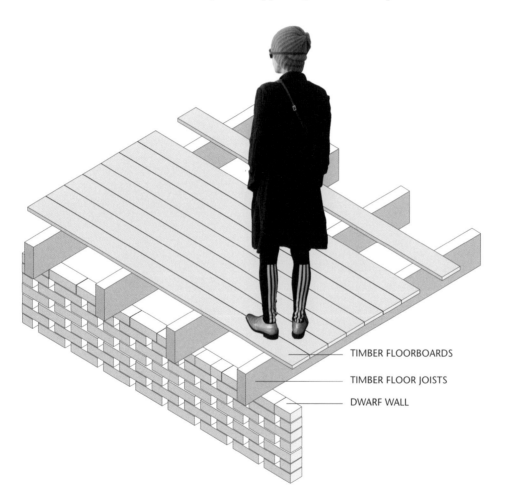

TIMBER FLOORBOARDS

TIMBER FLOOR JOISTS

DWARF WALL

DWARF WALLS
Dwarf walls reduce the span and therefore the size of joists needed for a suspended timber ground floor. The gaps in the brickwork allow air to circulate, reducing the risk of rot.

JOIST SPACING
Joists should be equally spaced, usually at 400mm centres for compatibility with standard composite-board sheets. The spacing of the final joists should be reduced in response to site dimensions (and should never be increased above 400mm).

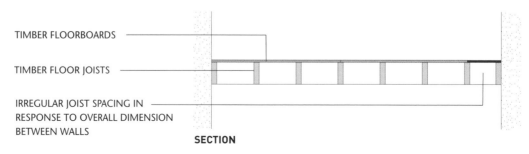

TIMBER FLOORBOARDS

TIMBER FLOOR JOISTS

IRREGULAR JOIST SPACING IN RESPONSE TO OVERALL DIMENSION BETWEEN WALLS

SECTION

Upper floors

Timber floors

Timber joists offer the simplest and most common method of constructing upper floors. Typically, joists span the shorter room dimension. They are normally at 400mm centres with wooden floorboards nailed to them at right angles to create a comparatively monolithic structure. The width of joists is normally 50mm but the depth varies – the longer the span, the deeper the joist. Longer, deeper joists normally have cross-bracing at approximately 1200mm intervals to prevent distortion along their length.

Altering existing timber floors
Even when an existing floor is sound, a designer will often encounter difficulties ensuring its suitability to support a change of use, either because its structural capacity is unknown or because the cautious statutory values ascribed to it for calculation purposes will fail to meet loadbearing requirements.

It is always possible to find a solution by making significant changes, but to do so will often require elaborate, costly amendments to floor structures and the elements that support them. Such changes will require the contribution of a structural engineer who will be able to suggest solutions and provide the calculations to satisfy local authorities, but the extent of work required may well make a project economically unviable.

Beams and columns
Deep timber joists can span up to six or seven metres comfortably. However, with greater spans or heavy loadings normal practice is to reduce spans with beams, which in turn may be supported on columns, each of which will require a foundation pad. Existing beams and columns are usually made of cast iron or steel, with timber joists resting on top of the beams or on their lower flanges. Again, it is difficult to justify ambitious loadbearing capacities for columns and beams.

Openings
When making openings in suspended timber floors, to insert a new staircase for example, it is sensible to contain the new opening within an existing 'bay' – the area contained within adjacent beams. Cutting through or removing existing beams will destroy the integrity of the whole structure and the symmetrical loading of existing columns, thereby distorting the forces within them. Generally it makes sense to remove as few joists as possible and it is therefore best to run the long side of any opening parallel to the direction of the joists.

Existing concrete floors

Two alternatives to structural floor timbers are reinforced-concrete floor slabs and shallow vaults, often with a core of hollow clay 'pots'. Both are constructed in situ and supported on beams along each edge.

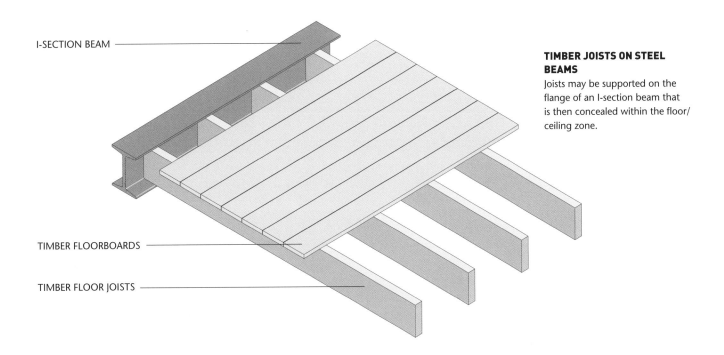

I-SECTION BEAM

TIMBER FLOORBOARDS

TIMBER FLOOR JOISTS

TIMBER JOISTS ON STEEL BEAMS
Joists may be supported on the flange of an I-section beam that is then concealed within the floor/ceiling zone.

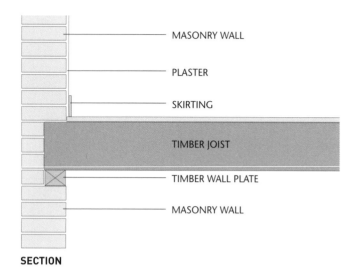

MASONRY WALL

PLASTER

SKIRTING

TIMBER JOIST

TIMBER WALL PLATE

MASONRY WALL

SECTION

Timber joists

Joists are the beams that support the components (such as timber floorboards and plasterboard sheets) that make up the planes of floors and ceilings. Their depth varies according to the distance between the structures that support them. Those used in ceilings are not as deep as those for floors, as they do not support the additional loadings of furniture and people. They are usually 50mm wide, but can vary from 38 to 63mm. Sizes for depth and width can be identified using tables issued by the statutory bodies controlling building standards.

In traditional timber construction, joists come into direct contact with the brick walls that support them. They may be built into the brickwork or carried on the projecting upper surface of a wider wall. If moisture permeates the brickwork, either directly from the exterior face or by capillary action from the foundations, it may transfer to, and cause rot in, the embedded end of joists. In modern timber construction, joists will normally be supported on 'joist hangers'. These are galvanized sleeves built into a mortar course in brickwork or blockwork to keep the ends of joists free from contact with exterior walls during construction, and to allow bricklayers and carpenters to work independently of each other.

RESTING JOISTS ON WALLS
The width of wall may be increased by half a brick thickness to provide a 'shelf' to support floor joists. These may rest on, and be nailed to, 'wall plates', which are lengths of timbers bedded in mortar on top of the projecting brickwork. While this allows air to circulate around the ends of joists, reducing the risk of rot, it does not eliminate the danger of rot spreading from the wall plate.

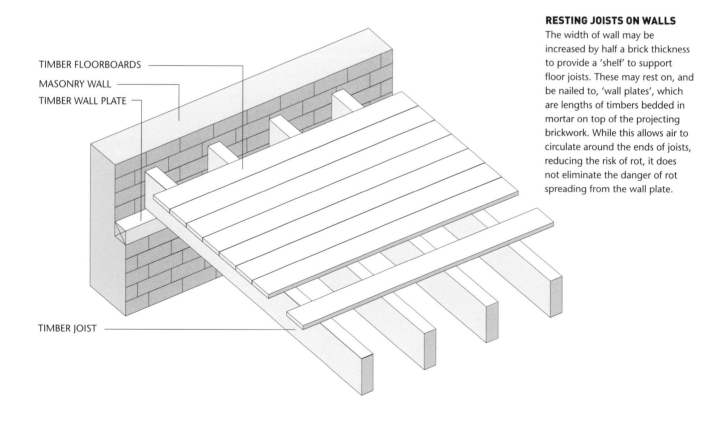

TIMBER FLOORBOARDS

MASONRY WALL

TIMBER WALL PLATE

TIMBER JOIST

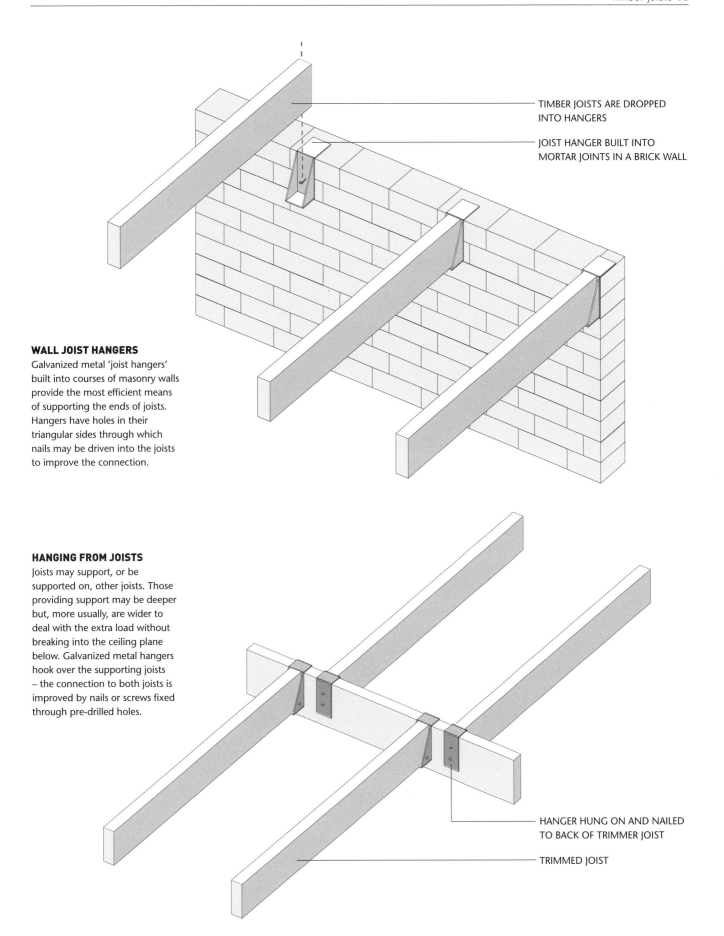

TIMBER JOISTS ARE DROPPED
INTO HANGERS

JOIST HANGER BUILT INTO
MORTAR JOINTS IN A BRICK WALL

WALL JOIST HANGERS

Galvanized metal 'joist hangers'
built into courses of masonry walls
provide the most efficient means
of supporting the ends of joists.
Hangers have holes in their
triangular sides through which
nails may be driven into the joists
to improve the connection.

HANGING FROM JOISTS

Joists may support, or be
supported on, other joists. Those
providing support may be deeper
but, more usually, are wider to
deal with the extra load without
breaking into the ceiling plane
below. Galvanized metal hangers
hook over the supporting joists
– the connection to both joists is
improved by nails or screws fixed
through pre-drilled holes.

HANGER HUNG ON AND NAILED
TO BACK OF TRIMMER JOIST

TRIMMED JOIST

Timber rot

One of the most important things to look for when assessing the condition of an existing building is evidence of wet and dry rot. Dry rot is perhaps more insidious since it can travel far into a structure, while wet rot is localized at a place where moisture has penetrated the building fabric. Since it is seldom possible to examine concealed areas of a building before it has been purchased, problems hidden within the depth of floor and ceiling voids often only come to light when work has started on a project, and are difficult to tackle without removing large areas of floor and ceiling finishes.

Treating the problem
Both wet and dry rot tend to start at points where timber joists are built into saturated solid masonry walls, which prevents moisture that had reached the timber from drying out.

When rot is identified, affected timbers can be cut out to a distance of about 1500mm beyond the last visible evidence of deterioration. This necessitates supporting, or 'shoring up', the unsupported ends of cut joists while new sections of clean timber are bolted, and reinforced with timber connectors, to the ends of the old joists with an overlap of at least 900mm.

Usually if joists are rotted then the wall plate on which they sit will also be affected and will need to be replaced, again cutting back 1500mm beyond any evidence of damage. All timber used in building should now be specified as having been treated against rot with a pressure impregnating process.

CUTTING BACK JOISTS
When rot has been identified, timber must be cut back at least 1500mm beyond any signs of damage. During work, sawn-off joists should be protected by props to the floor below.

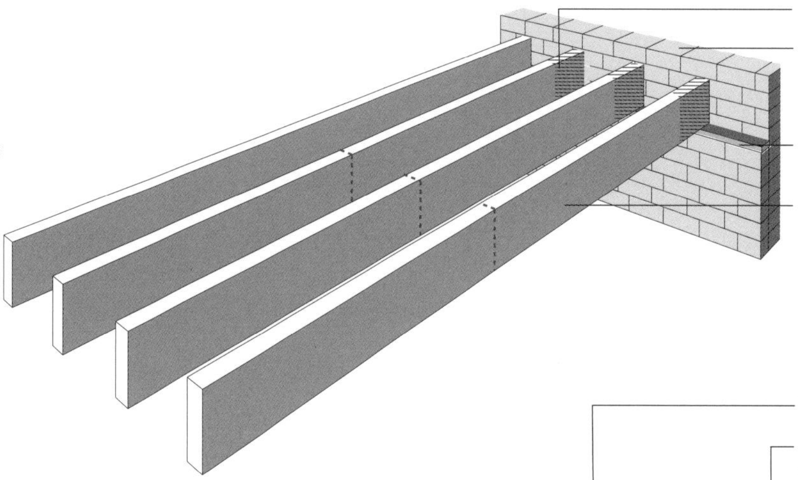

INSERTING NEW SECTIONS
Joists may be reinstated by using treated extension pieces bolted into the sound ends, overlapping by at least 900mm. Timber connectors should be used at bolt positions to spread and strengthen the connection.

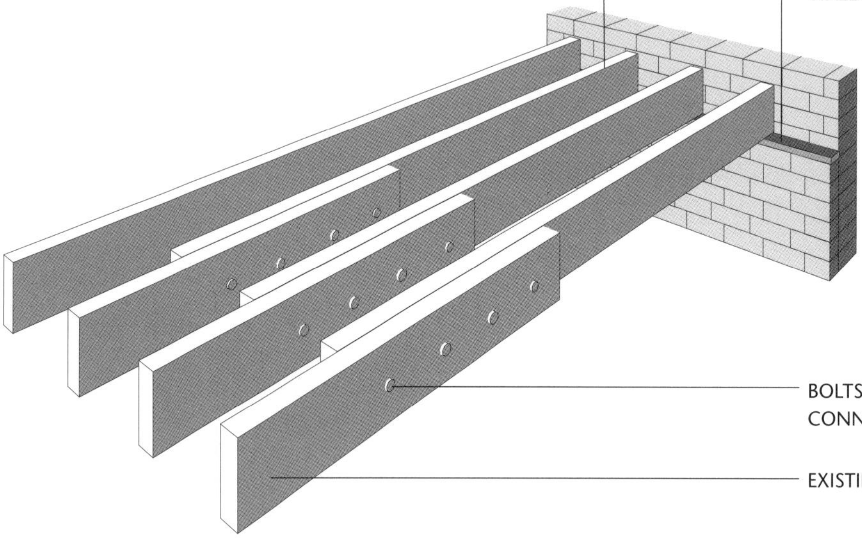

AREA OF ROTTED TIMBER

BRICK WALL

TIMBER WALL PLATE

TIMBER JOIST

NEW TIMBER JOIST

NEW TIMBER WALL PLATE

BOLTS WITH TIMBER CONNECTORS

EXISTING TIMBER JOIST

Construction tips for timber

Calculating depths

The depth of a floor joist relates to the distance it must span: the greater the depth, the greater the distance it can span. Dimensions can be calculated by a structural engineer based on distances to be spanned and loads to be supported. There are considerable variations within these calculations: the thickness of joists can vary for the same depth and for the quality of timber and its approved structural capacity. Tables published by statutory bodies responsible for approving building works set out figures on which calculations can be based. For simple jobs, these can be used independently by designers to size joists, as they relate different qualities of timber to the different categories of loads and identify required sizes. Variation is possible: a wider joist requires slightly less depth; a better grade of timber allows a reduction in dimensions.

Stabilizing structures

A timber floor becomes essentially monolithic when floorboards and ceiling panels are fixed to its upper and lower faces. However, with deep joists there may be a tendency for the joist to twist along its length, particularly because the materials used in most ceiling construction are not strong. The solution is to brace joists laterally to prevent the lower edges twisting. This can be done by inserting short lengths of cut joist at right angles between main joists, but this uses considerable amounts of timber. A more efficient solution is to use 'herringbone strutting', which braces the lower edges against the upper, which are in turn stiffened by the floorboards. The strutting, which need be no bigger than 50 x 50mm, significantly reduces the volume of timber used.

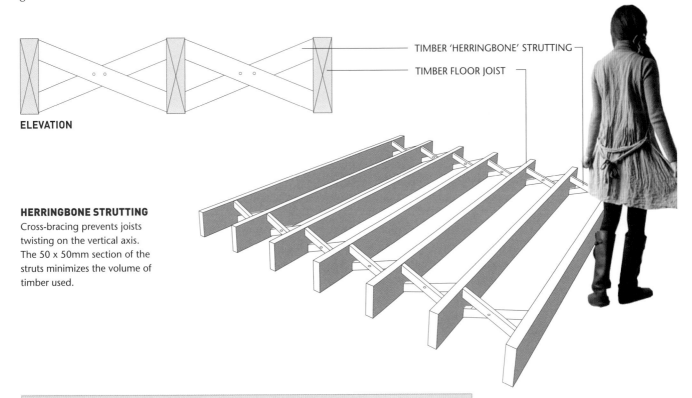

ELEVATION

TIMBER 'HERRINGBONE' STRUTTING

TIMBER FLOOR JOIST

HERRINGBONE STRUTTING
Cross-bracing prevents joists twisting on the vertical axis. The 50 x 50mm section of the struts minimizes the volume of timber used.

TIP READING THE CLUES

Upper floors, in the vast majority of cases, consist of long floorboards, usually about 100–150mm wide, laid across and nailed to floor joists, resting on walls or beams. More modern construction often substitutes oriented strand board (OSB) or particle boards that are usually 1220mm long and 600mm wide, but with both options the longer side will be laid at right angles to the joist. It is therefore possible to tell the direction of joists by looking at the boards and, since the joists will necessarily be supported on loadbearing walls, it is also possible to identify structural walls that are more complicated to remove or make holes in. It is not, however, safe to conclude that a wall is non-loadbearing simply because it is not supporting joists – it may have other roles.

Steel beams

The greater strength of steel beams is often used to reduce the span of timber beams. Their dimensions, including the thickness of the steel, should always be calculated by a structural engineer.

Timber joists may rest on top of the steel beam or, with the I-section beam (often known as rolled-steel joist, or 'RSJ'), between the top and bottom horizontal 'flange' elements.

Greater steel thickness can allow shallower or narrower dimensions. It is possible to equate the depth of the steel beam to that of the timber joists so that the projection of the beam below the joists can be eliminated to ensure a flat ceiling finish.

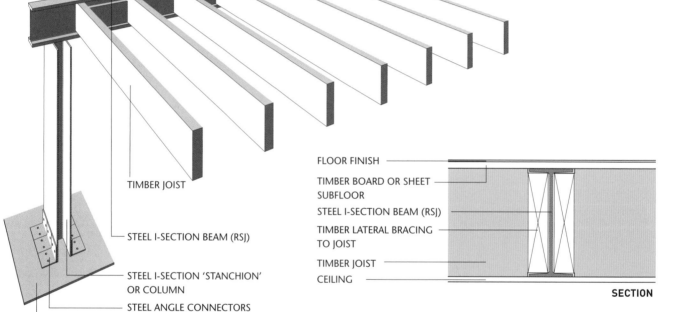

TIMBER LATERAL BRACING TO JOIST

TIMBER JOIST

STEEL I-SECTION BEAM (RSJ)

STEEL I-SECTION 'STANCHION' OR COLUMN

STEEL ANGLE CONNECTORS (BOLTED TO BASE AND STANCHION)

STEEL BASE PLATE (TO SPREAD LOAD)

FLOOR FINISH

TIMBER BOARD OR SHEET SUBFLOOR

STEEL I-SECTION BEAM (RSJ)

TIMBER LATERAL BRACING TO JOIST

TIMBER JOIST

CEILING

SECTION

TIMBER JOISTS ON LOWER FLANGE OF STEEL BEAM
Timber joists may be supported directly on the lower horizontal flange of an I-section beam.

TIMBER BRACING
Lengths of timber running parallel to the steel beam and nailed to the joists keep them securely located and vertical. Joists may be cut around the profile of the flanges to provide support for board, floor and ceiling finishes.

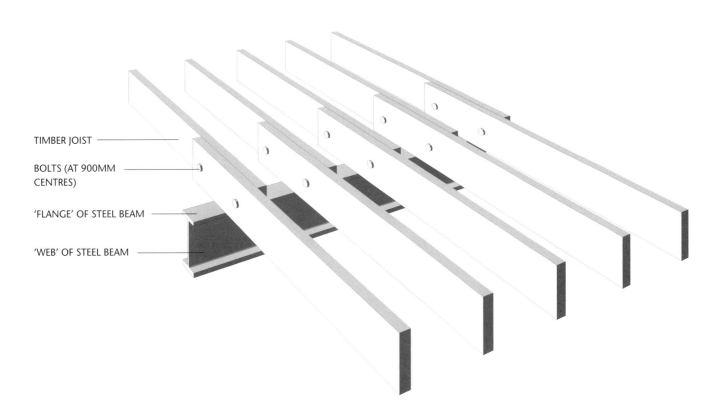

TIMBER JOIST

BOLTS (AT 900MM CENTRES)

'FLANGE' OF STEEL BEAM

'WEB' OF STEEL BEAM

JOISTS RESTING ON STEEL BEAMS

When timber joists rest on top of steel beams they should meet at the beam but be staggered, with sufficient overlap to allow a secure bolt and timber connector fixing between the two.

JOIST CUT TO PROFILE

Since traditional timber floorboards run at right angles to the timber floor joists, it is desirable to have continuity of support and fixing over the steel beam. This is provided if joists project at least 50mm above the beam and are connected by 600mm lengths of 25 x 50mm timber batten nailed to joists that line through.

SUPPORT FOR THE JOIST

Steel beams may be pre-drilled, usually off site, to allow lengths of timber to be bolted to the lower flange, to provide both support for the joist and to allow nail fixings to locate the bases of the joists securely. The connecting strips, fixed flat against the upper flanges, locate and fix the upper edge of the joist.

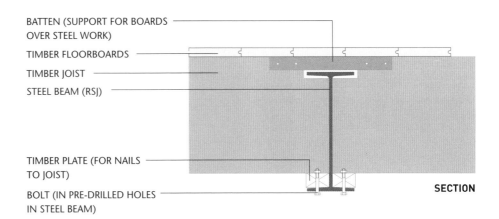

BATTEN (SUPPORT FOR BOARDS OVER STEEL WORK)

TIMBER FLOORBOARDS

TIMBER JOIST

STEEL BEAM (RSJ)

TIMBER PLATE (FOR NAILS TO JOIST)

BOLT (IN PRE-DRILLED HOLES IN STEEL BEAM)

SECTION

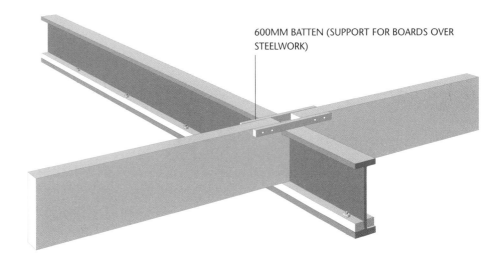

600MM BATTEN (SUPPORT FOR BOARDS OVER STEELWORK)

Planning new structures

Loadbearing capacities

New floors may be comparatively simple to construct, but it is essential to prove that existing walls, columns and foundations can support the increased loading to get approval for a proposal, whether it covers the whole or part of a building's footprint. Different activities have nominal loadings, and even if it is possible to demonstrate empirically that the structure can support the load, it is necessary to provide calculations based on the legally designated structural capacity of the existing materials, which veer towards the cautious.

In addition, building materials have designated loadbearing capacities, which new superimposed loads cannot exceed. These do not equate to the bearing capacity of foundations: the success of one to deal with new loadings does not guarantee the capability of the other.

Providing additional foundations

If it is not viable to prove the loadbearing capacity of existing structures, then new loadbearing walls or columns, each with appropriate foundations, must be introduced to support the new load.

The principles of these are simple. Any loadbearing stratum has a designated 'bearing strength', depending on its geological composition, which determines the weight it can support. The loading imposed by elements of the building, divided by the bearing strength of the ground that supports it, determines the area of the foundation. Generally a column creates what is known as a 'point load', where the weight of all the floor area it supports is directed on to a small area. This may well require a reinforced foundation pad to spread the imposed weight to a viable local loading. A wall will spread loading over a larger floor area, and it may be possible to support additional weight on an existing reinforced floor slab.

It is desirable that the pattern of loading for existing columns should not be altered radically. The addition or removal of floor areas can result in asymmetrical loading and, without balanced lateral support, this can set up untenable stresses within structural members.

If new foundations are required (most likely if new columns are introduced and the point load must be taken to a bearing stratum at least 900mm below ground-floor level), the damp-proof membrane will be pierced and must be made good – a potential source of water ingress. An even greater problem is if new foundation blocks, or 'pads', are located close to boundary walls with neighbouring properties, as they may undermine existing foundations. This may lead to significant complications during negotiations for permission to carry out the work.

PADSTONES
A padstone will distribute the load of a beam or joist over a greater length of wall.

PADSTONE WITHIN WALL

TIMBER JOIST

SUPPORTING WALL

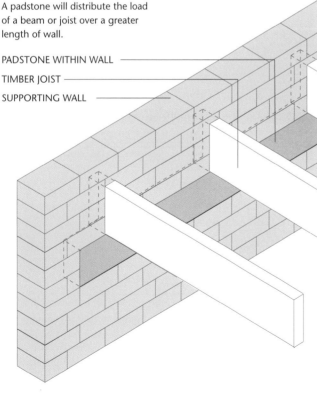

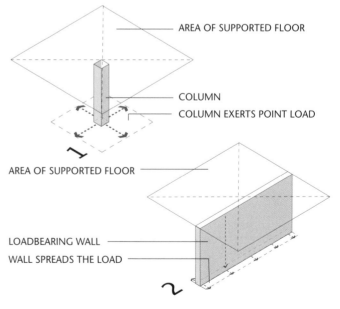

AREA OF SUPPORTED FLOOR

COLUMN

COLUMN EXERTS POINT LOAD

AREA OF SUPPORTED FLOOR

LOADBEARING WALL

WALL SPREADS THE LOAD

1 COLUMNS
Columns concentrate the loading on a small area of floor, and are likely to require additional foundations.

2 WALLS
Walls spread the loading over a larger area of floor, and may not require additional foundations.

Padstones

Where joists, or more particularly the beams that carry them, are supported on walls, it is usually necessary to create a 'padstone' within the width of the wall. This is in effect a beam, usually concrete, built or cast into the brick- or blockwork of the perimeter wall, which spreads the load over a calculated length of wall so it falls within the permissible bearing capacity of the walling material.

Party walls

Where a new loading is too great for the walling material (a problem particularly with some lightweight concrete blocks) it is necessary to take it down to a new foundation pad, either by cutting out and rebuilding a section in a more substantial material or by inserting new columns integral to or close to perimeter walls. It is not normally possible to cut into a shared wall to more than half its width, as the other half belongs to the adjoining property.

If structural work encroaches on such shared, or 'party', walls, the client will be responsible for damage to neighbouring property, so the implications are significant. The collaboration of a structural engineer is necessary to advise, produce the calculations and drawings needed for formal approval, and take responsibility for decisions.

It will also be essential to have a party-wall agreement with the owner of the adjoining property. This will provide a written, drawn and photographic record of the condition of neighbouring properties so that responsibility for damage will be clear. The adjacent owner would be compensated for damage caused by the building work, and the project client absolved from responsibility for damage that existed before work began.

Existing drawings

Often, particularly in new buildings when a floor-to-ceiling height is sufficient to allow the insertion of an extra floor level, the original designer will have ensured that existing elements can support additional loadings. Original drawings and calculations should provide the information needed to get formal approval for new work.

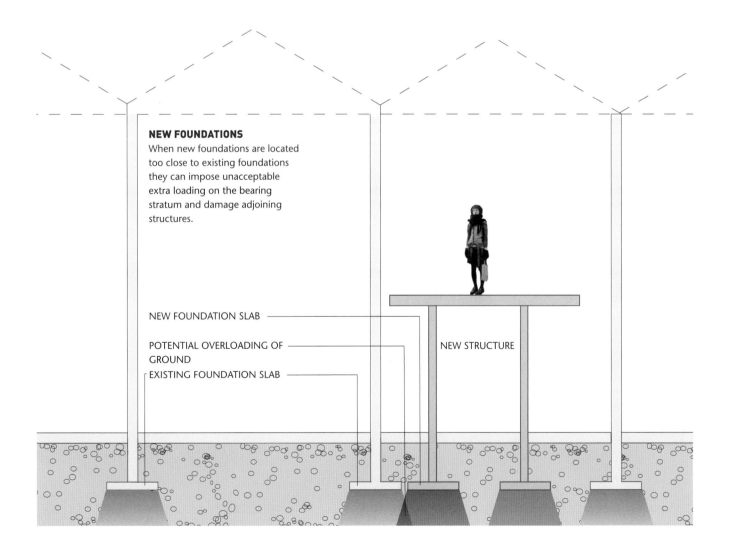

NEW FOUNDATIONS
When new foundations are located too close to existing foundations they can impose unacceptable extra loading on the bearing stratum and damage adjoining structures.

NEW FOUNDATION SLAB

POTENTIAL OVERLOADING OF GROUND

EXISTING FOUNDATION SLAB

NEW STRUCTURE

Installing mezzanines

If an existing shell has a floor-to-ceiling height that allows the insertion of an additional floor, preserving the full height over some of the floor area will retain some of the drama, and perhaps emphasize it, by adjusting the proportions of the high area in favour of the vertical.

Construction methods

Construction of such a 'mezzanine' level can be comparatively complicated but the impact usually justifies the effort. It is necessary to take structural advice from an engineer during development, and to justify the structure's viability to local authorities.

Any efficient solution should aim to use a minimum amount of material and simple construction techniques. Structural elements should be easy to install so that work on the rest of the project is not delayed. Wet construction – poured concrete or masonry walls – should be avoided as both require time to dry before work can continue.

Joists and beams

Timber joists A new floor using timber joists is generally simplest and easiest to build. Ideally, these should span between existing loadbearing walls. A joist 250 x 50mm can span in the region of 5000mm. If the stair that leads to a mezzanine runs in the same direction as the joists, then it will sit efficiently within a simple structural strategy. The joist on the outer edge will provide a suitable support off which to build the essential

protective handrail. If construction is coherent, then the balustrade can act as a deep beam spanning from wall to wall and contribute to the stability of the edge structure.

When joists cannot run between existing walls it will be necessary to support their ends on beams. For modest spans, these may be no more than bulked-up timber joists, perhaps 75mm rather than 50mm wide and supporting secondary joints on joist hangers. For more substantial lengths of edge beams, more is required.

Timber structural members need fire protection, often in the form of plasterboard or plaster casing. This can usually be incorporated in other aspects of construction.

Laminated timber beams These strips of wood glued together increase the potential of timber as a structural material. Their laminated construction – similar to, but significantly thicker than, the laminations in plywood – allows greater depth of beam with structural stability. They also have the increasingly important quality of being manufactured from a renewable source using an environmentally approved production process. They have a good-quality finish that does not require additional treatment, but there is no reason why they should not be clad to be compatible with the interior.

Steel beams Steel remains the most common solution for structural beams. Usually lengths are pre-drilled to accommodate fixing bolts before delivery to site. They

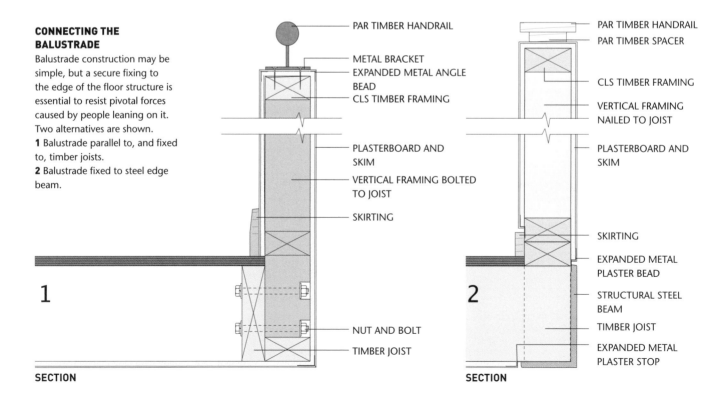

CONNECTING THE BALUSTRADE
Balustrade construction may be simple, but a secure fixing to the edge of the floor structure is essential to resist pivotal forces caused by people leaning on it. Two alternatives are shown.
1 Balustrade parallel to, and fixed to, timber joists.
2 Balustrade fixed to steel edge beam.

PAR TIMBER HANDRAIL

METAL BRACKET
EXPANDED METAL ANGLE BEAD
CLS TIMBER FRAMING

PLASTERBOARD AND SKIM

VERTICAL FRAMING BOLTED TO JOIST

SKIRTING

NUT AND BOLT

TIMBER JOIST

1

SECTION

PAR TIMBER HANDRAIL
PAR TIMBER SPACER

CLS TIMBER FRAMING

VERTICAL FRAMING NAILED TO JOIST

PLASTERBOARD AND SKIM

SKIRTING

EXPANDED METAL PLASTER BEAD

STRUCTURAL STEEL BEAM

TIMBER JOIST

EXPANDED METAL PLASTER STOP

2

SECTION

may also have short steel brackets and plates welded to them to facilitate fixing. They have the advantage of being comparatively easy to assemble on site and, once fixed, provide a stable and dimensionally accurate base for subsequent work.

They are useful when curved edges to mezzanines are proposed – precise radii can be pre-fabricated off site and, provided the survey of the existing shell is accurate, are a useful way of setting out and building complex geometrical forms. Standard sections provide useful support for timber joists and comparatively easy fixings for balustrading and finishes. Steel can be left exposed if a fire-retardant coating is sprayed on after installation, or can be lost in the depth of floors and balustrades.

Concrete beams Usually pre-fabricated, concrete beams do not have to dry on site, but do have to be laid in a bed of wet mortar and must be given time to set in position before further work can be carried out on and around them. It is possible to cast fixings for other elements and finishes into them during production, but generally they are not as easy to handle or as adaptable as steel. They do, however, have the advantage of being fire-resistant.

Columns

Concrete columns Where there are no suitable walls or it is expedient to reduce spans, it is necessary to introduce columns. Concrete is generally not suitable for columns as it must be cast in situ, requiring the construction of a formwork mould into which wet concrete can be poured and considerable drying time. Unless a concrete floor is also being cast in situ there is little to justify its use.

Stanchions A more viable option is to use a steel column or 'stanchion'. Comparatively modest loadings can be supported on an existing concrete floor slab when the concentrated impact of the stanchion is reduced by the addition of a flat steel base plate. This allows the loading to be spread over a large enough area to ensure that it will fall within the permitted bearing strength of the slab. The steel base plate is usually shallow enough to allow it to be contained within the the floor finish. An engineer's calculations will be necessary to specify for permissions, sizes, connection methods and grades of steel.

Posts It is possible to use timber columns, or posts, which are suitable for light loadings but will still require engineer's calculations to determine their size, the grade of timber and the nature of the connections. It is not possible to rest the end of a timber post directly on to a floor slab, and the section and nature of the material does not incorporate substantial fixings well – the end grain will tend to split under loading pressure. It is therefore good practice to provide a mild steel 'sleeve' to facilitate fixing to the floor and to allow a bolt fixing at an adequate distance from the end of the post.

TIP STRENGTHENING TIMBER JOINTS

Joints are critical to the success of any structure, including mezzanines, and standard methods of nailing and screwing timbers may not offer adequate performance. 'Timber connectors' increase the efficiency of contact when a bolt passes through aligned holes in the connector and timbers and is tightened, forcing the double circles of the steel teeth into the timbers. The circular plate spreads force over a wider area of the timbers, which would otherwise tend to deteriorate under a concentrated point load. The teeth eliminate any rotational effect.

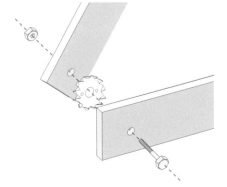
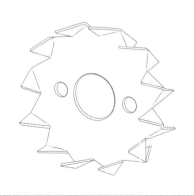

Raising the floor

When it is considered desirable to introduce changes of floor levels, typically within a comparatively high ground-floor space, it is again simplest and most economical to use timber construction. The principle is familiar. Joists at 400mm or 600mm centres support either traditional tongue-and-groove floorboarding – or more commonly tongue-and-groove chipboard or oriented strand board (OSB) sheet, which is better suited to take sheet or tile floor finishes.

The joists need not be deep because posts can be used at regular intervals to reduce long spans. The principle can also be used to create stepped floors for auditoria when the dimensions of seating and circulation zones will determine the setting out.

The obligation to ensure physical accessibility for all building users means that changes in levels require ramp or lift access. Both consume floor space, and in the latter case particularly may represent a substantial expense.

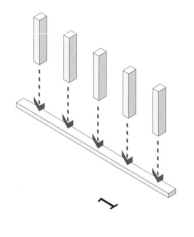

CONSTRUCTION SEQUENCE FOR A RAISED FLOOR LEVEL
100 x 50mm softwood posts, nailed to a 100 x 50mm softwood base plate, will normally provide enough support for a raised floor level. While joists will be spaced at conventional 400mm centres, the frequency of uprights will depend on the length of the raised floor. A 150mm-deep joist will allow a clear span in the region of 3000mm – joists may be sized using statutory tables.

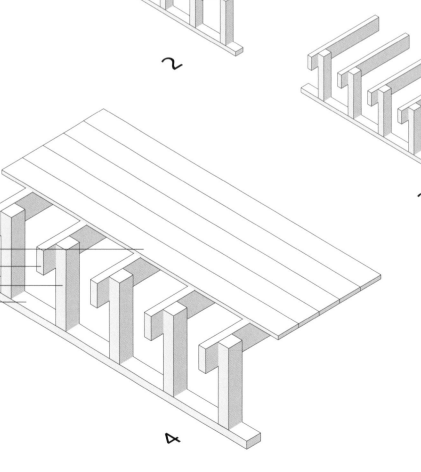

FLOORBOARDS

TIMBER JOIST

TIMBER POST

TIMBER BASE PLATE

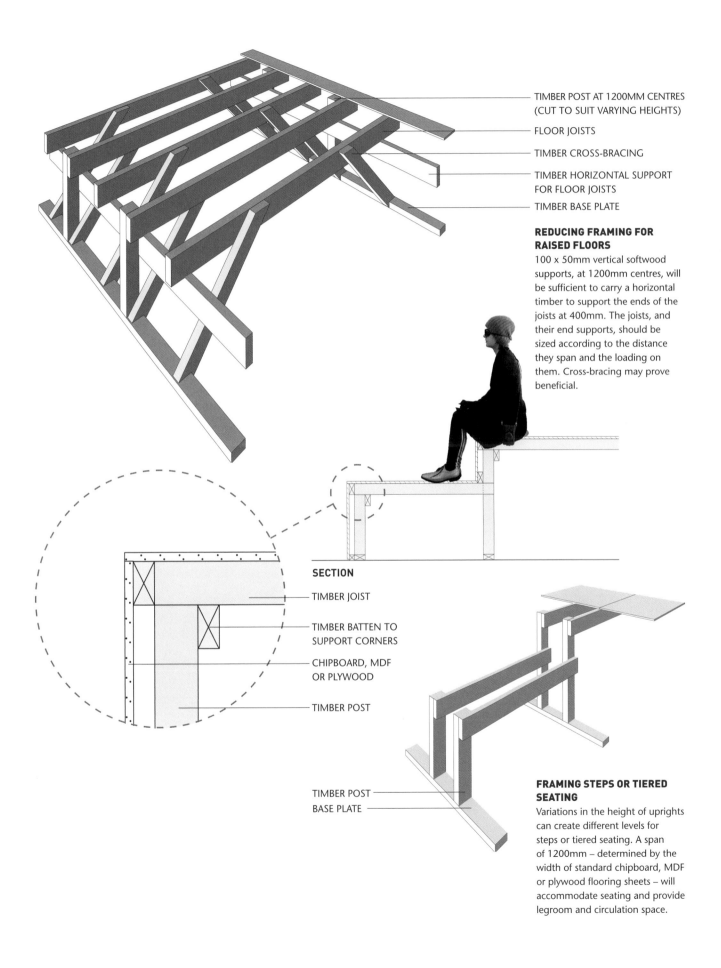

TIMBER POST AT 1200MM CENTRES
(CUT TO SUIT VARYING HEIGHTS)

FLOOR JOISTS

TIMBER CROSS-BRACING

TIMBER HORIZONTAL SUPPORT
FOR FLOOR JOISTS

TIMBER BASE PLATE

REDUCING FRAMING FOR RAISED FLOORS

100 x 50mm vertical softwood supports, at 1200mm centres, will be sufficient to carry a horizontal timber to support the ends of the joists at 400mm. The joists, and their end supports, should be sized according to the distance they span and the loading on them. Cross-bracing may prove beneficial.

SECTION

TIMBER JOIST

TIMBER BATTEN TO
SUPPORT CORNERS

CHIPBOARD, MDF
OR PLYWOOD

TIMBER POST

TIMBER POST
BASE PLATE

FRAMING STEPS OR TIERED SEATING

Variations in the height of uprights can create different levels for steps or tiered seating. A span of 1200mm – determined by the width of standard chipboard, MDF or plywood flooring sheets – will accommodate seating and provide legroom and circulation space.

Openings in floors

Existing floors

Generally, when making openings in existing floors the principle of minimal intervention makes sense. Structural elements are generally interconnected, and changes will require elaborate solutions when that interdependency – a crucial part of their effectiveness – is compromised.

The impact of new construction on existing elements, such as adjacent floors and walls, needs to be taken into account not only when the new structure is complete but also for the duration of the work, requiring as it may temporary support. The consequences of structural damage to the building shell and to adjacent buildings – where the most minor movement can cause expensive damage to finishes – demand elaborate supports. Such protection is expensive and the alterations that demand it can only be justified in more ambitious projects.

If it is necessary to make an opening – to accommodate stairs, ramps, lifts or simply to connect two levels visually – then the viability of the existing structure must be investigated, and supporting calculations by a structural engineer will be necessary.

JOIST HANGERS

Joist hangers provide a sleeve support for 'trimmed' joists, which have been cut short to make the opening. The hangers wrap over and are nailed into the back of the 'trimmer' joists that are, in turn, supported on hangers nailed to the 'trimming' joists. Both trimmer and trimming joists carry additional weight. To cope with this, their width can be increased, typically from 50mm to 75mm, or they may be doubled up and the hangers hooked over.

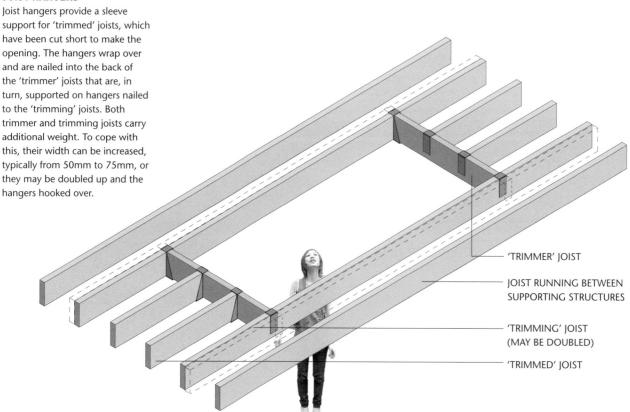

'TRIMMER' JOIST

JOIST RUNNING BETWEEN SUPPORTING STRUCTURES

'TRIMMING' JOIST (MAY BE DOUBLED)

'TRIMMED' JOIST

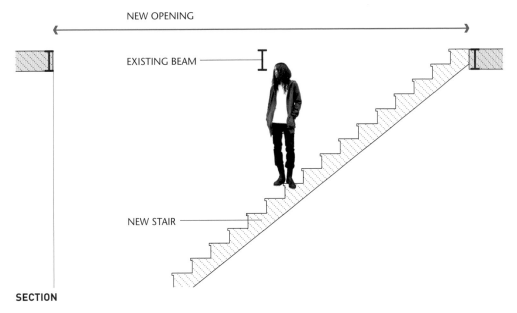

NEW OPENING

EXISTING BEAM

NEW STAIR

SECTION

ENSURING ADEQUATE HEADROOM

The necessary retention of structural beams can interfere with headroom on stairs or ramps. There are precise legal minimum requirements, so it is vital to check these are met at various points throughout a project's development. The beam itself may not cause problems but, if clad for fire protection, the minimal additional depth can mean it fails to get approval. Manipulation of the relationship between treads and risers should solve problems but it is quite easy, particularly if working solely on plan, to overlook the existence of an obstruction that cannot be circumvented.

Basic principles

While it is easier to insert openings into new floors than existing ones, the basic principles are relevant to both. Openings should, as far as possible, sit logically within the proposed grid of the floor structure, parallel to joists and within the confines of structural bays. The location and configuration of stairs is a crucial factor in how the plan of connected floors is resolved. The designer must balance the practicalities of construction with the practicalities of habitation.

Trimmed joints The simplest undertaking is the insertion of a straight staircase flight into a timber floor. If aligned parallel to the joists, it will seldom be necessary to remove more than two joists. This reduces the structural demands made on the joists alongside the opening, which have to take the load of the truncated, or 'trimmed', joists.

A joist supporting the end of the cut joists is called a 'trimmer'; those that support the ends of these 'trimmers' are 'trimming' joists. It is less efficient to make an opening with a longer axis at right angles to the direction of the original joists as this increases the number of 'trimmed' joists, and therefore also increases the load on the 'trimmers'. However, it is usually enough to increase the thickness of these supporting 'trimmer' joists, typically from 50mm to 75mm, to deal with the extra loading.

It is considerably more complicated to make an opening with sides that are not parallel or at 90 degrees to the direction of joists. It is difficult to make satisfactory connections, and the uneven loading on the trimming joists can cause distortion along their length and set up tensions at the point of their support that will not have been anticipated at the time of their construction.

Steel elements Where steel beams form an existing primary structure they usually have timber joists spanning between them to support the floor area. It is comparatively simple to remove all or part of this secondary structure, but more complicated to interfere with the steel elements as the removal of one section can weaken the whole structural network of the building, of which it is an integral component.

Concrete elements Where concrete beams support precast concrete 'planks', the principles for removing primary and secondary elements remain the same as the 'planks' have at most only a minor stiffening role to fulfil.

If the floor slab and beams are cast monolithically, usually with interconnected reinforcing bars, it is much more difficult to cut openings. It is necessary to introduce a secondary structure to support the edges of the opening during the work, and probably permanently.

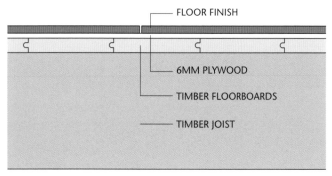

SECTION

SOLID TIMBER FLOORS
Traditional solid timber floorboards
are prone to warping and, over
time, seldom provide a completely
level surface. Therefore when
laying tiles, plastic, or even clay, it
is advisable and usually necessary
to lay sheets of 3mm, 6mm or
9mm plywood over them to
provide a smoother surface that
eliminates the stress caused by
uneven support and ensures a
more even distribution of adhesive
over the whole underside of the
tile.

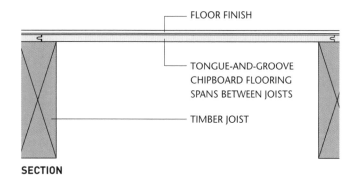

SECTION

TIMBER COMPOSITE FLOORING
The interlocking tongue-and-
groove joint and the more inert
nature of timber composite
flooring sheets, which are less
susceptible to atmospheric change
than solid timber, mean that the
resulting floor is significantly more
stable. Consequently it is possible
to lay new floor finishes, with or
without adhesives, directly on to it.

Floor finishes

The essential structural components of floor construction,
with the exception of good-quality tongue-and-groove
boarding or sheeting, do not offer an acceptable finish
for any but the most utilitarian contexts. It is therefore
necessary to introduce a 'subfloor' – a layer between the
structural floor and the finishing materials. The latter will
often be only a few millimetres thick, so vulnerable to
fracturing if laid on uneven or rough surfaces.

New buildings
Preparing for finishes In newly completed buildings,
the quality of structural floors may be acceptable for
many commonly used finishing materials. However,
minor variations in level, which may mean that areas
of sheet or tiles are not wholly glued to the subfloor,
can result in fracturing of brittle materials. Where
undulations occur, a 'self-levelling screed' can be used
– this is a very liquid compound that when poured
into shallow areas will spread to match the level of the
existing floor, and is capable of drying, where necessary,
in very thin layers that will adhere to the existing surface.

Concrete floors A 50mm smooth screed will often cover
the rougher 150mm of a concrete subfloor. Finished
screeds should be of a high enough standard to allow
finishes to be fixed to concrete floors directly. A good-
quality screed is achieved by mechanical vibration of the
newly poured concrete. The agitation prolongs its liquid
state and allows it to find its level.

Where the screed itself is intended to be the final
finished surface, or when adhesive will be used to fix the
finish, the concrete should be painted with a proprietary
liquid sealant to prevent the generation of dust from the
comparatively fragile surface of raw concrete. Sealant
darkens the flat, grey tone of raw concrete and brings
out the natural visual texture that is not apparent in the
untreated material.

Timber-based floors Tongue-and-groove timber
floorboards are increasingly being replaced by composite,
timber-based sheet materials as the preferred finish in
timber construction. Such sheets are cheaper than natural
timber, and the nature of their composition makes
possible a refinement of the tongue-and-groove joint to
provide an interlocking connection.

The resulting floor needs little fixing to the joists
since, once joined, sheets become essentially monolithic
and cannot move. The boards' size, generally 1200 x
600mm, also makes them easier to handle and quicker
to lay. Their composite structure makes them less

vulnerable to temperature and moisture variations. Even when the impression of conventional floorboards is required for aesthetic reasons it is now standard practice to first lay the sheeted subfloor before covering it with an 'engineered' board – a thin veneer of good-quality, decorative timber on a composite board base. These are essentially unaffected by atmospheric variation and, in this respect, are superior to solid timber boards.

Existing buildings

Preparing for finishes When new interiors are inserted into old building shells that were originally conceived for utilitarian functions or have become worn from long use, existing floors will usually require upgrading, as much for health and safety as for aesthetic reasons.

Concrete floors Existing screeds may be pitted, friable or crudely patched where new service pipes have been inserted. Undulating surfaces and holes may be repaired with self-levelling compounds. If the surface is worn it should be treated with a sealant to eliminate loose surface dust that would prevent effective adhesion.

Traditional timber boards Unevenness is a common problem with traditional floorboards, which tend to bow across their width over time. Where these have character and when the intention is to use them as the finish, then it is normal to sand and seal them. Sanding will remove most of the high spots. Sealing them will darken and tint the boards slightly, but will usually accentuate the grain pattern and give an improved impact resistance.

Over time, existing wooden floors are often damaged by the installation of electrical cables and heating and plumbing pipes. Old boards tend to have a different patina and width from new boards, so it is difficult to replace them convincingly – short of having boards especially made from the same wood and having them skilfully 'distressed', which is expensive and unlikely to be wholly convincing. The best tactic is to make a virtue of the discrepancy and to inlay areas of different size and grain pattern, to present them as a deliberate gesture, contrasting the characterful shortcomings of the existing with the perfection of the new.

Where there is serious bowing of boards it may be necessary to use a levelling compound or, particularly where thin sheet materials are used, larger sheets laid across and nailed to the boards to provide a more even surface. There is usually a requirement to use thin sheets – often 3mm hardboard – with this strategy because any increase in floor depth has repercussions when the new raised section meets existing levels. However, thin sheets themselves have a tendency to distort where there are significant undulations in the original subfloor.

INTERLOCKING BOARDS
Self-locking composite boards are now manufactured and eliminate the need for all but occasional perimeter nails. If solid timber boards are used as the floor finish, nails can be driven into the joist at an angle through the top of the tongue to be hidden by the next board when slid into position.

TONGUE-AND-GROOVE JOINTS
The traditional tongue-and-groove joint is used both for solid timber floorboards and for composite OSB or chipboard flooring panels. Its function is twofold: to ensure that abutting boards meet at the same level over their width, and that there are no clear gaps for draughts.

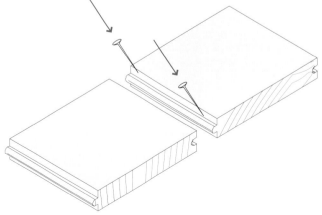

Finishing materials

A designer may be required to do no more than specify a floor finish, since the laying of this finish will usually be done by a specialist following a manufacturer's or supplier's instructions. However, it remains essential to consider practicalities and realities when selecting the finishing material.

The floor plane, although apparently a modest element in an interior composition, is crucial. Users of any space tend to move around with lowered eyes, and the floor is almost always in their peripheral vision. It contributes significantly to holding the other elements together visually. Its deterioration, if it is carelessly selected, will quickly devalue the whole.

It is also important to consider the acoustic and thermal qualities of materials – these can critically affect users' enjoyment of, and efficiency in, a space. There is always room for originality in the specification of finishes, but commonly used materials owe their popularity to their suitability and it is logical to look amongst them for a solution.

Stone and clay

Natural stone, reconstructed stone and fired clay tiles are best laid directly on to a smooth, level screed, using proprietary brands of adhesive and 'grout' – the material used to finish the joints between tiles. It is possible to lay tiles on a wooden subfloor if existing timber-boarded floors are covered with a sheet material, which will provide a more effective surface for adhesive and ensure a more level finish. Tiles require very little maintenance, apart from regular cleaning, and withstand wear from foot traffic very well.

Stone and clay tiles come in a variety of sizes, up to 600mm square, and are comparatively thick, typically 10mm. The adhesive layer adds an extra 2 or 3mm to the overall depth of a new floor. This can cause difficulties where new and existing finishes need to be aligned. A sloping threshold will provide a smoother transition, eliminating the danger of tripping and, since the level change is likely to occur at a door opening, the visual impact is minimized. With a wooden subfloor, it is possible to remove the existing boarding and replace it with thinner sheet material that minimizes the variation in level – this is likely to require subtle packing to achieve a wholly level transition.

Stone colours, textures and tile patterns can be accurately reproduced with plastic laminates. These are available on engineered baseboards, usually 100 x 200mm, with interlocking jointing systems that eliminate visible joints. They also have the advantage of being easier to maintain.

Plastic and rubber

Thinner, more flexible tiles are manufactured from various plastics, rubber and linoleum. The last two varieties are increasingly favoured because they use renewable, sustainable sources. A consequence of this, however, is that they, and rubber in particular, are more susceptible to surface wear than the best-quality plastics.

All come in a variety of sizes, with 300mm square the most common. They are fixed with proprietary adhesives and, because of the precision of manufacture and their stability under atmospheric variations, they can be tightly butt-jointed and require no grouting. Joints will, however, be discernible and will become more obvious with age. It is possible to get pure colours in rubber tiles and some plastics, but linoleum and most plastics have a flecked pattern that is reminiscent of, and can be made to resemble, stone texture and graining.

These materials are also manufactured in sheet form, which is wide enough to eliminate the need for joints in most interior spaces (particularly useful in areas where hygiene is important). Joints between sheets can also be heat bonded during laying to eliminate gaps entirely.

Timber

Timber floor finishes are popular because they are perceived to be clean and natural. They offer a range of grain pattern and tones, but all are inevitably variations on beige and brown. Some colour tinting of the basic hue is possible. The most popular variation replicates or mimics the liming process that tints the wood white.

It is now unusual to rely on traditional loadbearing plank-like boards to provide the finished floor surface. While old, worn boards are usually enthusiastically retained because of their perceived character, it is now standard practice to lay thin boards – usually 10 or 12mm thick – on top of a sheeted subfloor.

While some of these boards are strips of solid wood, most consist of a thin veneer of good-quality wood glued to a composite baseboard, which can cope with atmospheric variations. This reduces the quantity of expensive timber required. The boards are usually manufactured in 'planks', typically 1200mm long and up to 200mm wide. The width is usually made up of three strips of the wood.

There is a significant discrepancy in the prices of boards, which directly reflects the quality of their manufacture and the finishing veneer. The price of the most expensive examples is linked to the quality of the real wood veneers used and of the engineered baseboard.

The cheapest 'wood' flooring consists of a very thin photographic veneer glued to a correspondingly cheap baseboard. It wears badly and the repetition of wood grain in the photograph can be obvious. A top layer of plastic laminate, which can accurately replicate all timber varieties, offers a more convincing, and durable, substitute. It is visually convincing but lacks the kudos of real wood. In descriptions of wood or quasi-wood flooring products the term 'veneer' refers to real timber and 'laminate' to plastic or paper replications.

Most boards have a locking joint system, eliminating the need for nails, screws or adhesives. They ensure a very tight joint, indistinguishable from those between the strips that make up the basic plank component. They should be laid on a soft underlay to absorb slight local irregularities in the subfloor and reduce sound travelling between floors. They are laid to stop a few millimetres short of perimeter walls, allowing for thermal expansion and contraction. It is desirable to remove existing skirtings, refixing or replacing them after the new floor has been laid. The solution of fixing an additional quadrant moulding to cover the joint when skirting has not been removed looks unacceptably expedient.

Carpets

Carpets offer the widest range of colours, patterns and textures and are produced from natural wool and artificial plastic-based yarns. They are available in rolls up to 4500mm wide, and tiles, usually 400 or 500mm square.

The latter are normally made from artificial fibres and are primarily intended for working environments. They are usually fixed with an adhesive, and although the length of fibre is not great it is sufficient to disguise joints and give a visually monolithic appearance.

Selection of carpet type must be partly determined by location and intensity of traffic, and all types of carpets are classified according to their durability. Carpet in rolls should be laid on to underlays. Tiles can be laid directly on to a floor screed or on to composite timber sheets, which may be subfloors in their own right or coverings to uneven floorboards.

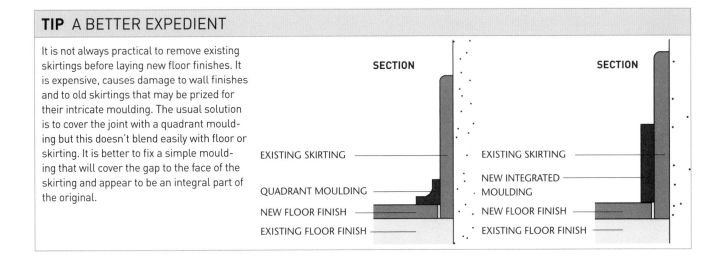

TIP A BETTER EXPEDIENT

It is not always practical to remove existing skirtings before laying new floor finishes. It is expensive, causes damage to wall finishes and to old skirtings that may be prized for their intricate moulding. The usual solution is to cover the joint with a quadrant moulding but this doesn't blend easily with floor or skirting. It is better to fix a simple moulding that will cover the gap to the face of the skirting and appear to be an integral part of the original.

SECTION

EXISTING SKIRTING

QUADRANT MOULDING

NEW FLOOR FINISH

EXISTING FLOOR FINISH

SECTION

EXISTING SKIRTING

NEW INTEGRATED MOULDING

NEW FLOOR FINISH

EXISTING FLOOR FINISH

Other considerations

Conduiting

The floor provides an important zone for the distribution of electrical cabling and of pipework for both plumbing and heating.

New concrete floors With new concrete floors, it is normal for all wiring and pipes to be laid on the structural floor and the finer mix of the screed (which contains no large pieces of stone) poured over them. Pipes are in effect buried and unreachable, but if the systems are tested before the screed is poured they should perform satisfactorily because burying protects them against casual damage.

The only threat will come from future interference with the screed, but if record drawings are retained showing the location of service elements this may be avoided. Electrical wiring is normally enclosed in a shallow metal conduit that allows old wiring to be pulled through and discarded. If new wiring is attached to the old, it can be drawn through the length of the conduit in the same operation.

Existing concrete floors With existing concrete floors it is possible to cut 'chases', or small trenches, in screeds to make routes for service distribution. It is not difficult to make good the physical damage, as long as the damp-proof membrane has not been affected and visual evidence of the work can be lost under the floor finish.

Timber floors In timber construction the void spaces between joists provide generous circulation zones, and when wiring and pipework (usually of a modest 12mm diameter) must cross joists at right angles they can be drawn through holes drilled in the centre of joists. Holes should be in the centre because this is the least structurally stressed area in the joist – the top experiences the most compression, and the bottom the most tension.

Soundproofing

Mass and density of flooring is the most significant component in sound transference. The heavier the construction the less likely it is to vibrate or act as a sounding board for the transmission of noise, so concrete construction is inevitably effective.

Filling voids With traditional timber floors, voids between joists and the discontinuity of construction where floors meet walls create the greatest problems of sound transference. The accepted solution was to increase mass by filling the spaces between joists with loose material, usually clinker or sand, known as 'pugging', laid on top of the lath-and-plaster ceiling plane, and this is still used with limestone chips replacing clinker or sand.

'Floating' floors Another technique for soundproofing is to 'float' new floor planes. Resilient strip materials such as mineral fibre can be laid on top of joists. Battens rest on the quilt nailed to the joists, and receive nails fixing the floorboards. This breaks the continuity of structure.

New floor finishes on top of existing boards or new subfloors may be laid directly on a mineral-fibre quilt and, if joints are interlocking, do not need to be fixed to the joists – which further improves performance.

SOUNDPROOFING: FILLING VOIDS

'Pugging' – loose material poured between joists – increases the weight of a floor and cuts down the vibration and transmission of sound waves through the void. A secondary floor finish, laid loosely over existing boards, will further reduce transmission.

SOUNDPROOFING: 'FLOATING' FLOORS

A mineral-fibre quilt laid over joists will absorb sound waves and, by cushioning the connection of flooring to joists, softens the direct transmission of sound through the structure.

Fireproofing

As with walls, standards of fire resistance are legally required for floors to protect escape routes within buildings and adjoining property. Different building uses and numbers of occupants will determine requirements and solutions, which can be identified in guidelines produced by the responsible statutory bodies.

A concrete floor deep enough to satisfy structural demands will almost certainly meet those for fire resistance. With traditional timber construction, an acceptable barrier can be achieved by upgrading the specification of both the floor and the ceiling beneath it. For example, a 'half hour' rating – which means that the construction will be capable of retaining its integrity for

a minimum of half an hour when subjected to fire – may be achieved with 21mm tongue-and-groove flooring on 37mm-thick joists and 12.5mm plasterboard with taped and filled joints. A 'one hour' rating can be achieved with 15mm tongue-and-groove flooring on 50mm joists with 28.5mm of plasterboard, which is achieved by using three layers of 9.5mm board, laid with staggered joints.

Pipes or ducts that pass through floors represent potential weaknesses. The problem is overcome by enclosing them in a non-combustible vertical duct; making them in non-combustible materials; packing the void between pipe and floor with non-combustible material; and reducing the size of elements that penetrate the floor to minimize their impact on its strength.

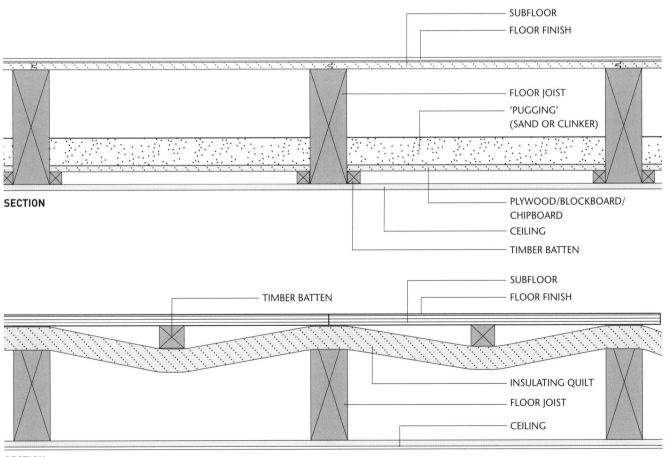

SUBFLOOR
FLOOR FINISH
FLOOR JOIST
'PUGGING'
(SAND OR CLINKER)
PLYWOOD/BLOCKBOARD/
CHIPBOARD
CEILING
TIMBER BATTEN

SECTION

TIMBER BATTEN
SUBFLOOR
FLOOR FINISH
INSULATING QUILT
FLOOR JOIST
CEILING

SECTION

CHAPTER 6 CEILINGS

Basic principles

Traditional construction methods

Ceilings were almost invariably an integral part of floor construction. Thin timber laths nailed to the underside of the timber floor joists formed a key for the three coats of plaster that built up the final smooth surface.

Timber was the only other finishing material used in ceiling construction, most commonly as tongue-and-groove boarding, thinner than floorboards (usually 12mm) and nailed to the underside of joists. In more ambitious projects, wider boards were glued together on a timber frame with butt joints to make an apparently seamless panel, usually functioning as a neutral backdrop for the elaborate, hand-carved decorative elements, which also served to cover or distract attention from joints.

Joists that only support ceilings carry a lighter load than floor joists, and can therefore be shallower. Regulatory authorities also produce tables that relate size of ceiling joist to span.

Secondary structures Occasionally a secondary ceiling structure was introduced, usually either to reduce the height of smaller rooms or to give a distinctive profile to a ceiling. This used the same principles as floor construction, with regularly spaced joists that either formed an independent structure or were hung from the joists of the floor above.

Modern techniques

Modern techniques for ceiling construction are essentially the same as those used for stud partitions. Plasterboard sheets (skimmed or drywall), nailed or screwed to the underside of floor joists, have replaced plaster and lath. The sheets have the same composition as for stud partitions but smaller sheets are sometimes favoured as they are easier to handle overhead, although they require more joint filling.

Light fixings It is easy to cut plasterboard with a thin, serrated saw blade and simple to make openings for light fixings, whether pendant or flush. A hole smaller than the fitting will allow connections to wiring and, after fixing, the fitting will cover rough cut edges.

With pendant lights, which can be heavy, a plate of timber board or composite sheet spanning between joists can provide support to which the fitting may be screwed. Light fittings that are designed to finish flush with the ceiling usually have a mechanism that locks into the edge of the cut plasterboard and a rim to cover rough edges.

Concrete floors The underside, or 'soffit', of concrete floors can be finished with three coats of plaster. Wiring can be enclosed in flat aluminium or plastic conduit, which can be plastered over or run on the surface.

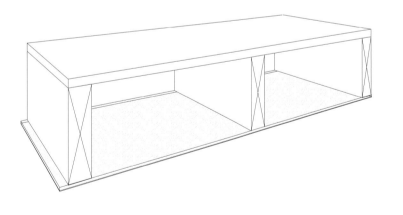

BASIC CEILING CONSTRUCTION
In multi-level properties, the joists that support floors will also carry the ceiling finish. In single-storey buildings or top floors, lighter joists may support only the ceiling finish.

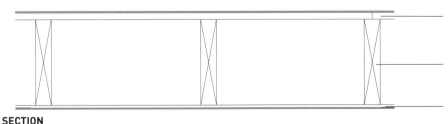

FLOORING ABOVE
(ON INTERMEDIATE FLOORS)

TIMBER JOIST

CEILING (PAINTED PLASTERBOARD AND SKIM OR PAINTED PLASTERBOARD WITH FILLED JOINTS)

SECTION

Suspended ceilings

In modern interiors, the requirements for service circulation are often greater than can be accommodated in the depth of floor joists or surface-mounted conduits. A suspended ceiling creates a void that allows for freer circulation of more complicated electrical and plumbing provisions and larger pieces of equipment, such as heating and ventilating units and ducts.

Lowered ceilings also offer practical options for the designation of different areas within an interior space. This is usually more practical than raising floor levels, which requires substantial construction including access stairs, ramps and lifts, which are expensive and consume valuable floor space.

Construction

Suspended ceilings may be supported off timber floor joists. Existing ceiling material need not be removed since it is simpler to fix through it than to remove it. If the existing ceiling is undamaged it will constitute a fire barrier between two separate areas, reducing the statutory requirements made of the new construction.

Lengths of softwood, known as 'hangers', are fixed directly to the floor joists above (or, if a ceiling is retained, to battens screwed to the original floor joists) and support light joists. Hangers may be as thin as 50mm square – they are in vertical tension, so do not need to resist bending. The structure is comparatively

fragile so it is better to screw pieces together, since nailing will destabilize work already completed. The same rules for spacing of framing members applies as for any plasterboard cladding, and every joint should have framing behind it to eliminate hairline cracking and to ensure the even junction of sheets.

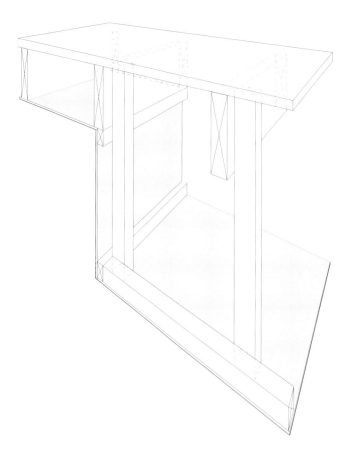

STANDARD SUSPENDED CEILING
Hangers, which need be no more than 50 x 50mm, are nailed to the joists supporting the original ceiling and dropped to the height of the lowered ceiling. Horizontal secondary joists support the new finished surface.

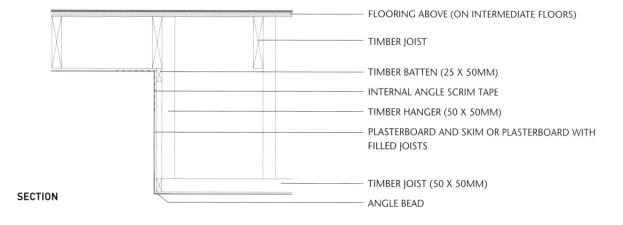

FLOORING ABOVE (ON INTERMEDIATE FLOORS)

TIMBER JOIST

TIMBER BATTEN (25 X 50MM)

INTERNAL ANGLE SCRIM TAPE

TIMBER HANGER (50 X 50MM)

PLASTERBOARD AND SKIM OR PLASTERBOARD WITH FILLED JOISTS

TIMBER JOIST (50 X 50MM)

ANGLE BEAD

SECTION

Angled and curved ceilings

A flat ceiling is the simplest option to construct, but given a ceiling's modest practical obligations it is comparatively easy to shape its profile, producing something more positive than the minimum boxing that is required to accommodate services.

Construction

Support hangers can be cut to appropriate drop lengths to set up the skeleton form. Plasterboard is suitable for cladding squared and angled forms but for curves it is more effective to use expanded metal lath, which can be nailed or screwed to the formwork and finished in three coats of plaster.

Smaller curved forms With smaller curved forms it is more efficient to use a smooth composite timber board,

such as plywood or MDF, which, when painted, will adequately match a painted plaster finish. Both materials are produced in sheets specifically designed to bend, with grooves cut into the convex face.

Larger curved areas When the area of curved surface exceeds that of the largest standard sheet then it will obviously be necessary to consider the nature of joints and, although they may be filled and rubbed smooth, it is worth considering a recessed joint and the pattern it might create.

Wiring for suspended light fittings can be fed through open panel joints although care must be taken during installation to align the suspension point precisely above the joint, so that the wiring passes cleanly through the gap and does not lie against one edge.

LARGE CURVED CEILING
The shaded area represents a plywood rib, cut to define the profile of a curved, dropped ceiling and fixed with softwood hangers to the existing ceiling. The plywood cladding panel is screwed to the ribs and the screw heads are driven below the surface of the plywood. The indentations are then filled, sanded and painted. Since it is difficult to achieve an invisible joint with butting sheets, joints are expressed as gaps through which electrical cable may be dropped.

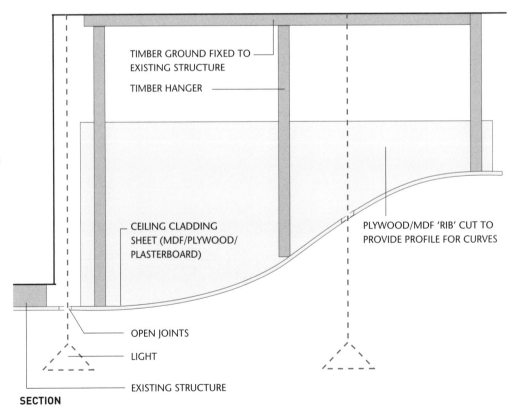

TIMBER GROUND FIXED TO EXISTING STRUCTURE

TIMBER HANGER

CEILING CLADDING SHEET (MDF/PLYWOOD/ PLASTERBOARD)

PLYWOOD/MDF 'RIB' CUT TO PROVIDE PROFILE FOR CURVES

OPEN JOINTS

LIGHT

EXISTING STRUCTURE

SECTION

TIP MAKE A VIRTUE OF NECESSITY

It is common practice to lower an area of ceiling to contain utilitarian elements, such as air-conditioning ductwork. If only the necessary minimum area is lowered (as in **1**) the redefinition of the space is unlikely to be sympathetic to its practical organization or visual coherence. If the lowered area is extended in response to the particular use of the space (as in **2** or **3**), an expediency can make a positive contribution.

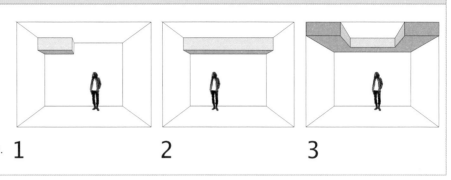

1 2 3

LIGHT FITTING IN A CURVED CEILING

If any details that are prompted by considerations of the most efficient construction can fulfil a second function, a virtue can be made of the expedient.

Proprietary ceiling systems

Proprietary suspended ceiling systems represent an economical solution to finishing large ceiling areas, particularly in offices and other spaces where their somewhat utilitarian appearance is considered acceptable. They also offer an easy and quick way of providing a fairly uninterrupted void for substantial service elements like air-conditioning ducts.

Most systems consist of lightweight tiles that are between 300 and 600mm square and manufactured from mineral fibres, inserted into a grid suspended by wires

from the underside of the structural floor above. The wire suspension system offers a comparatively simple fine-tuning system to establish a level surface over an extensive area.

The lightweight tiles are usually finished with a random, slightly indented, surface pattern that has some limited acoustic qualities and serves to camouflage the lines of butt joints. The systems also include edge trims that will generally create a narrow recess at the junction of the ceiling and the wall.

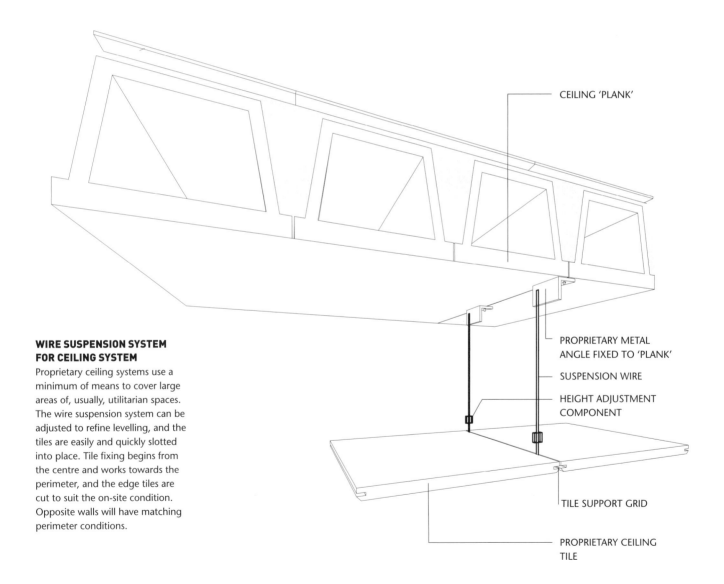

CEILING 'PLANK'

PROPRIETARY METAL ANGLE FIXED TO 'PLANK'

SUSPENSION WIRE

HEIGHT ADJUSTMENT COMPONENT

TILE SUPPORT GRID

PROPRIETARY CEILING TILE

WIRE SUSPENSION SYSTEM FOR CEILING SYSTEM

Proprietary ceiling systems use a minimum of means to cover large areas of, usually, utilitarian spaces. The wire suspension system can be adjusted to refine levelling, and the tiles are easily and quickly slotted into place. Tile fixing begins from the centre and works towards the perimeter, and the edge tiles are cut to suit the on-site condition. Opposite walls will have matching perimeter conditions.

TILES FOR STANDARD CEILING SYSTEM

A suspended ceiling with a visible supporting grid. The individual tiles, trimmed to fit at the wall junction, are visible. The system offers light fittings that fit the grid precisely. Tiles are easily cut to receive smaller fittings.

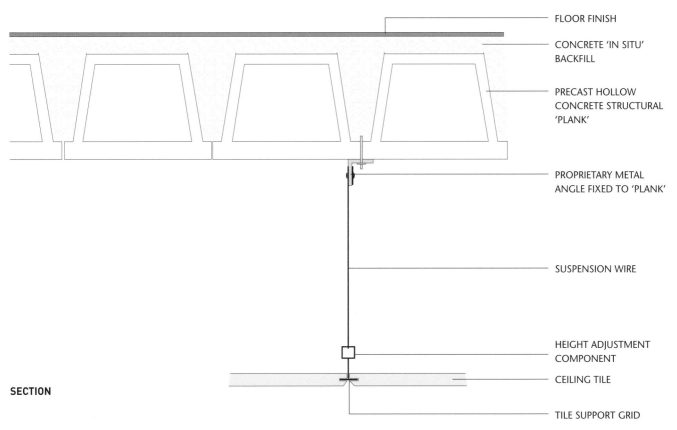

FLOOR FINISH

CONCRETE 'IN SITU' BACKFILL

PRECAST HOLLOW CONCRETE STRUCTURAL 'PLANK'

PROPRIETARY METAL ANGLE FIXED TO 'PLANK'

SUSPENSION WIRE

HEIGHT ADJUSTMENT COMPONENT

CEILING TILE

TILE SUPPORT GRID

SECTION

Hanging methods for proprietary systems

Exposed square grids

In the simplest hanging methods, the square grid on to which square-edged tiles are set is exposed. Tiles can be pushed upwards for access to services or replacement.

Chamfered tiles

If an exposed metal grid is unacceptable, a chamfered-edged tile, with a slot that is pushed over the flat metal grid member, retains a square grid pattern. The 45-degree chamfer will allow the tile to be removed fairly simply.

Slotted tiles

The third basic type of hanging method uses a tile with a square edge and also a slot into which the supporting grid is inserted. To install this system, it is necessary to work progressively from one line of grid – usually in the centre of the ceiling area to be covered – so that the cut tiles are evenly spaced around the perimeter. When the whole ceiling has been installed and the tiles are butted tightly together, there should be no remaining evidence of the grid pattern.

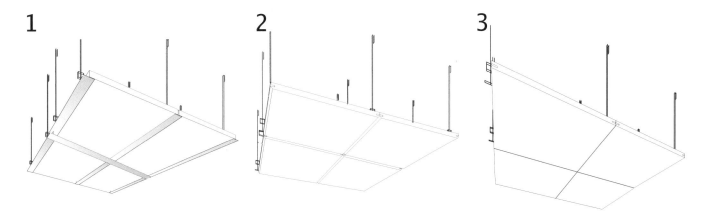

1   **2**   **3**

EXPOSURE OF GRID JOINTS
There are three basic types of grid system, each with a different attitude to disclosure of the grid.
1 Exposed square grid.
2 Chamfered tiles creating a visible v-joint grid.
3 Slotted tiles creating an invisible grid.

Other considerations

Sound insulation

Since the most serious sound problems will be caused by noise from floors above, the most satisfactory remedies are those discussed in the flooring section (see page 110). Where it is not possible to carry out work to a floor above, it is possible to achieve a degree of reduction if a secondary, lower ceiling can be built. If the mass of this can be increased by 'pugging', the reduction will be significantly improved.

The potential for a lowered ceiling may be limited by an already restricted height, but since the effectiveness depends on separation rather than distance there may be some scope for improvement in existing properties.

Fire resistance

Ceilings and floors operate as a single unit in fire separation, and their requirements have already been discussed on page 111. It is, however, important to consider the possibility of the spread of fire in what regulations refer to as 'concealed spaces' – the areas above a suspended ceiling. Large areas will often need to be subdivided to prevent the spread of fire by the continuation of appropriate walls to the underside of the floor above.

EXPOSED DUCTWORK
Some designers are happy to dispense with suspended ceilings, and to expose ductwork (above). Others prefer a compromise, and hang an empty grid below ducts to establish a notional ceiling plane and to have the ducts recede perceptually (below).

Exposing service elements

In some contexts, and in conformity with a prevailing aesthetic, it is acceptable to expose ducts and cabling. A compromise position between this and a suspended ceiling is to hang a skeleton grid, of timber or metal, below the servicing elements to create a perforated plane that will partly obscure them. Painting service elements and the soffit of the floor above the same colour, usually dark, produces a more coherent visual composition.

CHAPTER 7 FURNITURE, FIXTURES AND FITTINGS

Basic principles

It could be argued that there is little need to have items such as tables, chairs or sofas custom-made, given the plethora of options available from manufacturers, and it is seldom economically viable to do so. It is also likely that pieces in mass production will have been more thoroughly tested than is possible in batch manufacture.

However, there are certain elements that consistently occur in interiors that are designed and manufactured as one-off installations. Examples are reception desks, which are the first point of contact for visitors and serve to establish an identity, and built-in seating and storage units, as they are designed for a specific physical context.

Joinery

Some of these bespoke elements will be constructed on site, often largely from wood and wood-based materials because these are more easily worked within the limitations of site conditions. Such woodwork is referred to as 'joinery', as opposed to 'carpentry', which is larger, less refined and more structural – in effect, the first fix of timberwork. Joinery will almost invariably use smoothly planed or prepared timber.

Fabricating furniture off site

It is generally sensible to pre-fabricate as much furniture and detailed construction as is possible in a specialist workshop, dedicated to either high-quality generic items or specialist production using a particular material, away from the confusion and unsympathetic conditions of a building site. Joinery work requires both precision and a high level of finish that will need protection up until the moment it is used by the occupants of the interior.

A good workshop will contain the required range of specialist machinery and tools, in a well-planned and tidy working environment. While hand-crafting is often prized, for most interior projects it is only with machine production that the required quality, quantity and price can be achieved.

Exploring new materials

It is always good practice when working with unfamiliar materials or unfamiliar techniques to discuss possibilities with the specialist maker, or when working with new makers to discuss their preferred methods of production. This can ensure a more refined outcome and can also act as a stimulus to the designer's imagination. Such collaboration also allows designers to add to their specialist knowledge and to their repertoire of options for future projects.

Drawings

The designer is not necessarily required to describe the making process in detail. It is increasingly common for a drawing setting out the dimensions and material specification of the designed object to be given to the maker, who will then produce a set of drawings which determine how the designer's intentions can best be achieved using the specialist techniques available. These drawings will be sent to the designer for approval before manufacturing begins.

Installation and responsibility

It depends on the nature of the work whether it is necessary for the maker to install on site – this consideration can apply to all or parts of the piece. Generally it is better that installation be done by the makers, who will be more aware of how pieces should be handled. If they do so, responsibility for any faults will also be clear.

With such an arrangement the maker is responsible for ensuring that the quality of the work is satisfactory, but the designer remains responsible not just for the aesthetic quality but the specification of finishes appropriate to the practical obligations of the object. This requires knowledge of the performance of materials – whenever a material, familiar or not, is being considered for an unusual context, consultation with manufacturers and suppliers is important to ensure that the product can meet the particular requirements.

Other considerations

Like every aspect of an interior, the key to a successful piece of furniture lies in creative consideration of detail, of the way different materials relate and are connected. The construction process can often be intricate, and a good specialist maker will usually be able to achieve the desired result. However, it is counterproductive to demand something that will be difficult to clean and maintain because, no matter how pristine the newly finished piece may be, dust and wear and tear will undermine the perceived quality. Natural materials such as wood and stone tend to acquire character when worn; manufactured materials do not.

WORKSHOP SAWS

The radial arm saw (left) is used for cutting timber to length. Cuts may be made at angles and the extended bench offers support to the timber, allowing one-person operation. The band saw (below) can be used to cut intricate two-dimensional curves, while the table saw (bottom) is used for cutting sheet materials. The extending grid elements support the sheet over its entire area and allow one person to operate the saw.

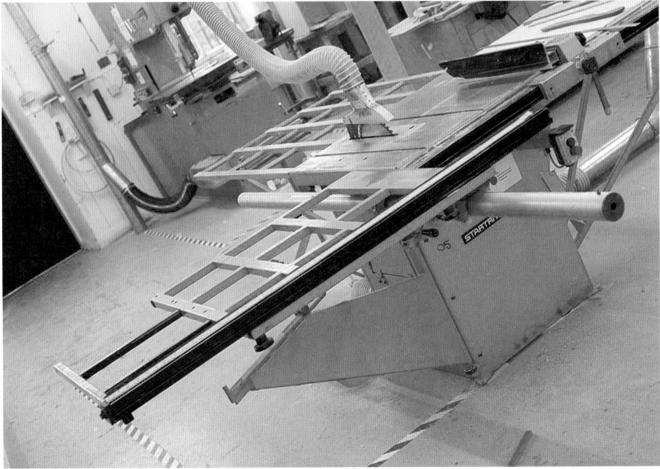

Portable workshops

It is difficult to produce refined objects away from a workshop but not unusual for simpler joinery work to be carried out on site, particularly on small jobs carried out by small contracting companies.

Some power-tool manufacturers are now producing what are, in effect, portable workshops that deal with most essential operations, including dust extraction. If a reasonable working area can be established and if the contractor has good-quality power tools and some proven expertise there is no reason why modest elements cannot be made on site.

The great advantage of working on site for an interior project is that the fine-tuning that has frequently to be done in response to the eccentricities of site conditions (and which may not be noticeable until all or most of the construction has been carried out) can be done in situ.

PORTABLE WORKSHOP
In the chaos of a building site the guide plate for the circular saw, which slots together from modular sections, allows perfect accuracy (top right). The wheeled base contains a vacuum cleaner that connects directly to cutting and sanding tools, removing sawdust at its source (right). Power tools are transported in clip-on boxes (far right).

Base structures

The base structure of any piece of furniture – also referred to as the 'carcass' – on to which final finishing materials are fixed, is usually not visible and is therefore manufactured from utilitarian materials. It was until recently standard practice to build a softwood skeleton in a specialist workshop, with machine-cut joints (typically, simple interlocking mortices and tenons)

that were glued together to create a carcass. This was then made more rigid by the panels of veneered plywood or other composite board that were screwed and glued to it. This method of construction has now largely been superseded by one that makes use of the developments in manufacturing techniques to utilize the panels as both structure and cladding.

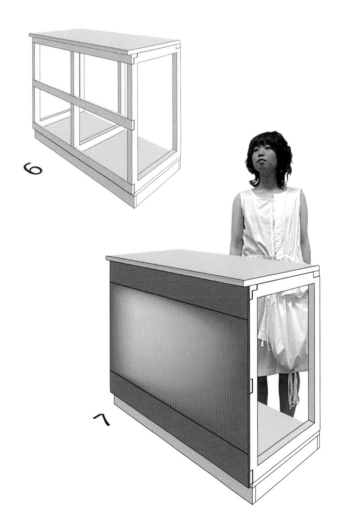

BUILDING A SITE-SPECIFIC CARCASS

1–2 A solid wood plinth forms a separate base that will be set back on the front elevation to form a toe recess.

3–4 The base board make the plinth rigid and provides a base on which wooden ribs are built.

5–7 Horizontal wooden ribs give lateral rigidity and provide fixings for the cladding panels that also increase rigidity and consolidate angles.

Jointing techniques

While manufacturing technologies have made the menu of traditional wood joints – evolved under the constraints imposed by hand tools – redundant for the production of utilitarian connections, the principles of traditional joint-making have retained an important role in the production of solid softwood or hardwood elements. While the joints are now likely to be made by machine,

their form, defined by an understanding of the structure and capability of natural wood, remains an important component in the visual vocabulary of furniture construction. The visible expression of connections and practical detail is inherent in modern design philosophy, and the expression of traditional joint forms may be used to signal a commitment to raw function.

CROSS JOINT

1–3 The cross joint locks both pieces at right angles, and when glued is very rigid. It can be repeated to make three-dimensional grids that serve as storage elements.

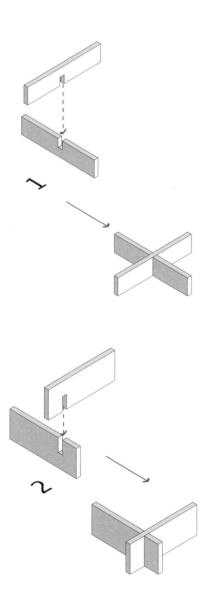

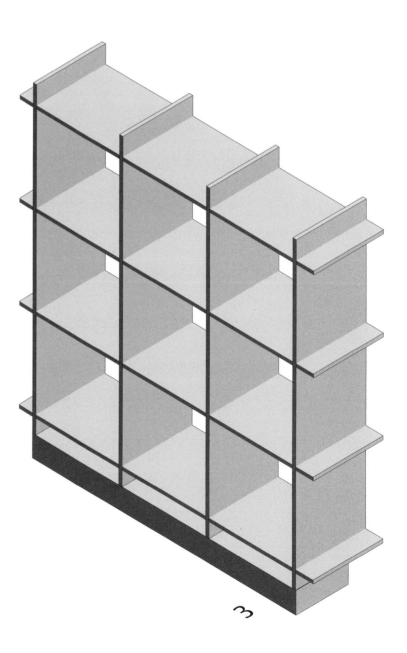

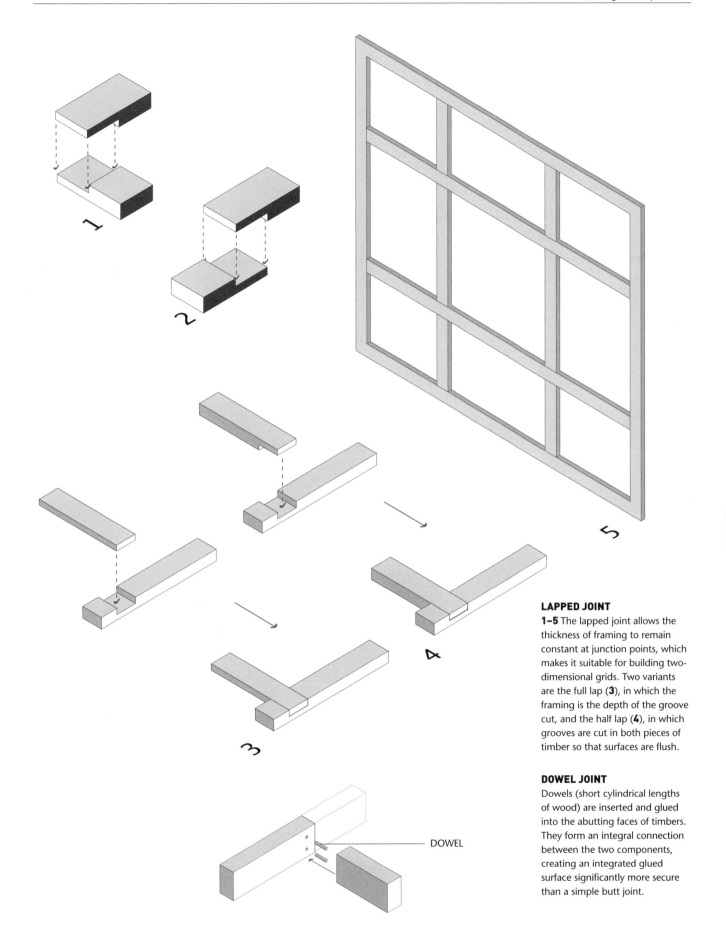

LAPPED JOINT

1–5 The lapped joint allows the thickness of framing to remain constant at junction points, which makes it suitable for building two-dimensional grids. Two variants are the full lap (**3**), in which the framing is the depth of the groove cut, and the half lap (**4**), in which grooves are cut in both pieces of timber so that surfaces are flush.

DOWEL JOINT

Dowels (short cylindrical lengths of wood) are inserted and glued into the abutting faces of timbers. They form an integral connection between the two components, creating an integrated glued surface significantly more secure than a simple butt joint.

DOWEL

Decorative joints

Some of the most interesting traditional jointing devices worth considering for contemporary detailing are those, like simple mortice and tenons, in which the slotting together of components generates patterns akin to inlays on the surfaces of the finished construction. Visual definition of the different pieces is the result of the rougher end grain appearing in the smoother longitudinal grain. Once the decorative potential of such traditional jointing is accepted, the use of such details can exceed the number that is strictly necessary for practical purposes.

1 SINGLE MORTICE-AND-TENON JOINT
The tenon is cut to fit the mortice tightly and the abutting surfaces of both are glued. This increases the area of glued surface and the interlocking, if accurately cut, ensures that the two components meet at the desired angle.

2 DOUBLE MORTICE-AND-TENON JOINT
The additional tenon increases the area of glued surface and provides another decorative element.

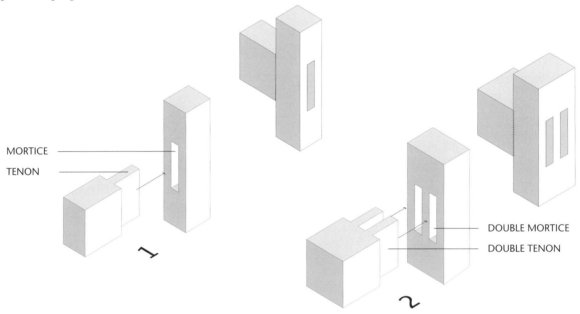

MORTICE

TENON

DOUBLE MORTICE

DOUBLE TENON

TIP HIDING SCREW HEADS

Wooden plugs, to cover sunken screw heads, also create differentiation of colour and grain.
1 A hole with a diameter less than that of the thicker end of the plug is drilled in the cladding strip or sheet.
2 The cladding sheet is screwed in position and the plug hammered into the hole until it fits tightly.
3 The projecting section of the plug is removed with a chisel or plane, and the cut end is sanded smooth.

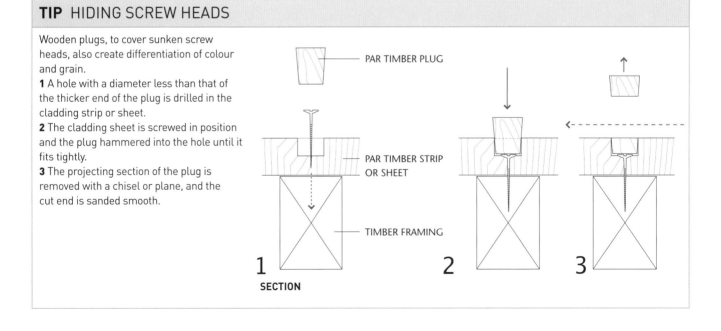

PAR TIMBER PLUG

PAR TIMBER STRIP
OR SHEET

TIMBER FRAMING

SECTION

Joining sheet materials

In joinery, solid timber carcassing pieces have now largely been replaced by MDF, plywood and chipboard. This is primarily the result of improvements in specialist machinery and the emergence of highly specialized workshops that can process large quantities of sheet material with precision.

Routed joints

Sheet materials can be cut to make stable angles, and a 45-degree mitre joint presents no problems. It is also easy to cut sharp-edged channels with great precision. The process of cutting channels is known as 'routing' and the machine that carries out the operation is a 'router'. Minimal but robust joints can be achieved when a channel cut in one sheet exactly matches the thickness of the sheet to be slotted into it, providing a tight, fitted housing for a secure, glued joint.

Advantages This capacity to produce precise elements and angles establishes the configuration of the finished object. The two-dimensional elements that make up a storage unit can double as its structural members. Each rib is an identical template for the unit's cross-section. The monolithic nature of sheet materials makes them inherently stronger and easier to construct than the traditional wooden skeleton frame, which relies on comparatively complex joints and remains fragile until made rigid by the fixing of cladding panels.

ROUTERS
A hand-held router makes a precisely dimensioned slot in sheet materials (top right).

SHEET WITH ROUTED SLOT
The slot exactly matches the width of the sheet to be inserted into it. Gluing creates a rigid connection (above right).

ALTERNATIVE ROUTING TECHNIQUES
1 The edge of the upper panel fits exactly into the slot made by the router. The joint is glued.
2 Stopping the routered slot short of the edge of horizontal panels allows these to maintain a consistent depth.

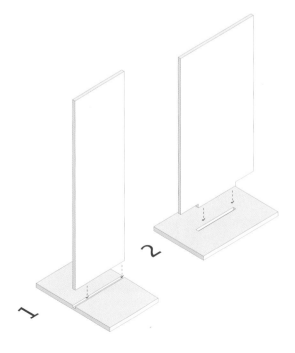

STEP BY STEP BISCUIT JOINTING

Furniture-making requires precision. Pieces are subject to close scrutiny and joints must be perfect. While a shadow gap may provide one answer to the alignment of elements, it is not a viable option when planes and faces need to be butted together. Traditional solutions – like tongue-and-groove joints for the edges of panels, and mortice and tenons for connecting solid timber framing – are being superseded as a result of the greater use of composite sheet materials and the development of specialist machinery and techniques.

It has increasingly become standard practice to use elliptical 'biscuits' for glued joints in all wood and wood-based

elements. The biscuits, made from wood-based composites, are designed to hold together the components of a joint exactly and to increase the area of the joint that may be coated with glue. They also integrate glue more deeply into the core structure of the pieces to be bonded.

Biscuits replace the more traditional dowel insertions, and, because they are thinner, are easier to insert in the thin edges of board materials. Recesses to receive them are cut with a specialist tool that ensures perfect alignment in adjacent components, and these are clamped together to close the joint and eliminate movement while the glue sets.

1 Glued butt joints in sheet materials should be reinforced by elliptical composite timber 'biscuits'.

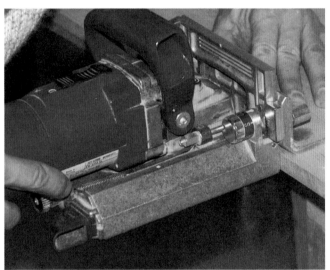

2 A handheld machine, which fits precisely against the edges of the butt joint and which can be adjusted to suit the thickness of the boards, ensures that slots in the two pieces are perfectly aligned.

3 Biscuits are glued and inserted in each board. Glue is applied to the slots and edge of the second board.

4 The two boards are then pressed together and firmly clamped until the glue sets.

Veneers

Veneers are thin sheets of timber, usually no more than 1mm thick, shaved in a sawmill from a rotating tree trunk to make a continuous roll in which the natural grain of the timber provides a strong decorative pattern. They are normally cut from comparatively expensive timber, valued for the complexity of its grain and colour.

The precision of the production process, which maximizes the number of thin slices that can be shaved from the same tree, means that the pattern of a batch from a single source will be very similar and so can be combined to give a mirrored or repetitive effect. Similar configurations of grain are often exploited in the production of door and wall panels to create visual unity.

CONSISTENT GRAIN
Veneers can provide strong patterns, and when from the same tree can also suggest continuity between panels.

Edging veneers

Veneers were traditionally glued to poorer-quality timber as an economical means to ensure stability and strength. Today the base layer is more likely to be plywood or another composite board, which will be even more economical and resist distortion when exposed to damp or heat. However, when good-quality materials are also used in the baseboard, the layered pattern of the edge may be exposed as a decorative motif. This is an intrinsically modern solution, where the inherent qualities of basic construction materials are prized.

Plywood edging

Even where a base sheet is not plywood, or is poor quality, made out of thick porous veneers, it is not unusual to use a thicker, high-quality plywood edge to increase the perceived thickness of the top sheet. This technique can be applied to all edging strips. The deeper edge will also increase the rigidity of the sheet.

Solid wood edges

In traditional construction, exposed edges of sheets were veneered almost invariably in the same wood as the top veneer. However, the thinness of the veneer made it vulnerable to impact damage, so it is more usual for a robust solid wooden strip, usually about 25mm wide with mitred corners, to be glued to the edge of the veneered sheet, flush with the surface of the veneer. If dowels are then inserted and glued into holes in both the sheet and the edge piece, the connection can be further strengthened.

It is normal to use the same timber for the edge as is used for the surface veneer but, because of different production methods for veneers and solid timber lengths, and because both will be from different trees, variation in tones and grain will be clear. However, it is possible to use different woods and to make a virtue of the variation.

Other veneers

It is also common to retain the wooden edge strip when using other surface-veneering materials such as plastics and metals, or leather for traditional desktops. The solid wood strip provides protection for the edge of the veneer and also reduces the likelihood of it being separated from the base panel.

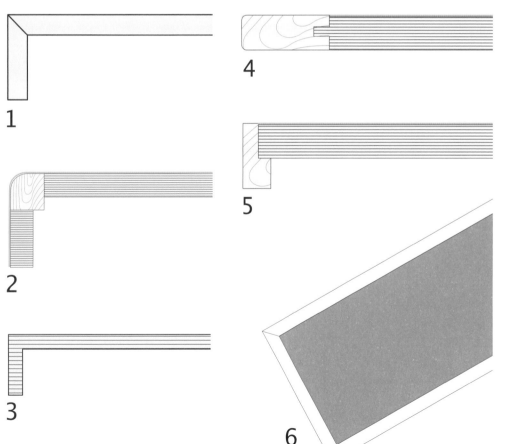

1 MITRED JOINTS
A mitred joint allows the top veneer to turn down over the visible edge, implying solidity and thickness (the increased depth stiffens the edge and increases the potential span of the top).

2 ROUNDED EDGES
Edges can be rounded, and veneer dressed continuously over a curve.

3 THICK PLYWOOD EDGE
The pattern of exposed layers in the plywood edge suggests solidity and thickness to contrast with the thin top veneer. Depth may be increased by thin strips of plywood with the same layer pattern glued to the edge of the sheet, also increasing resistance to bending.

4 SOLID WOOD EDGE
A solid wood edge strip flush with the veneer's surface gives protection.

5 SOLID WOOD EDGE
The edge may be fixed vertically to increase resistance to bending.

6 EDGING OTHER MATERIALS
The veneer can be timber, plastic laminate, metal or leather.

Aligning furniture edges

It is always difficult to line through the faces of furniture components precisely. The treatment of edges or junctions in furniture is crucial as it can determine perceptions of solidity or fragility. When the faces of components that make up a detail are lined through, there is a likelihood of misalignments. It is better to make a virtue of this and allow abutting faces to project or recede.

Cover strips and shadow gaps

The traditional cover strip – usually wooden and decoratively moulded – adequately covers junctions and raw edges. It also encourages perception of the object as a single piece, in which the relatively large expanses of unadorned surfaces are secondary to the motifs and patterns defined by the cover strip.

Shadow gaps

Using a shadow-gap solution, on the other hand, allows the constituent elements of a piece to be given their own significance, and it is also compatible with the modern predilection for acknowledging both simple forms and natural materials.

Finishing with a mechanical saw

It is sometimes practical, when a number of elements has been bonded together and when an allowance has been made for a slight reduction, to pass the new layered face through a mechanical saw. If the material is cut cleanly, the process will shave a sliver from the original conjoined faces and leave a perfectly aligned cut face that can then be sanded.

This process will avoid the minor misalignments that can make joinery look unrefined, but the junction line between elements will continue to be visible and, with timber, the layering will be further emphasized by variations in the grain. It is possible to make a virtue of this layering – the priority in detailing is to make it clear that that is a deliberate intention.

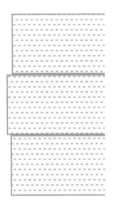

MISALIGNED EDGES
It is difficult to line through the faces of abutting elements. Minor discrepancies make the finished piece appear poorly constructed.

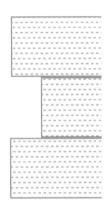

PROJECTING AND RECEDING FACES
One solution is to make alternate faces project or recede to signal that the misalignment is deliberate.

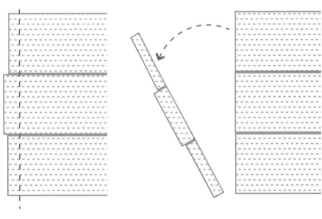

CUTTING FIXED EDGES
An alternative, if elements are securely fixed together and their configuration allows it, is to cut through the composite and to create a single plane.

TIP CREATING THE ILLUSION

For aesthetic reasons one may wish a horizontal surface to appear deeper or thinner than it need be. This is simply done by adding a vertical edge to increase depth (**1**) or tapering the edge to reduce it (**2**). However, both can only work if the surface is below eye level.

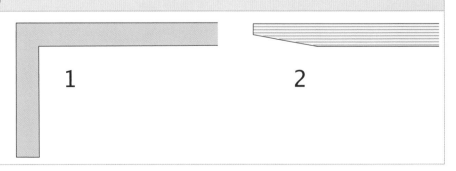

Fabricating elements on site: built-in seating

While pre-fabrication in a workshop will ensure the highest quality of finish, it is sometimes more practical to build pieces on site, particularly where a location may necessitate a series of precise one-off adjustments. The following method of producing and assembling the components of built-in seating illustrates the principles.

It is simple to cut the required structural ribs, fix them to a wall for support and connect them with the linear planes of horizontal seating and vertical backrests. The connection between vertical and horizontal elements can be precise and secure if the backrest and seating planes are routed to receive the edges of the ribs.

Use of a template

Perfect precision is possible if a 'jig' or template is set up that is used in the marking and cutting of all identical elements. Minor and frustrating variations will occur if each is marked out individually and cut out by hand.

Structural ribs

It is easier and quicker to use sheet material and a power saw on a solid working bench to cut structural ribs if the same angles, recesses and routings are needed (traditional softwood-frame construction would produce a series of what are, in effect, one-off skeleton frames in situ). Each identical component cut from sheet material becomes a template for the setting out of the whole, establishing the precise configuration and the location of joints.

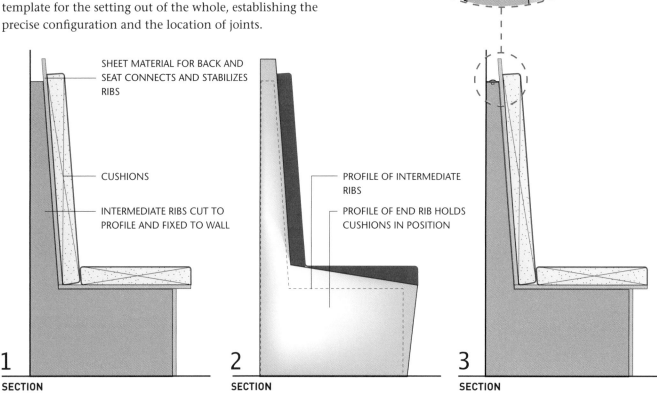

CUSHIONS

SHEET MATERIAL FOR BACK AND SEAT CONNECTS AND STABILIZES RIBS

UPLIGHTER (OR GRILLE FOR HEATING SYSTEM)

CAPPING TO SECURE AND CLOSE TOP OF RIBS

4

SHEET MATERIAL FOR BACK AND SEAT CONNECTS AND STABILIZES RIBS

CUSHIONS

INTERMEDIATE RIBS CUT TO PROFILE AND FIXED TO WALL

PROFILE OF INTERMEDIATE RIBS

PROFILE OF END RIB HOLDS CUSHIONS IN POSITION

1
SECTION

2
SECTION

3
SECTION

On-site adjustments

It is important in on-site installation work to anticipate the likelihood of floor and wall surfaces not being vertical or level, but variations are seldom apparent until installation begins. It is therefore likely that it will be necessary to carry out minor adjustments when, for example, a line of ribs have been provisionally set in position.

Some may need to be shortened and others 'packed out' with slivers of wood inserted between them and the floor in order to provide continuous contact and support. Packing out is not entirely satisfactory but it is acceptable for occasional, minor local variations. If it is efficiently done, the fit between floor and object should be snug enough to prevent its moving. There is always likely to be some insignificant settlement as new elements are subjected to their final loadings.

Finishing work

The degree of finessing necessary to achieve a satisfactory standard will depend on anticipated finish. If, for example, upholstery is to cover most surfaces, the substructure need not be finished to a high standard and, indeed, should not be since that will only add time and money to the contract.

Upholstery All upholstery work should be carried out by specialists. Even the simplest fabric-covered foam seat will be more successful if made with expertise. It is also important to anticipate the need to clean upholstery – specialists can provide solutions. It is perfectly acceptable, particularly where a fairly rigid foam core is used, to fix cushions, both horizontal and vertical, with strips of high strength Velcro.

ALTERNATIVE APPROACHES TO BUILT-IN SEATING (LEFT)
1 The intermediate ribs are cut to size and angled to provide support for the seat and backrest panels.
2 The end rib, which will be butted to an intermediate rib, may be cut to a different height.
3 The back and seating panels can project beyond the end ribs by up to 100mm to contain the cushions.
4 The space between rib and wall may be adjusted to conceal a light fitting or radiator.

ORDER OF WORK (RIGHT)
1 Structural ribs set out the profile of the seating, screwed to softwood battens that are screwed and plugged to wall and floor.
2 Routing on the backs of panels that form the seat and back receives the edges of the ribs. The joint is glued.
3 The cushions for back and seat are contained within the end ribs and fixed with Velcro strips to allow removal for cleaning.

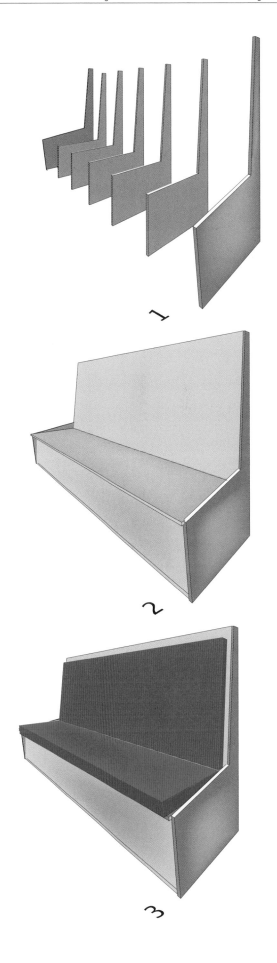

Furniture legs

In traditional furniture-making, legs were predominantly of the same material as the rest of the piece and were integral to it, so that the connection was secure. Modern methods, however, favour lighter construction, for reasons that are both aesthetic and economic. It is necessary, therefore, when detailing connections to maximize the area of contact.

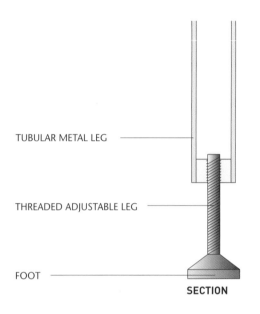

TUBULAR METAL LEG

THREADED ADJUSTABLE LEG

FOOT

SECTION

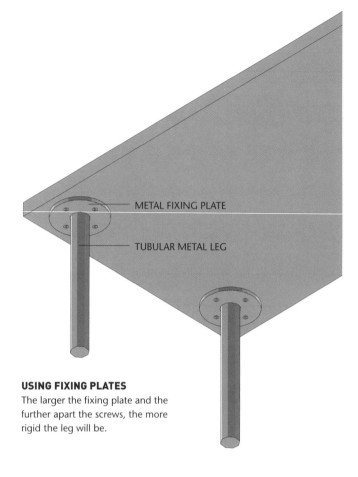

METAL FIXING PLATE

TUBULAR METAL LEG

USING FIXING PLATES
The larger the fixing plate and the further apart the screws, the more rigid the leg will be.

STANDARD ADJUSTABLE FOOT
Floors, particularly in old buildings, are seldom level, and when a table has one designated location it is useful to be able to make on-site adjustments.

ADJUSTABLE FOOT WITH FIXING NUT
The threaded connector allows the foot to be adjusted to variations in floor level. When tightened, the nuts prevent further movement.

THREADED CONNECTOR

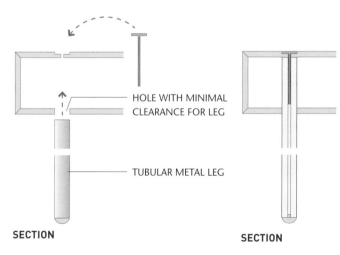

HOLE WITH MINIMAL CLEARANCE FOR LEG

TUBULAR METAL LEG

SECTION

SECTION

DOUBLE FIXINGS
With a comparatively deep top (75–100mm) it is possible to fix the leg on the upper skin after passing it through a hole, which provides minimum possible clearance, in the lower skin. The double fixing gives rigidity to the leg.

SECTION

SECTION

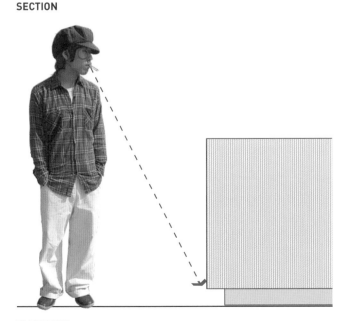

ELEVATION

'Floating' furniture

Suspending and 'floating' furniture items may have novelty value, but it is important to consider some practical implications before committing to them.

Position of legs

If the intention is that the piece should appear to 'float', it is worth considering setting legs as far back from the edge of the base as is possible without destabilizing it. This works well with seating or low display units, and when a higher upper surface is required deep sides will help disguise, or draw attention away from, the legs.

Number of legs

Four legs will provide secure support. Three legs, carefully placed, will be adequate if they do not result in overhangs that are unstable when loaded or sat on. Two legs or one provide no stability unless they are attached to a wide base plate, which may sit, either freestanding or securely bolted, on the floor. This last stratagem can only be employed when the location of the object is fixed and flooring layers are thick enough to allow concealment.

Additional benefits

Floor finishes are frequently uneven, particularly if existing finishes are kept. The lower edge of pre-fabricated joinery, made perfectly straight in workshop conditions, will act as a line against which the most minor variations in the evenness of the floor will be visible to viewers. The solution is to raise the piece on a plinth, recessed at least 75mm, so that the lower edge of the upper unit holds the eye and distracts attention from imperfections. The recess will also protect the piece against damage from feet.

ALTERNATIVE FLOATING UNITS
Concealed legs will give the impression of floating. Where a plinth is preferred (bottom), the uneven junction between the floor and the plinth can be obscured by the projecting straight edge of the plinth.

TIP WHAT GOES IN COMES OUT

If one element can be pushed inside another, there can never be enough grip to hold the two together. A tight fit will not be enough to secure legs, brackets or anything else. A secure mechanical or glued connection is essential for rigidity.

Shelving

Cantilevered shelving

Shelving supported on legs is comparatively simple to design, but frequently – for aesthetic ambitions or practical considerations, such as leaving floor areas free of obstructing legs – it is desirable to support shelves off a wall. The simple, inverted L-shaped bracket will fulfil practical needs but usually offers too utilitarian a solution for public interiors.

Cantilevered wall brackets can provide a solution. They may be utilitarian if concealed within the depth of the supported shelf, but when exposed – as with a glass shelf – need refinement, with fixing carried out early in the construction of the wall.

Suspended shelving

It is seldom easy to get adequate fixing to an existing ceiling. Timber joists are unlikely to be conveniently located and it may be impossible to fix to concrete floor soffits.

Hanging wires, usually preferred because they are least visually obtrusive, will not prevent oscillation of the shelf, which is particularly problematic when displaying fragile objects. Tensioning wires with a floor fixing will not eliminate trembling, and applying tension needs strong fixings that may damage existing surfaces. Rigid rods may reduce swinging but will be visually obtrusive and will not eliminate vibration.

1 CONCEALED CANTILEVERS

The wall bracket allows frequent fixing and refixing. A screw through the underside of the shelf into the supporting arm will hold it in position. Shelves and brackets may be inverted when above eye level so that screws are not visible.

2 VISIBLE BRACKETS

A threaded bracket, cantilevered from a back plate, will support a threaded tube that will conceal rough edges of the hole cut in the wall cladding. Glass shelves are normally on short spacers, often capped with rubber pads for adhesion.

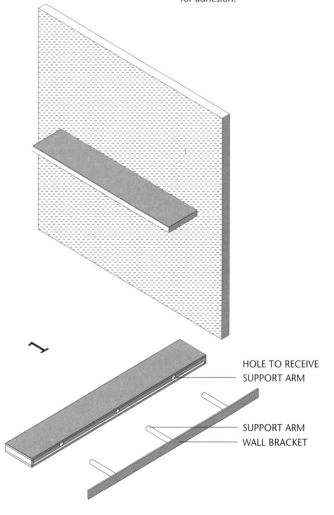

HOLE TO RECEIVE
SUPPORT ARM

SUPPORT ARM
WALL BRACKET

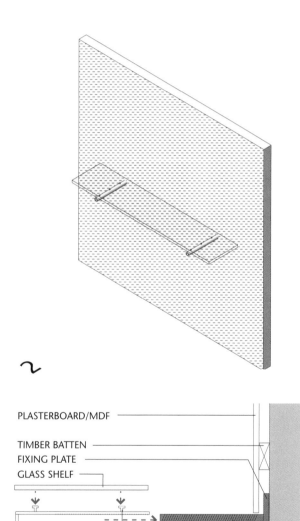

PLASTERBOARD/MDF

TIMBER BATTEN
FIXING PLATE
GLASS SHELF

THREADED TUBE
METAL SPACER
THREADED ARM

SECTION

Supporting heavier loads

The conventional cantilever will support light objects, but with heavier loading, greater depth of shelf against the wall will brace it against the rotational movement to which the thinner shelf or bracket will be subjected. A split-batten fixing, although not essential, will allow secure fixing and easy fitting – particularly, as with the triangular section, when the shelf is solid on all faces.

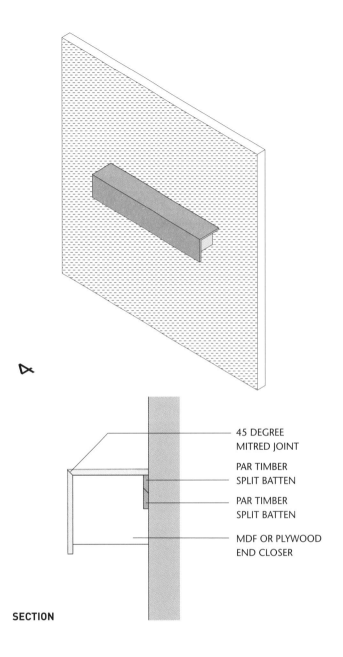

45 DEGREE
MITRED JOINT

PAR TIMBER
SPLIT BATTEN

PAR TIMBER
SPLIT BATTEN

MDF OR PLYWOOD
END CLOSER

SECTION

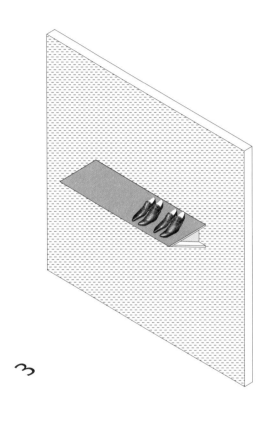

PAR TIMBER
SPLIT BATTEN

PAR TIMBER
SPLIT BATTEN

MDF OR PLYWOOD
TO CLOSE ENDS

ANGLES UNDER 45
DEGREES ARE TOO
ACUTE FOR MITRES

SECTION

3 THE TRIANGULAR-SECTION SHELF

The upper half of the split batten is glued to the top and side panels, the lower screwed to the wall, with appropriate plugs for solid or plasterboard walls. In a shelf with an angle of less than 45 degrees, the very acute leading edges of a mitred joint will be particularly vulnerable to impact. Each of the planes must be cut to the appropriate angle – a join will be less apparent on the underside and should disappear with filling and painting.

4 THE SQUARED SHELF

While a triangular section offers the most direct response to the forces acting on the cantilevered shelf, the principle applies to any deep shelf section. Others, like the square, will allow a mitred upper edge, therefore allowing use of materials such as plywood without filling and painting.

CHAPTER 8 STAIRS

Basic principles

Stairs respond directly to a practical requirement, but they can also offer the interior designer an opportunity to create a three-dimensional set piece that encapsulates and embellishes the aesthetic intention of the areas that the staircase connects.

When stairs are located within the volume of a multi-level interior space, the importance of their being visually integrated is self-evident. However, when stairs provide the primary link between levels but are contained within a separate stairwell – as is normally the case when they act as fire-escape routes – it is still important that they sustain aesthetic coherence.

Stairs that only act as escape routes may be treated in a more utilitarian fashion. While stringent rules, set out in building regulations, provide clear information about the dimensions and construction criteria required, a designer will find scope for ambitious interpretation. Those who use any stair necessarily interact with it, physically and visually.

TYPES OF STAIRS
Stairs may be rotated through
any angle – as long as there is
headroom for users.
1 Straight flight
2 Dog-leg
3 Angled
4 Spiral

Types of stairs

There are a number of standard configurations for stair plans. The decision about which one to use is likely to be based on findings about the impact of their plan on layouts and how each affects circulation between, and around, linked levels.

It is always essential to test the layout of stairs on section, since a minimum headroom of 2000mm is vital. While the height of individual steps varies, 12 or 13 risers will usually ensure sufficient clearance.

Straight flight This is a single flight of stairs between two floors. There are legal restrictions on the number of steps that may be included in one flight. When the legally permitted number needs to be exceeded, a flat landing may be inserted – this can be added at any position, not necessarily after the permitted maximum.

A straight flight running parallel to the longer dimension of a narrow plan will eat less into the room than a dog-leg or spiral, but if connecting more than two levels will require a circulation zone for those walking directly to the next flight.

Dog-leg This configuration doubles back on itself at an intermediate landing, often providing support for the top and bottom of the flights that serve it. It need not necessarily be at the midpoint of a stair. It is perhaps the most efficient option where more than two floors are

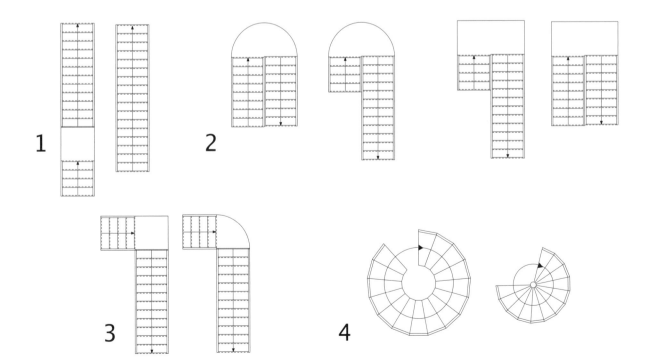

connected, as the circulation space for users bypassing a floor is thus minimized.

Angled Flights of stairs frequently alter direction through 90 degrees but may be turned through any angle, in response to site conditions or design choices, as long as landings have a minimum width equal to that of the stair.

Spiral This has a circular plan with fan-shaped steps that are either supported on a central column or cantilevered from the wall so the stairwell has an open central void. A quarter of the plan area is devoted to a landing, but since this still allows space for 13 risers, acceptable headroom is easily achieved.

Terminology

For efficient communication and credibility, it is important to use the recognized terms, both generic and technical, relating to stair construction and components.

String The sloping structural component that supports treads. There are usually two – one on each side of the flight – but one, three or more are possible.

Flight A single continuous run of stair. It may span between floors or be one of a number of flights, joined at horizontal landings, that combine to connect levels.

Rise The overall height of a flight.

Going The length of a flight measured on the horizontal.

Tread The horizontal surface on which a user steps.

Riser The vertical surface between treads. These may be eliminated to create an 'open tread' stair.

Nosing The projection of the front edge of the tread to increase its length. It is usually designed to withstand greater impact and loading and also to offer improved grip for safety purposes.

Landing The horizontal area on the length of a flight that may allow users to change direction. Its minimum length is determined by building regulations; its width should not be less than that of the stairs. It is usually permissible to use quadrant or semicircular plan forms as long as the radius of the curve is not less than the width of the stairs.

Stairwell The volume within which a stair is contained.

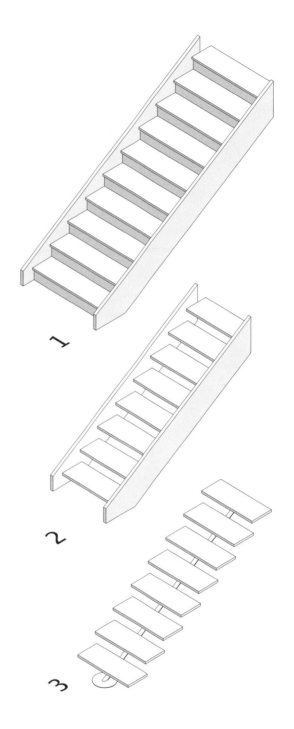

STRINGS AND RISERS
1 Traditional stairs are usually of timber construction and have two sloping edge beams or 'strings', timber steps or 'treads' and timber uprights or 'risers'.
2 Risers may be eliminated to make an 'open tread' stair if treads are designed to cope with the stresses of spanning between the strings when under use.
3 Edge strings may be replaced by two strings set back from the edge of the treads, a single central string (as above) or one asymmetrical string.

Timber stairs

The traditional stair is a pre-fabricated wooden structure, made in a workshop and brought to site at an appropriate time in the contract. If it is installed at an early point, it will be important that it is protected as delicate edges, particularly nosings, are easily damaged by heavy use.

Construction

Timber stairs are reasonably complex pieces of joinery, using routings, wedges and glues. Treads, risers and two-edge strings form what is in effect a complex three-dimensional beam sloping between the lower floor and the joist that trims the opening in the floor above.

It is standard practice in all but the widest treads for the front edge – the nosing – of the tread to project about 25mm in front of the face of the riser. In traditional timber construction the nosing was rounded to eliminate vulnerable sharp edges; in more modern construction where greater use is anticipated, or where the quality of timber is poorer, it is normal to rout out a slot on, or close to, the nosing to receive a metal insert that increases its strength. The insert will usually incorporate a rubber strip to improve grip.

The nosing increases the length of the tread without increasing the going. There is little room or need for variation on this standard model. Perhaps the only crucial decision that needs to be made is about the quality of timber from which it will be built, and that may be determined by the anticipated finish. Elaborately carved timbers were integrated in grand historical examples of wooden stairs, and persist as simple fretwork patterns in historicist work.

Open-tread stairs

Traditional stair construction tends not to offer the visual potential required in many modern installations. The most frequently used variation is the open-tread stair. This involves omitting the riser, which has a significant structural role in standard timber construction and contributes to the integrity of the overall structure.

Where the riser is omitted, treads are liable to critical bending under loading because they do not have the depth, conventionally provided by the riser, which is necessary to span the distance between strings. There are a number of solutions for various materials.

Reinforcement for timber treads

Various means of reinforcing treads are available. As in any other area of the design process, considerations of materials are persistently prompted by practicalities. It is unlikely that there will be a single, entirely objective, right answer. The final decision is most likely to be based on aesthetics.

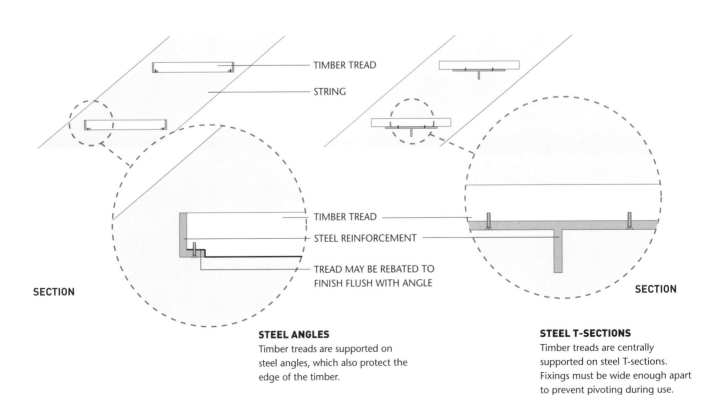

TIMBER TREAD

STRING

TIMBER TREAD

STEEL REINFORCEMENT

TREAD MAY BE REBATED TO FINISH FLUSH WITH ANGLE

SECTION

SECTION

STEEL ANGLES
Timber treads are supported on steel angles, which also protect the edge of the timber.

STEEL T-SECTIONS
Timber treads are centrally supported on steel T-sections. Fixings must be wide enough apart to prevent pivoting during use.

Steel strips Wood can be supported along its length, usually midway between front and back, by a steel strip in a 'C', 'T' or hollow section, to which the timber may be screwed. The steel sections may be comparatively shallow because of the material's superior loadbearing capacity, so need not register visually on the tread's front edge.

Steel angles Timber can also be supported by steel angles on the front and rear edges of the tread. An angle with an upstand of 20–25mm will usually be enough to provide the necessary additional support. Timber treads may be routed to create a recess into which any metal supports may be set, flush with the face of the timber.

Setting in strings When the strings are set in from the edge of the stair, the reduction in the unsupported span of the tread may fall within its bearing capacity. Support brackets should be pre-drilled to allow screw fixings into the timber, and the screw can be countersunk if the hole is tapered to receive it.

Lamination Timber can begin to match the structural capacity of steel if it is converted into laminated beams, which are bulkier than steel but, because they are manufactured to exploit the appearance of the material, do not require further cladding or decoration.

Stone and concrete stairs

Stone
Historically, the grandest stairs tended to be cut from stone with pre-fabricated, usually interlocking, tread and riser units spanning between masonry walls, or, in the case of dog-leg plans or flights within large spaces, cantilevered from walls enclosing the well.

Concrete
Reinforced concrete offers an equivalent solidity to the stone stair and may also be constructed of precast tread and riser units built into one or more supporting walls. It is, however, more common to use a single precast flight to span the distance between floor levels.

While the concrete may be polished, the normally rough surfaces of the precast unit require the addition of better-quality finishes. Timber or ceramic and plastic tiles are commonly used for treads and sometimes risers. Sides and soffits are usually plastered.

Stairs with a polished-concrete or tiled finish usually incorporate a ribbed strip close to the nosing for safety.

RUBBER NOSING
A steel strip provides a strong front edge while the rubber insert behind supplies grip.

NOSING IN CONCRETE STAIRS
A series of grooves cut into the leading edge of concrete stairs can provide extra grip.

Steel stairs

As steel often provides support for treads it may be more practical, and visually consistent, to switch to steel strings also. That, in turn, may lead to consideration of metal or glass treads. In addition, the structural capacity of steel allows greater freedom, for instance in the configuration of flights and in the placement of strings. Steel members will normally require a corrosion-resistant finish.

Single strings

Two edge strings are often replaced by one, normally in the middle of the flight, to create symmetrical loading. It is feasible to offset the string, or to use only a single edge string with cantilevered treads, but with asymmetrical loading the structure will have a tendency to distort. If steel sizes, joints and connections to floor planes are properly engineered, the structure will be stable.

WOODEN TREADS ON A STEEL STRUCTURE
Wooden treads, screwed to steel flats, are welded to steel tubes, which are welded in turn to a tubular steel string. This separates elements and minimizes the bulk of the stair.

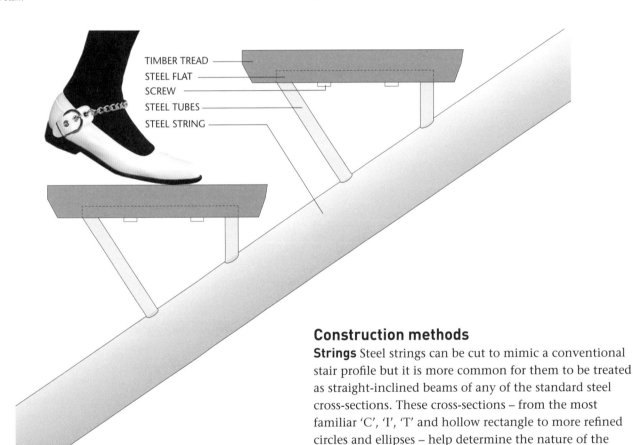

TIMBER TREAD
STEEL FLAT
SCREW
STEEL TUBES
STEEL STRING

Construction methods

Strings Steel strings can be cut to mimic a conventional stair profile but it is more common for them to be treated as straight-inclined beams of any of the standard steel cross-sections. These cross-sections – from the most familiar 'C', 'I', 'T' and hollow rectangle to more refined circles and ellipses – help determine the nature of the bracket that connects tread to string.

String and bracket construction Brackets will usually be steel, connected to the string by welding, riveting or nut and bolt. The last option is particularly suitable for assembly on site. Welding is usually done in a workshop; if a weld is to be visible in the final construction, the join may be smoothed using a power grinder.

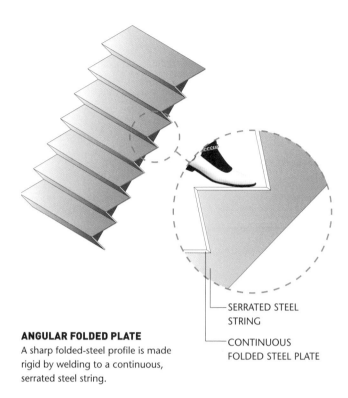

ANGULAR FOLDED PLATE
A sharp folded-steel profile is made
rigid by welding to a continuous,
serrated steel string.

SERRATED STEEL
STRING

CONTINUOUS
FOLDED STEEL PLATE

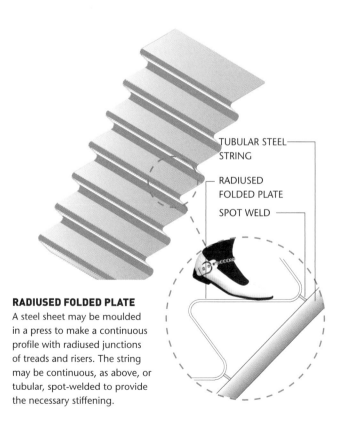

TUBULAR STEEL
STRING

RADIUSED
FOLDED PLATE

SPOT WELD

RADIUSED FOLDED PLATE
A steel sheet may be moulded
in a press to make a continuous
profile with radiused junctions
of treads and risers. The string
may be continuous, as above, or
tubular, spot-welded to provide
the necessary stiffening.

The shape of a bracket will depend on how it is
required to support the tread. In its simplest form it
need be no more than an angle, welded or bolted to the
string, to which the tread is in turn bolted or screwed.
In other situations, some understanding of how loads
are transmitted through materials and how stresses are
created in structural members will suggest the most
effective shape for a bracket – this can be refined in
collaboration with a structural engineer.

With this construction it is possible to use a range
of materials for the tread as long as they are capable of
withstanding wear, which will be concentrated in a few
localized areas. Steel treads can be moulded or textured to
improve grip.

Direct welding or screwing Steel treads may be directly
welded to strings, and the weld ground smooth. This
is satisfactory if the stair is to be pre-fabricated. Steel
components can also be screwed and bolted together –
the selection of screws and bolts becomes aesthetically
crucial. Pre-fabrication allows great precision in the
drilling of fixing holes and this can ensure accuracy in
site assembly and installation, although it is usual for
holes to be enlarged or elongated during site adjustment.

Folded-plate stairs The thinnest tread-and-riser profile
is achieved by a folded-plate stair – either pressed
from a continuous steel sheet, with the angles slightly
rounded, or welded for a more angular profile. The three-
dimensional element formed by the monolithic sequence
of treads and risers needs stiffening along its length to
prevent sagging. This can be done discreetly with one
or more serrated plates fixed, usually by welding, to the
underside of the folded profile. One or more beams,
welded or bolted to the profile, will fulfil the same
structural role.

Steel rods Steel treads may be welded to strings and steel
rods. These are used to create complex three-dimensional
skeletal beams, which provide the necessary structural
depth but eliminate visual bulk. When creatively
engineered such structures can employ a combination
of thin, stiff compression members and even thinner
tension wires. The visual permeability of such a structure
makes it particularly appropriate for stairs using glass
treads. It is usual for the steel to be highly polished or
chromed to create a reflective finish sympathetic to the
glass. While it will be necessary to have the support of
a creative engineer, it is the designer's role to initiate
discussions and to ensure the quality of the solution.

Handrails and balustrades

Handrails

Even in the narrowest flights between two full-height walls, it is normal to provide a handrail, usually fixed on wall-mounted brackets, to help users pull themselves up and steady themselves on the way down. A handrail must run parallel to the slope of the stair and should be sized to be comfortable to grip. A rail that is too small in diameter is as uncomfortable as one that is too big. Safety legislation determines the distance between the individual elements that support the handrail, and this obligation in turn influences structural options.

A handrail can usually only be fixed at its base, and the chief loading exerted on it is lateral and at the point furthest from the fixing. It is therefore essential that the connection of vertical handrail support and stair structure be capable of withstanding significant pivotal loading.

Balustrades

In traditional timber construction handrails are supported on thin timber posts, usually moulded and referred to individually as 'balusters' or 'banisters'. Safety regulations usually result in two uprights per tread – this frequency creates a combined strength capable of resisting all but the most extreme, unanticipated lateral loadings. A baluster, glued into a precisely cut mortice, will become an integral component of the string.

Advantages of steel components

A steel structure not only offers components with an inherently greater strength, but also fixing methods – whether welding, bolting or screwing – that add to this. If the longer dimension of a baluster is used at right angles to the direction of the load applied to the handrail, it will have a better resistance to bending. Such robust elements may be fixed at comparatively wide centres, determined by engineering calculation.

Safety legislation, however, will normally require that the intervals between components be no greater than 100mm, but the steel members necessary to achieve this can be significantly reduced in size – to thin metal rods or thinner wires. The latter will normally pass through holes drilled in the centre of the structural uprights, and are tensioned after installation with a turnbuckle.

These two methods have the aesthetic advantage of introducing linear elements that run parallel to the slope of the stair. The malleability of steel also makes it easier for components to be shaped to maximize resistance to lateral loading.

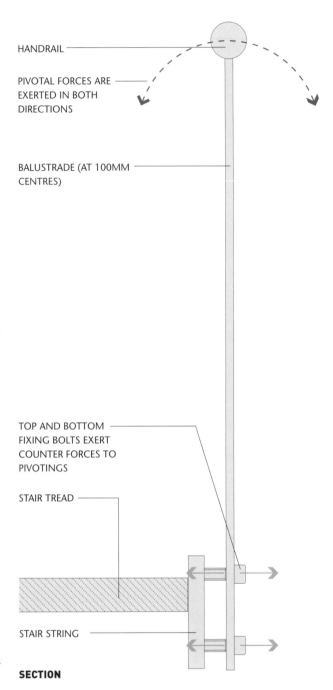

HANDRAIL

PIVOTAL FORCES ARE EXERTED IN BOTH DIRECTIONS

BALUSTRADE (AT 100MM CENTRES)

TOP AND BOTTOM FIXING BOLTS EXERT COUNTER FORCES TO PIVOTINGS

STAIR TREAD

STAIR STRING

SECTION

PIVOTAL FORCE ON HANDRAILS
Handrails are subject to significant pivotal forces as stair users lean against, and pull, them. For stability they need secure fixing at base level – regular fixings need to be evenly spaced to avoid the tendency to pivot.

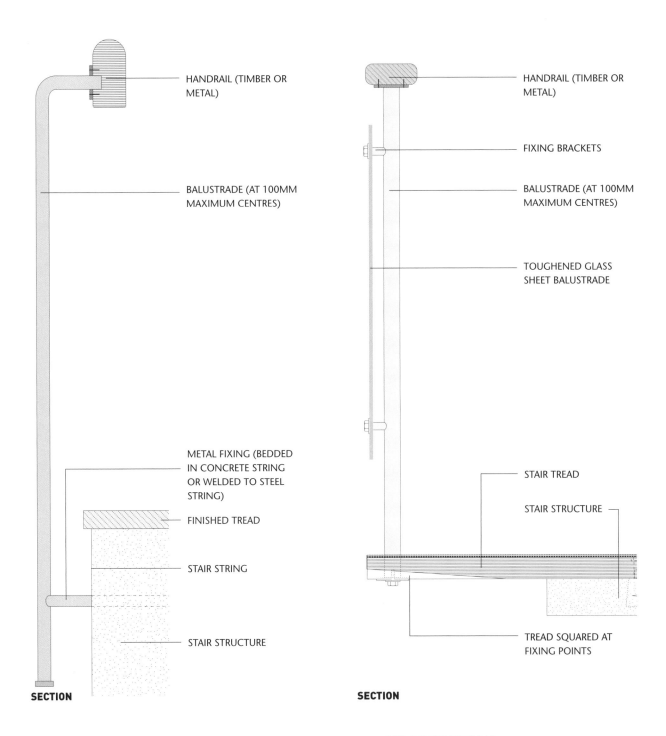

HANDRAIL (TIMBER OR METAL)

BALUSTRADE (AT 100MM MAXIMUM CENTRES)

METAL FIXING (BEDDED IN CONCRETE STRING OR WELDED TO STEEL STRING)

FINISHED TREAD

STAIR STRING

STAIR STRUCTURE

HANDRAIL (TIMBER OR METAL)

FIXING BRACKETS

BALUSTRADE (AT 100MM MAXIMUM CENTRES)

TOUGHENED GLASS SHEET BALUSTRADE

STAIR TREAD

STAIR STRUCTURE

TREAD SQUARED AT FIXING POINTS

SECTION

SECTION

HANDRAIL FIXING IN CONCRETE TREAD

Fixings for handrails may be cast into concrete treads or into floors and the handrail uprights then screwed or bolted to the fixings.

HANDRAIL BOLTED TO TREAD

Holes may be cast or drilled into treads to accommodate bolts or screws that engage with the threaded core of the vertical hollow rod. The tread's underside may be shaped to allow a square-on fixing and the load further spread by large-diameter washers.

Cantilevered treads

It is possible to cantilever the treads of straight or curved flights, but this makes serious demands on the structure of the supporting wall. The pivotal action of the tread when stood on will require a substantial fixing and will transfer significant asymmetrical loadings to the wall.

An engineered, well-built masonry wall, or an in-situ concrete wall, should have the cohesion and stability necessary to support cantilevers either built in during construction or securely fixed later. Where such heavy construction is not possible or desirable, a supporting structure, normally pre-fabricated steel, may be hidden in the thickness of a lightweight, non-structural wall.

Structure of treads

A cantilevered tread must itself have substantial structural strength to support the loadings imposed on it. This can be achieved by increasing its depth; understanding forces acting within a tread determines its profile. With concrete treads this usually constitutes a tapering away from the wall. With steel treads it will be sufficient to turn down the edges, which then may or may not be tapered.

End plates

If a tread cannot be inserted into a wall, a wall plate, fixed with expansion bolts and lying flat against the wall's face, works as efficiently as an embedded connection. Bolts need only be located at the top of the plate – they support weight, while the plate spreads the stress of rotational movement over an area of wall capable of absorbing it.

Finishing

If treads are built into a wall, detailing of the finish around the tread as it emerges is crucial. There is likely to be flexing in any cantilever tread; if this is not allowed for, adjacent finishes will crack. A cover piece can be fixed to the tread, which moves independently of the wall surface, or to a recess provided at the connection point so that the tread can flex without touching visible finished surfaces.

CONCRETE TREADS
Smooth precast treads are supported on a central string, cast in situ. Holes cast in the treads at manufacture accommodate expanding bolts that are tightened into holes cast in the string for secure fixing.

STEEL TREADS
Cantilevered steel trays, whose upturned edges contain concrete treads, are welded to right-angle brackets that are, in turn, welded to I-section strings.

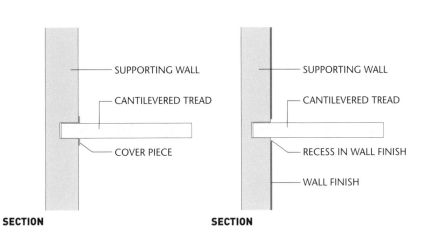

SUPPORTING WALL

CANTILEVERED TREAD

COVER PIECE

SECTION

SUPPORTING WALL

CANTILEVERED TREAD

RECESS IN WALL FINISH

WALL FINISH

SECTION

COVER PIECE
A cover plate will mask any limited damage to finishes around the junction of a cantilevered step and wall. Visually the tread and plate will be perceived as a unit fixed to the wall.

PRESERVING FINISHES
If finishes are stopped short on all sides of the cantilevered tread (as above) they will escape damage from movement of the tread under use. Visually the recess suggests that the tread is penetrating or emerging from the wall (right).

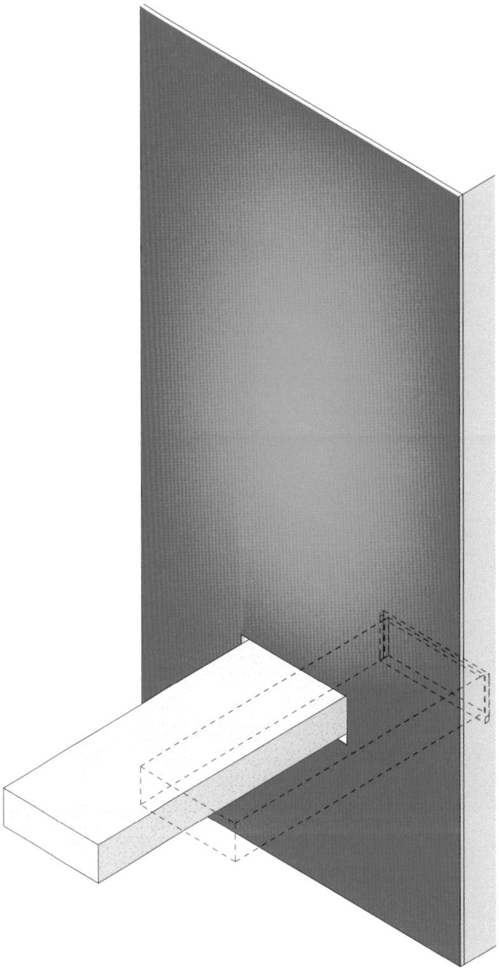

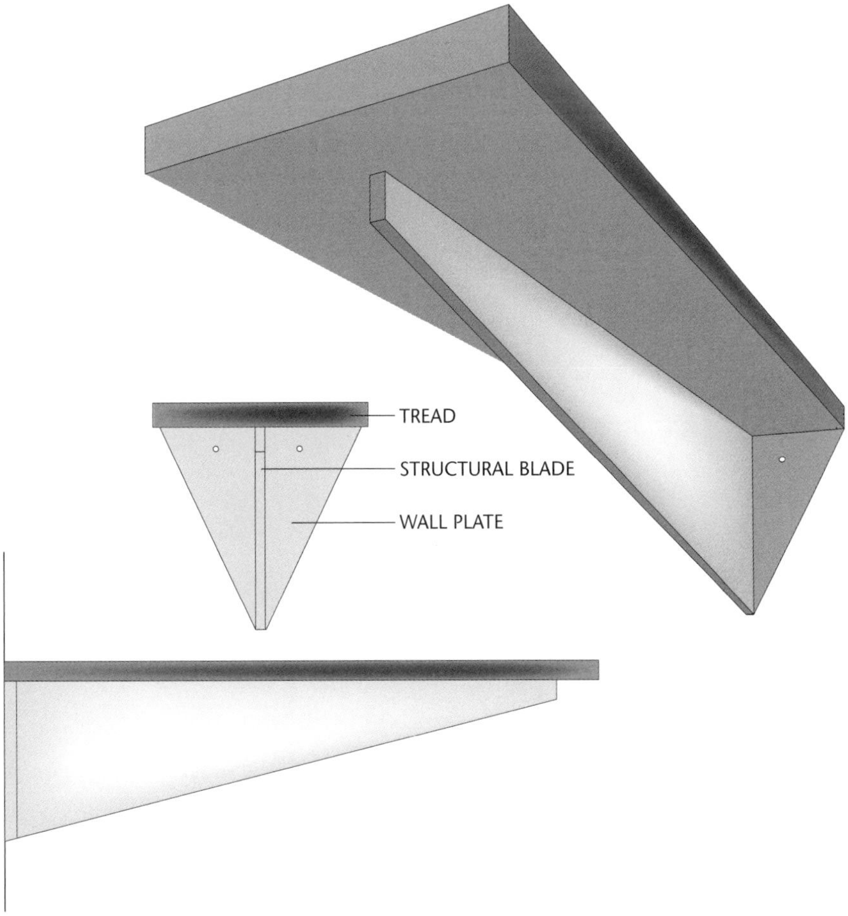

TREAD

STRUCTURAL BLADE

WALL PLATE

WALL PLATE
As well as allowing treads that cannot be inserted into a wall to be cantilevered, wall plates can allow comparatively thin treads to be cantilevered. The tread is strengthened by a central blade, increasing its depth and transferring loading forces back to the supporting structure. The wall plate, pre-drilled for fixing bolts, spreads the load and may be tapered, since the greatest resistance to bending is at the pivoting point.

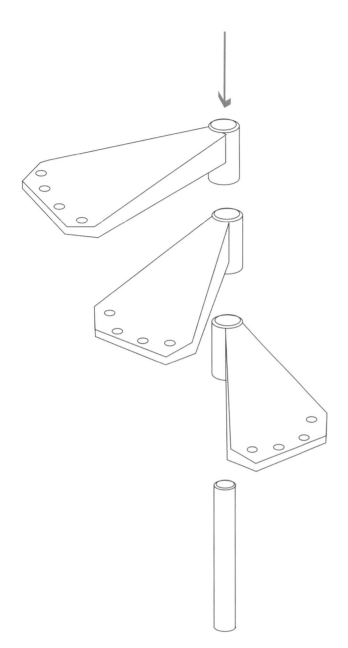

Spiral stairs

With both steel and laminated timber it is possible to curve strings. However, the curved or spiral stair is not necessarily a space-saving option. It cannot be located in the comparatively narrow zone of the straight flight, which makes minimal demands on surrounding floor structures. A spiral requires at least a two-metre-square area, and significantly more in public buildings. The area of tread next to the centre of the staircase is too constricted to be usable, and is discounted in the statutory formula for calculating the width of spiral flights – a greater radius is therefore required.

Spiral stairs are almost invariably pre-fabricated, often as individual tread elements that thread over or are bolted on to a central vertical support. Since each tread is, in effect, a cantilever, the flight is subject to complex asymmetrical loadings and requires very secure fixings at top and bottom. The involvement of a specialist engineer at an early stage is recommended.

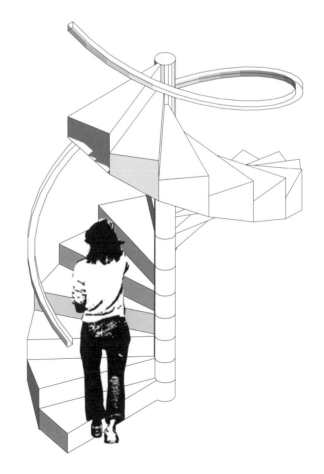

STEEL PRE-FABRICATED UNITS
In the construction of a steel spiral stair, pre-fabricated units are threaded over a structural post that spans from floor to ceiling. They are fixed in position by screw or bolt. In this example the edges of the tread are turned down to give greater resistance to bending under use, and drilled to receive the handrail uprights. One edge of each tread is positioned below the tread above it and an upright is shared by the two, which increases the rigidity of the whole stair.

CONCRETE PRE-FABRICATED STAIRCASE
If the visual effect of the steel spiral is usually that of a lightweight structure, concrete pre-fabricated and reinforced units suggest a more solid and monolithic object. Concrete units may be threaded over a structural spine, but it is more usual to assemble them, with the necessary temporary support, and to pour concrete into the tube created by the hollow cores of the central pivots. Tread units may be moulded to create either a stepped or a continuous soffit, which may also be plastered to eliminate joints for a smoother curve.

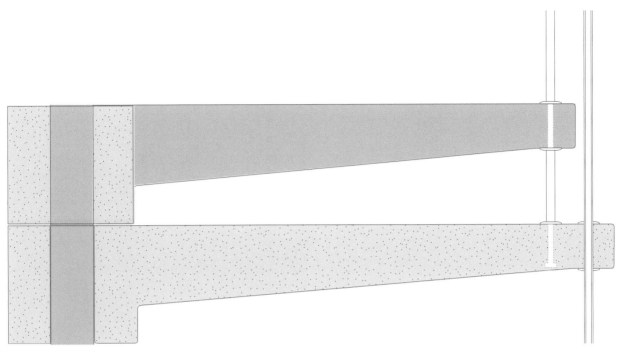

SECTIONAL ELEVATION

CONCRETE PRE-FABRICATED TREAD UNITS

Such pre-fabricated tread units may also taper in section and create an 'open tread' effect. If fixing holes are made in each unit then they may be connected by the upright supports for the handrail for greater rigidity.

TIP GETTING IN LINE

The height of a handrail on a landing or mezzanine is required to be about 100–200mm higher than that on a stair. Therefore, if the last riser is in line with the edge of the floor a visually awkward connection will result. One solution is simply to leave a gap between the two, although this may not be allowed by building regulations. Another, if there is space on the plan, is to project a portion of the floor, corresponding in width to the stair, back to allow the stair handrail to gain the height necessary to meet the horizontal rail without any adjustment to its angle.

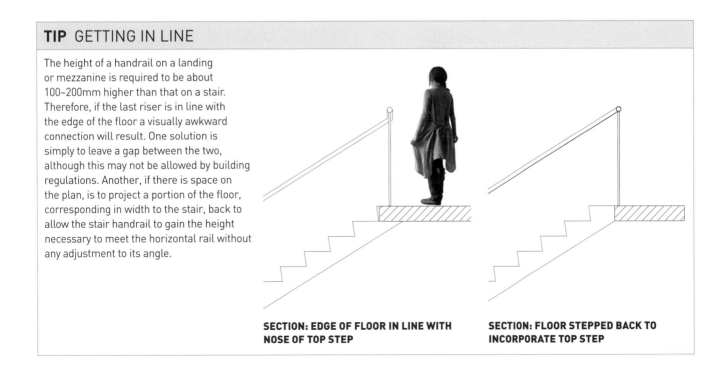

SECTION: EDGE OF FLOOR IN LINE WITH NOSE OF TOP STEP

SECTION: FLOOR STEPPED BACK TO INCORPORATE TOP STEP

Glass stairs

Stairs are frequently used to provide visual drama, often through the simplification of form and erosion of solidity exemplified by the use of glass as the tread material.

Steel troughs

Toughened glass can easily fulfil the load-carrying duties of a stair tread. The simplest application is to provide an edge support on each tread's sides so that it is essentially dropped into and securely held by its own weight in a shallow steel 'trough', which in its turn takes on a further structural role of connecting strings. There is no reason why strings should themselves be steel other than that hard, sometimes reflective, metal surfaces have some affinity with the surface qualities of glass.

Variations on the trough principle can evolve to complement a range of ambitions. The structural support can be located under the width of the tread, and its cross-section selected to fit aesthetically. Glass is normally pre-drilled to allow for fixing with bolts to the structure – fixing details, which are likely to be visible from most angles, must be carefully considered.

Rods and wires

The most extreme option is to combine glass treads with a skeletal steel structure in which the solid plate of the string is replaced by a complex matrix of rods and wires in compression and tension. This moves furthest from the idea of the stair as elemental form, creating a visual complexity in which the expression of form and structure is obscured. Such solutions take engineering possibilities to extremes; the glass treads can take on a structurally significant role as plates that can brace angles and stiffen the 'web' of rods and wires. The glass may be pre-drilled to accommodate fixing bolts, or clamped in place.

Treads

There are a number of considerations relevant to the use of glass treads. Whenever glass comes into contact with steel or hard material, whether laid in a supporting tray or bolted into position, the junction should be cushioned by a resilient strip, such as rubber or silicone. Transparency can be embarrassing in some circumstances, but it is possible to specify an obscured glass finish that will not prejudice the sense of fragility too critically.

Glass is robust but extremely smooth, and can therefore be slippery, especially when wet, so its location in an interior needs consideration. It is possible to provide some surface texture but this tends to collect dirt and stain permanently. Conventional metal and rubber solutions, which may be bonded to the surface, are at odds with the material's transparency.

Fire regulations

In any multi-storey building, stairs are crucial to the fire-escape strategy. They must provide a route, protected from fire and smoke, that allows a building's occupants to escape from, and bypass, outbreaks of fire. Escapees must not be required to re-enter the main volume of the building. The escape stair should lead directly to the open air. It cannot, for example, deliver escapees to an internal entrance lobby. Lifts and escalators may not be used as a means of escape because they rely on electrical power supplies that will fail in a fire.

Local building laws will have a significant impact on details of escape-stair construction. The regulations governing dimensions of treads, risers and landings, the fire-retarding capacity of materials and construction techniques will all have a significant impact on the palette of materials and impose restraints on planning and elevational treatments of the stairwell enclosure.

This will be particularly problematic when an escape stair also acts as the primary connecting stair between separate floors – it often makes sense to combine circulation and escape routes to avoid the loss of useful floor area. However the mandatory physical separation of escape stairs makes visual integration of vertical circulation routes difficult. While glass with an acceptable level of fire resistance is available, it is too expensive for all but the most extravagant interiors.

The complexity of the permutations of permitted options makes consultation with the body responsible for approving proposals important from early in the design process.

GLASS AND STEEL STAIR
Glass components for the
stair treads and balustrades
are supported by a precisely
engineered steel structure.

STRUCTURAL DETAIL
Elements within the steel structure,
in compression or tension, support
the glass treads.

Ramps, lifts and escalators

Ramps

Ramps provide disabled access. Their length is determined by legislation, which means that it is usually difficult to connect full storey heights – particularly because the longer the ramp the shallower the gradient permitted in order to reduce the physical strain on wheelchair users. Legislation also limits inclined length. A flat landing must be provided on long runs to allow disabled users an opportunity to rest.

A long ramp takes up a significant floor area and obliges users to walk significant distances. It is sensible to provide a stair also, to give able-bodied users the option of a more immediate link between floors, but a ramp does solve the access problem for modest changes in level and, if strategically placed to complement circulation patterns, can eliminate the need for stairs.

Ramp structure is similar to that for a raised floor with joists, which normally run parallel to the length of the ramp and are installed at the gradient of the ramp. The subfloor and finishes are applied as for a conventional floor. Balustrade and handrail construction follow principles appropriate to stairs and balconies.

Lifts and escalators

Where ramps are impractical, or where it is considered appropriate to offer a more direct method of circulation between levels, lifts offer the most effective option. While expensive to install, they use very little floor area and technical improvements have significantly reduced the area required for machinery.

Designing, building and installing lifts is a specialist activity; a designer is likely to be responsible only for the selection of finishes for the internal surfaces of the lift car. The decision is likely to be made in collaboration with the lift manufacturer, and may involve no more than making a selection from the standard options on offer.

Similarly, the design, construction and installation of an escalator will be carried out by a specialist manufacturer. There is some room for selection of materials for balustrades and the cladding that conceals the underside of treads and machinery. Revealing these through glass panels is an option. Designers do need to give thought to the junction of the underside of an escalator and a floor.

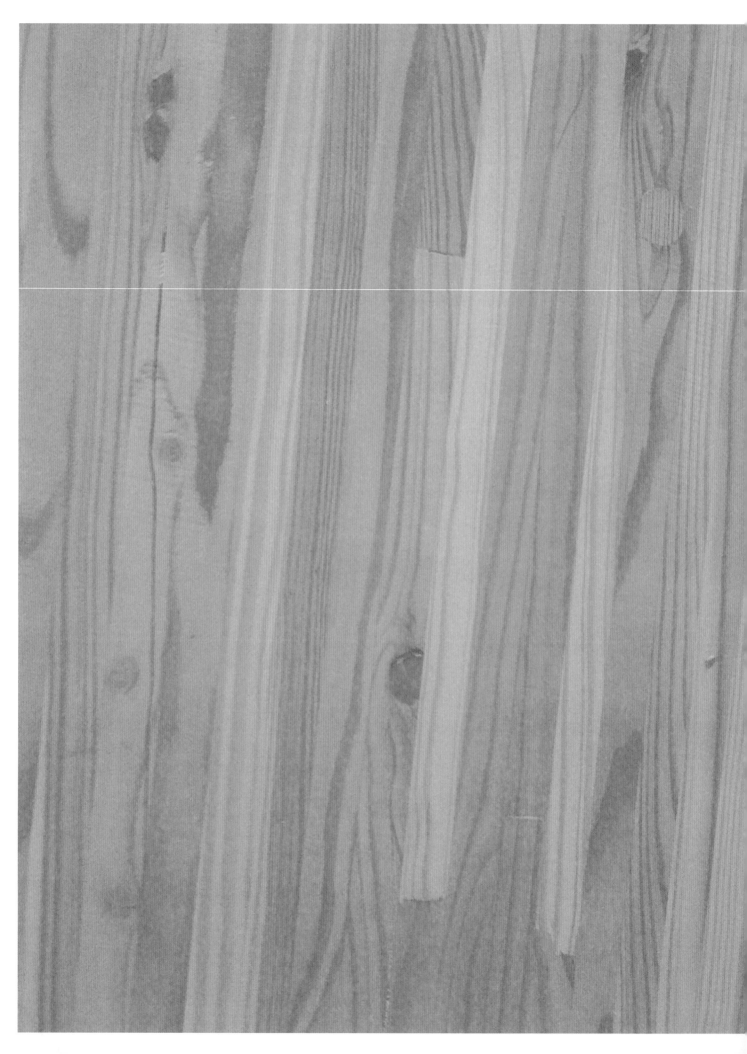

CHAPTER 9 MATERIALS

Timber

Timber is the most versatile building material – it can be used to make the crudest, hidden structural framing or to provide a finishing material of the highest quality. It is easy to work, durable and also offers a wide range of aesthetic options.

Softwood and hardwood

There are two categories of timber: softwood and hardwood. Softwood comes from fast-growing, usually coniferous, trees with widely spaced annual rings. Hardwood comes from slow-growing, usually deciduous, trees with closely packed rings. It is the latter that is most prized as a finishing material because of its rich range of tones and visual textures. The most exotic examples are frequently the product of rare trees, and their felling is now severely restricted or illegal. It is the designer's obligation to reject or minimize their use and to check that any wood from such sources, if it is to be used, has been legitimately felled.

Types of timber

When a tree is felled, branches are stripped from its trunk and, unless they are very substantial, are converted into the strands and fibres that are in turn transformed into the various building boards, such as oriented strand board (OSB) and medium density fibreboard (MDF). The trunk generally goes towards the timber used in building, in two different forms, as below.

Sawn timber The trunk is sawn along its length and converted into various-sized planks, the largest coming from the centre of the trunk and the smallest from the outer extremities. Cutting is done on a large circular saw. The resulting faces of the planks will be rough, torn by the teeth of the saw blade.

Softwood can be used in this state for structural elements – most commonly for floor joists. Most timber produced for the building industry will be treated for rot prevention, and it is important to check that structural timbers in particular have been impregnated under pressure with wet- and dry-rot-resistant liquid products.

PAR timber All other timber used in the construction of interiors is planed smooth on all its sides so that it offers precise surfaces for intricate assembly and finishing. It is described as PAR – an abbreviation of 'planed all round'.

Preparing the sawn pieces, which are cut to standard dimensions, involves shaving 3mm off each face so that a 100 x 50mm sawn cross-section is reduced to 94 x 44mm. These dimensions are generally accurate but, because of the organic nature of the material and its susceptibility to environmental conditions, there can be some, very slight, variation and this must be borne in mind when detailing. In recognition that exact precision cannot be guaranteed, PAR timbers are described as 'ex', followed by the original dimension – a 94 x 44mm PAR timber would thus be described as 'ex 100 x 50'.

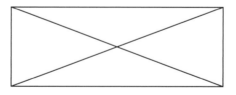

FORMS OF TIMBER
Sawn timber (on top) has the rough finish left by the blade of the saw that cut it from the tree trunk. It is suitable for framing. When sawn timber is 'planed all round' (PAR) to give smooth faces suitable for joinery (below) it is reduced by 3mm on each face.

GRAPHIC CONVENTIONS
It is normal and useful to indicate in drawings the category of timber being specified. The graphic convention for sawn timber, which is deemed to include the crudely planed CLS (Canadian Lumber Size) stud framing, is to draw the diagonals of the cross-section (top) and for PAR to suggest the lines of the wood grain (bottom).

Composite timbers

Because the basic rectangular lengths of timber are cut from a tree trunk, there are, inevitably, off-cuts and other residual materials, such as sawdust and the thin shavings created in producing PAR lengths.

Economic incentives have encouraged the development of composite timber products that utilize this potential waste material, bonded with specialist glues, to produce sheet materials that meet specific requirements within the building industry.

Plywood and MDF are the most common, but they also include blockboard, chipboard and OSB (oriented strand board). The last two are produced with a locking tongue-and-groove edge, and are used widely in place of traditional tongue-and-groove boards in floor construction. They are less suitable than timber floorboards as a finished surface but are superior as a subfloor for tiles and carpets. They are normally produced in 1220 x 600mm panels that are compatible with the spacing of timber floor joists.

Laminated beams

While timber has good structural properties, whether used as beam or column, its use is limited by both the natural size of tree trunks from which structural elements may be cut and the tendency of long lengths to split and warp over time when exposed to atmospheric variations. This has led to the development of laminated beams, which are manufactured from short lengths of timber glued together and frequently shaped in manufacture to create structural elements that fulfil aesthetic and practical requirements.

CURVED LAMINATED BEAM
Curved laminated beams supporting secondary beams – these in turn carry a glazed roof.

LAMINATED BEAM DETAIL
This detail of a laminated beam shows both the individual laminates that allow the beam to be precisely shaped during manufacture and the rich pattern created by variations in grain and colour.

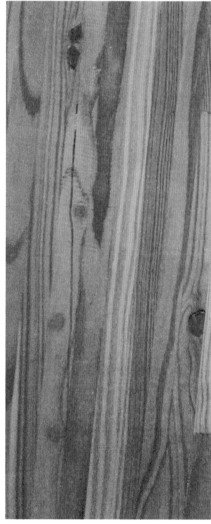

MDF

MDF (medium density fibreboard) is a board made from wood fibres glued together under heat and pressure. Its composition and manufacture make it very stable, with comparatively hard and very smooth surfaces on its 1220 x 2440mm faces.

Workability MDF has no true grain and can therefore be cut and machined with great accuracy and without surface damage. This simplifies the making of sharp precise angle cuts, or 'mitres', for the production of seamless corners, which can be glued and reinforced with 'biscuits' (see page 132) or dowels.

Although it is heavier than other wood-based building boards, MDF's workability and stability give it significant advantages over plywood, blockboard, chipboard and OSB (oriented strand board) for the on- or off-site manufacture of furniture pieces and wall panels. It is also used increasingly to produce simple moulded elements like skirtings and architraves.

Finishing MDF faces are a good base for paint finishes, but the softer core, which is exposed on all four edges, is more absorbent and should be filled or sealed to provide a non-porous surface to ensure a colour tone consistent with the primary faces. While MDF does not have a strong surface grain, a clear sealant coat will bring out a rich ginger tone with a slight, lighter fleck pattern. It also provides a stable base for veneers and laminates.

Specialist boards There numerous specialist varieties of MDF. Waterproof sheets are coloured green and fire-resistant sheets are pink. Some manufacturers are now producing decorative coloured boards that are pigmented through their whole thickness. Others produce sheets grooved on one side so that they bend easily and evenly.

Disadvantages The density of the board means that it is necessary to pre-drill screw holes. Nailing is difficult and can cause the material to split, particularly if too near the edge of the board. Edges can also crumble under impact – nails and screws should be at least 25mm from the edge.

It is, however, in the machining and construction process that the greatest problem with MDF occurs. It contains urea formaldehyde, which is released during cutting and sanding and can damage eyes and lungs. Working areas, whether in workshops or on site, need to be well ventilated, and masks and goggles should always be worn. Urea formaldehyde will continue to be released throughout the life of the product, so it is good practice to paint or varnish all surfaces to create a containing seal.

REPLACING TIMBER MOULDINGS
MDF is used to produce skirting mouldings that are more consistently stable than timber equivalents, although their edges are more easily damaged. They are supplied ready-primed for final painting. The green core indicates a waterproofing to withstand dampness at floor level.

REPLACING PLASTER
The smooth surface of MDF makes it suitable for comparatively delicately scaled work. This example of an internal window shows how a simple mitred frame can be pre-fabricated with great precision. If painted the same colour as the wall, it will be indistinguishable from the plaster.

Plasterboard

Plasterboard consists of a core of gypsum contained between two sheets of stiff paper. One side, the back, is coloured grey. The other, coloured cream, may be finished with a skim coat of 3mm plaster or, in 'drywall' construction, painted directly, once its joints and fixing points have been filled and sanded. The long edges of the cream face are often tapered to create a recess that can both receive filler and facilitate levelling during sanding.

Sizing Plasterboard comes in a number of sizes: 1200 x 2400mm is the standard but 1200 x 1800mm and 1200 x 900mm are also common. The smaller sizes are better suited for work in confined spaces or for single operatives. Although 1200 x 3000mm can be obtained for taller, usually older, spaces, the dimensions of the standard 1200 x 2400mm sheet are an important factor in determining ceiling heights and plan dimensions in new interiors, particularly in cellular layouts where reduction of waste in repetitious elements brings significant economies.

Specialist boards Colour-coded specialist boards with increased performance are available for specific applications. A green face identifies improved moisture resistance; yellow indicates better impact resistance; red a higher level of fire resistance; and blue indicates increased sound reduction. Other specialist boards, usually used for lining external walls, have foam insulation and vapour barriers glued to their backs in order to improve thermal performance.

Workability The comparative softness of the gypsum core allows the sheets to be cut to size with a handsaw. However, this can damage the gypsum, which is brittle and can disintegrate, making jointing – particularly in drywall construction – more difficult.

It is therefore more effective to cut the sheet using a specialist trimming knife and a metal straight edge. An incision through the paper into the gypsum provides a weakened line that may be snapped by bending backwards along the cut, giving a clean break through the gypsum; the paper surface on the reverse may then be cut.

Loadings When sheets are securely fixed with nails or screws at 150mm centres they will be robust enough to deal with significant impacts. It is also possible to support substantial loadings, such as shelves and cabinets. Where possible, fixings should be made directly into vertical studs. Where this is not practical because of the dimensions of the supported element, a plug – preferably metal, with a raised thread that cuts precisely into the gypsum core to produce a tightly integrated connection – will provide sufficient fixing for most loads.

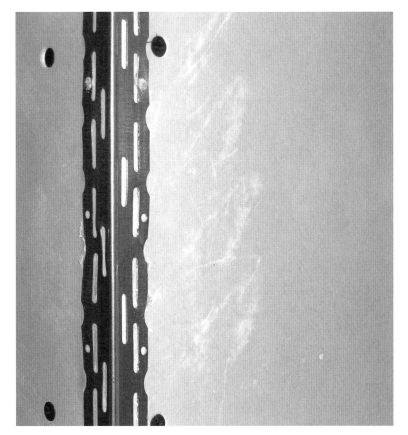

PROTECTING EDGES
External corners in plasterboard construction require reinforcing with expanded metal beads. These, nailed to the stud frame, provide a straight impact-resistant edge against which the skim coat of plaster may be finished.

BOARD COMPOSITION
Plasterboard consists of a brittle core of gypsum plaster sandwiched between two sheets of paper.

Plywood

Plywood consists of thin veneers of timber glued together, with the grain of each layer running at right angles to those next to it. This means that the tendency of individual veneers to bend in response to environmental conditions is neutralized, and the resulting product is a very stable board.

Manufacture The manufacturing process involves logs being stripped of their bark and subjected to steam and hot water to improve their 'peel' quality. Peeling is the process in which a continuous sheet of veneer is cut from the rotating log before being oven dried. Varying numbers of veneers are glued together to produce differing thicknesses of boards, and the glue is 'cured' in a hot press. After pressing, the panels are cut into standard 1220 x 2440mm sheets and graded.

Performance Grading identifies the performance capability of each sheet. Generally, the better the quality of the original timber the thinner the individual veneers and the better the quality of plywood.

Cheaper boards have little graining on their facing veneers and comparatively thick core layers. This is because they are produced from the fastest-growing wood, and the blade peeling the log slices few of the widely spaced growth rings. Cheap boards are only suitable for carcassing and temporary constructions, such as the 'shuttering' moulds for poured concrete.

Good-quality plywood has thin, dense veneers and their edges have a clearly defined linear pattern, which is good enough to be exposed as a finished edge.

Workability and finishing Plywood is relatively easy to cut, although the extant timber grains in each veneer mean that the cut edge of the poorer-quality boards may fray. When plywood is used as a finished surface, staining will enhance its grain pattern. Even a clear stain will darken plywood's natural colour.

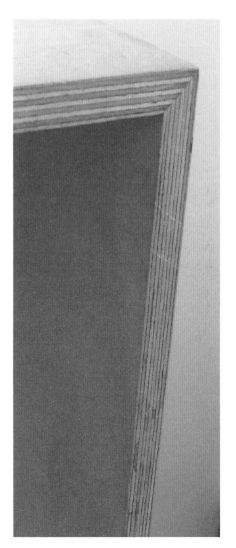

PLYWOOD VENEERS
Good-quality plywood has multiple layers of thin ply, which have a decorative quality and work well on a mitred corner.

VENEERS
A small selection of high-quality timber veneers.

Steel

Steel can be cut with mechanical hacksaws and curved by rolling between formers. This makes it a particularly suitable material in complicated edge-beam conditions. There are a number of types of steel used in the construction of interiors.

Mild steel This is obtainable in a number of hot- and cold-rolled sections, whose profiles enhance their structural capacity, and is primarily used in the construction of skeleton structures. Sections may be welded or bolted together. The latter technique, in which holes for the bolts are pre-drilled before the sections are brought to site, while not as strong as welding, allows for some adjustment on site.

Stainless steel For smaller steel elements, which are visible in detailing, stainless steel (an alloy with a minimum of 10 per cent chromium content) can be used. It is resistant to rust but can still suffer a degree of corrosion. It is produced with a range of surface qualities.

Alternative protections against rusting Painting provides the simplest way of protecting steel. Other more complex techniques, such as galvanizing with a film of zinc and other reactive coatings, provide more permanent protection. Chrome coating of mild steel, which is applied by an electroplating process, provides a highly reflective, corrosion-resistant surface.

Aluminium

While capable of fulfilling a structural role, and thus used extensively in the aerospace industry for lightness and durability, aluminium is more expensive than steel so its structural use in building is limited. However, as its density is around one third that of steel it is extensively used for lightweight framing or as a finishing material. It is protected from corrosion by a thin surface layer of aluminium oxide that forms when it is exposed to air.

Workability Its comparative malleability makes it easy to machine. It is frequently extruded into profiles similar to those for steel, but miniaturized for its more modest structural obligations. Because of its workability and lightness it can be rolled to produce thin laminates that may be glued to timber composite boards for rigidity. It is easily formed using a cold-pressing process, so thin sheets may be stiffened by folding. One of the most common applications of this is framing for drywall construction – the lightness of the material also makes handling easier.

Finishing In its natural state aluminium is similar to the silvery grey of steel, with variations caused by relative roughnesses of surface. It may be coloured, usually by a powder-coating process in which powdered pigment is applied electrostatically, then heat cured to create an even skin that is tougher than conventional paints.

Recycling It may be recycled easily and economically without losing its inherent qualities. This requires only five per cent of the energy used to process raw, natural ore. Recycled material, described as 'secondary aluminium', is used extensively in the production of extrusions.

ALUMINIUM STUD FRAMING
The very thin, very light sheet of aluminium is folded for strength and rigidity as framing.

ALUMINIUM STOPS AND BEADS
Expanded aluminium sections are vital components in the plastering process, here providing a stop bead for three-coat work.

PRE-FABRICATED ALUMINIUM
Aluminium is used extensively in the production of interior furniture elements.

Glass

Manufacturing clear float glass

Made using the modern method dating from 1959, which produced clear glass without distortion of vision or reflection, 'clear float glass' superseded 'plate' and 'sheet' production (although these two terms are still used to describe high-quality and thin glass respectively).

In the manufacturing process, molten glass is poured on to a bed of molten tin, on which it floats and spreads out to form level surfaces on each of its sides. It is 'annealed' (hardened) by precisely controlled cooling, and has almost perfectly parallel surfaces that eliminate visual distortion. Clear float glass can be manufactured in thicknesses from 2mm up to 25mm; for building purposes it is normally restricted to 3, 4, 5, 6, 8, 10 and 12mm with a maximum sheet size of 3180 x 6000mm. 15, 19 and 25mm thicknesses are restricted to 3180 x 4600mm.

Green, grey, blue and bronze colours can be created by variations in the proportions of ingredients used in manufacture, which result in selective absorption of parts of the light spectrum. However, since changing the proportions of the basic composition of a glass mix is a lengthy operation, modifications to basic clear glass are usually produced by surface coatings applied during manufacture ('on line') or afterwards ('off line').

Secondary manufacture

Glass can be further modified during what is known as 'secondary' manufacture to produce different specifications. These include:

Toughened glass This is made by heating and rapidly cooling glass after primary manufacture. The process makes it four times stronger, and better able to deal with impact, loading or thermal stress. When broken it disintegrates into small, smooth-edged fragments, making it particularly useful for glazed doors and screens.

It cannot be cut or worked after manufacture as any modification to the coherent compressive strength of its surface will cause it to fracture. Edges must be refined before the toughening process is carried out, and when drilling holes their size and possible positions are limited.

The size of toughened sheets is restricted to 4200 x 2400mm for those produced in a horizontal furnace and 3500 x 2500mm in a vertical furnace – thicknesses range from 4 to 19mm. A variety of glass types – including tinted, reflective and patterned – may be toughened.

Laminated glass This comprises sheets of glass bonded together with layers of clear plastic to which the glass adheres when broken, providing a significant safety factor. Varying thicknesses of the plastic interlayer can provide protection against physical attack from hammers, bullets and bombs. It can also improve sound insulation by dampening higher frequencies.

There are two principal manufacturing methods. In PVB laminating, a sandwich of polyvinyl butyral is heat-bonded in an autoclave between sheets of clear glass. Sheet sizes can be up to 5000 x 2500mm. In resin-lamination, an edge tape forms a space between two sheets of clear glass, which is then filled with liquid resin until all air is expelled. The resin sets to form a rigid interlayer, the thickness of which can be varied from 0.38mm to more than 6mm and the number of laminations from 3 ply (giving 4.4mm thickness) to 25 ply or more. Patterns printed on to glass can be protected within the laminations.

Multiple glazing This refers to hermetically sealed units, where panes of glass are bonded to create a single panel. Panes are separated by a hollow tube, usually aluminium, and filled with desiccant to keep the cavity dry. The sealed edge allows some slight movement of the glass sheets to prevent cracking, but should exclude moisture from the cavity. Most thicknesses and types of glass can be incorporated into multiple units, and the cavities can vary from 6 to 20mm.

While such units are principally used for thermal insulation they can also improve sound insulation and with the appropriate combination of glass thickness and gases in the cavity can attain a reduction of 40 decibels.

Fire-rated glass The fire resistance of some glasses is greatly increased by their chemical makeup or, in laminated glass, by the introduction of an intumescent gel between the glass sheets.

Wired glass This is produced by embedding wire within the thickness of glass (usually 6 or 7mm) during manufacture. It is very effective for fire resistance and security in door panels and screens, as the wire sustains the glass's integrity. Periods of 90 minutes fire resistance can be achieved in panels that are up to one square metre in area.

Glass blocks These are essentially transparent or translucent components that are bonded with mortar joints to create a wall or part of a wall. They are hollow and hermetically sealed and have good acoustic and thermal properties. Their thickness and the consequences of the manufacturing process mean that, even with transparent examples, there will be considerable visual distortion. There is a good range of sizes: 80mm wide blocks are 115 x 115mm, 190 x 190mm, 240 x 115mm or 240 x 240mm. The 300mm square block is 100mm wide.

Curved glass Curves are created by placing flat glass on top of a metal mould – or refractory – inside a kiln, which is heated until the glass softens, sags and takes on the shape of the mould. The kiln is cooled slowly for between 12 and 24 hours to avoid stressing the glass. Normally the maximum sheet size is 3000 x 2500mm. Toughened and laminated glass can also be bent.

Decorative finishes

Sandblasting The surface of clear glass is pitted by sand particles hitting it at high pressure. Areas of the surface may be 'masked' off to allow varying degrees of intensity of pitting or to create tonal patterns, or protected wholly to leave transparent areas. The process is not easy to control and works better if fine detail is avoided.

Acid etching This technique allows much greater control than sandblasting and is better suited to finely detailed decoration. The surface of the glass is eroded by hydrofluoric acid to produce degrees of translucency.

Brilliant cutting Patterns are cut into the thickness of the glass and edges are smoothed and polished. The facets exploit the effect of light.

Opal glass A pre-finished decorative glass, available in white, coloured or variegated form and ranging from a translucent white or 'flashed opal' to opaque or 'pot opal'.

Cutting and shaping glass

While all glasses, except toughened, can be cut after production, it is not recommended that this be done on site for any but the simplest operations.

For comparatively simple straight-line cuts information on dimensioned drawings will be sufficient for scoring, but for curves and irregular shapes a template is needed to guide the cutting tool.

Acute internal corners should be avoided where possible because they represent points of weakness. If they are unavoidable then a radiused corner, as large as possible, should be incorporated into the shape to be cut. The centre of any drilled holes should be at least four times as far from the edge as the thickness of the glass.

Acrylic

Transparent, translucent and opaque plastic sheets can offer more practical, and sometimes more economical, alternatives to glass; the most common of these is acrylic. While trade names, such as Perspex and Plexiglas, are in common use, it is perhaps better to use the generic label since these, and all similar products, are derived from acrylic acid. While their cost may make them impractical as an alternative to float glass in conventional applications, when specialist glasses are required acrylic-based products are often viable.

Manufacturing methods There are two main methods. Extruded, or continuous-cast, production is less expensive but the material is softer, more easily scratched and contains impurities that affect strength. Cell cast is more expensive but better quality and more reliable. The standard clear sheet may be coloured by the addition of dyes during manufacture.

Properties Acrylic's transparency rating of 92 per cent, with a 3mm thickness, makes it the clearest material available and it remains clear regardless of its thickness, while glass will develop a green tint as thickness increases. In addition, acrylic products do not turn yellow, become brittle or fracture with age.

It is significantly stronger than unreinforced glass, with a high resistance to impact damage. It has better insulative properties than standard glass and less than half its weight. This, with its less brittle character, makes it easier to work. It will not shatter but will break into large pieces without sharp edges. It can be cut with a saw and easily drilled to receive screws.

Applications Acrylic is particularly useful because it is easy to bend and therefore better than glass for curved screens. Although softer than glass and therefore more susceptible to scratching, marks may be removed by polishing or surface heating.

It is particularly useful for display and exhibition cabinets. It has a low reflectivity and its inherent strength and flexibility copes with viewers leaning on it. Resistance to impact also means that it is more secure than cheaper forms of glass. It can be easily shaped, and components can be joined by heat or solvents. It dissolves at the joint, fuses and sets, forming an almost invisible weld.

Fixings

Gluing

The options for fixing the basic materials used in interior construction are simple. They are nailing, screwing or gluing. The last is becoming more popular, particularly in carpentry and joinery work, since adhesives specifically designed to replace nails and screws have become more efficient and widely available. Gluing provides an invisible fixing but rules out the possibility of future disassembly and recycling, and there are difficulties in most existing buildings where surfaces are uneven and an even spread of the adhesive is impossible. A good glued joint will, however, be stronger than the timbers it connects so that if it fractures it will be due to a failure in the wood, which will split under the pressure of the joint.

Nails

When nails are hammered into timber they are forced between the wood fibres, which close back and grip them. They are the least strong of joining options, but are also the most common as they are simple and fast to use.

There is a wide range of types, covering the specialist requirements of carpentry and joinery. They normally remain visible, although their heads may be driven below the surface of timber using a 'nail punch', a small chisel-like tool with a flat, round head that transfers the impact of a hammer to the nail head without damaging the wood. The small indentation created will disappear if filled with a specialist compound, sanded and painted.

Types of nail

Round wire These are used for carpentry work and can vary in length from 15 to 200mm. The round head remains visible after fixing.

Oval wire From 20 to 150mm long, these have oval heads that may be driven a little below the timber surface, which is useful when other elements are to be fixed flat against the nailed surface.

Lost head These are from 15 to 75mm long, may be driven easily below the timber surface and the indentation filled and sanded for an invisible repair.

Panel pins From 10 to 75mm long, these are used for fixing thin board materials to framing and for the initial securing of joints while glue sets. The small heads have little visible presence against wood grains and are also easily driven below the surface of timber, with the indentation filled, sanded and painted.

Clout These, from 15 to 50mm long, are used to fix plasterboard sheets to timber stud framing. The large heads effectively clamp brittle plasterboard by spreading the connection. The head sits on the surface of the board but is covered by the final 3mm skim coat. The nails are galvanized to prevent rusting, which would cause swelling and damage the plaster.

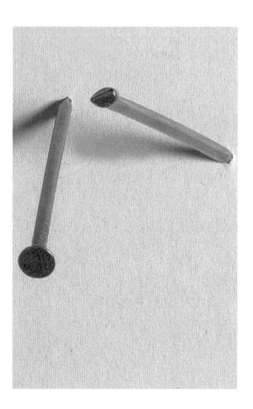

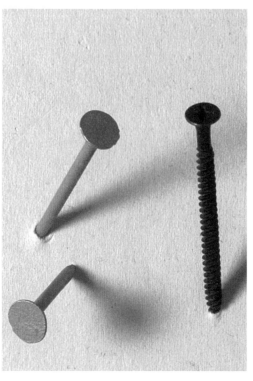

CARPENTRY NAILS (LEFT)
The round-headed nail is on the left. The head of the oval, on the right, can be hammered below the surface of the wood.

PLASTERBOARD FIXINGS (RIGHT)
Galvanized clout nails, on the left, secure plasterboard sheets to be finished with skim coat. Large heads increase the point of contact. The countersunk plasterboard screw on the right fixes plasterboard sheets for drywall construction. The head is sunk below the surface of the board and the indentation filled and sanded before painting.

Screws

The raised thread that distinguishes screws is designed to cut into timber, so that the thread ridges are integrated into, and locked in position by, the material that surrounds them. Screws, therefore, provide a more secure connection than nails and are more easily removed, although they do leave holes. Battery-powered screwdrivers and drills make the use of screws, instead of nails, simpler and faster. Pre-drilling, with a bit diameter smaller than that of the screw, will speed the process and reduce surface damage.

Types of screw

There is an extensive selection for use with different types of materials and in different conditions. Some are purely utilitarian but others are intended to make a positive visual contribution. All are classified by size: shaft thickness, length, material and type of head (for example: 'size 6, 50mm, steel countersunk'). The greater the size, the thicker the shaft and therefore the stronger the screw.

Countersunk The head of a countersunk screw, which tapers towards the shaft, can usually be screwed tight enough to finish flush with the surface of the timber or board it is fixing. It is possible to ensure a wholly flush finish by making an inverted cone-shaped recess in the timber surface, using a countersinking bit. This will also eliminate the possibility of damage to the wood surface as the screw is forced home. A screw 'cup' inserted over the shaft before fixing will also limit damage and provide a positive visual transition between screw and wood.

Round-headed or dome-headed The heads of these screws, which have a flat underside that finishes tight to the surface of the wood, sit on top of the wood and will cover minor damage caused in the fixing. A washer under the screw head will cover local damage.

Self-tapping This is a screw with a hard, sharp thread that can cut into and find a secure grip in thin metal. Its most common use in construction is with metal-stud framing where the screws are also coated to prevent rust.

Nuts and bolts

Bolts, like screws, are threaded, but have a flat rather than a pointed end and wholly penetrate through pre-drilled holes in the elements they are connecting. They are secured with a threaded nut on the reverse side. They are used in a wide range of applications – large diameter and heavy examples are utilized to connect structural elements; smaller, lighter sections are used to fix metal glazing beads. Pre-drilled holes normally have a bigger diameter than the bolt to allow some tolerance for fixing, and washers that fit neatly over the bolt cover the gaps that are left. When timbers are bolted, washers spread the load and prevent the head of the bolt and the nut biting into the softer surface of the wood.

NUT, BOLT AND WASHER
The washers cover the edges of the pre-drilled hole made for the bolt and spread the load of both the nut and bolt over the surface of the timber.

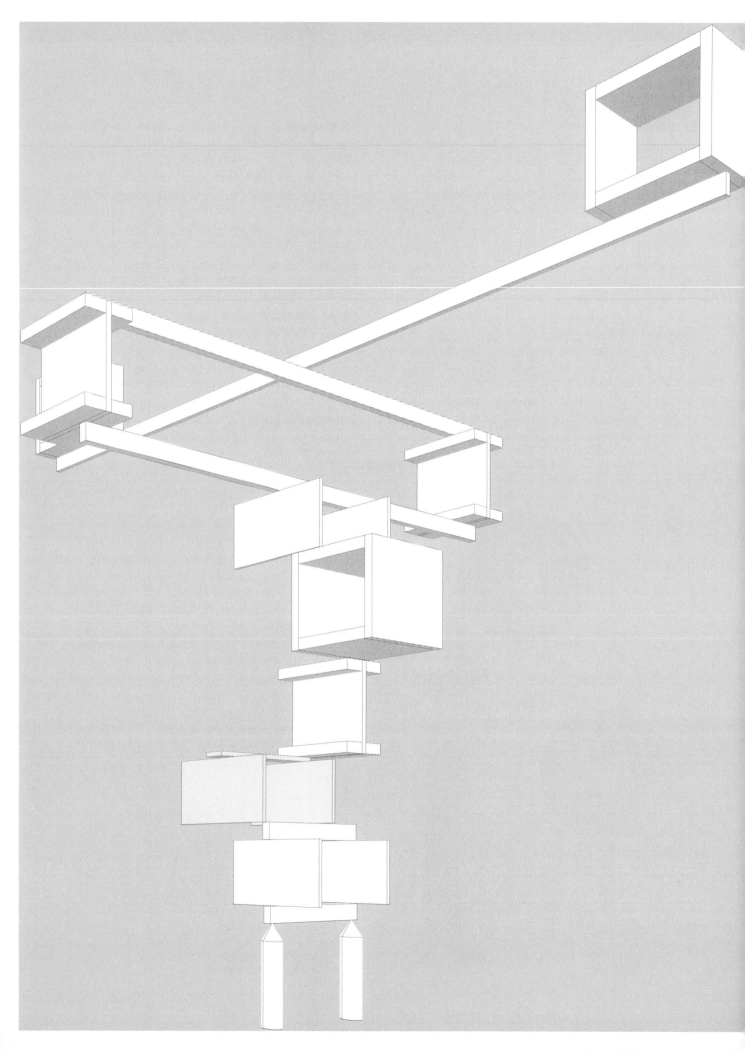

CHAPTER 10 STRUCTURAL PRINCIPLES

Introduction

Interior-design projects seldom involve building significant new structures or major additions or amendments to existing buildings. When these do prove necessary, it always makes sense to have properly qualified engineering advice to ensure the most effective solution and to provide the calculations necessary to gain local authority approval – their minimum standards tend to be demanding, with very conservative estimates given for the structural capacity of materials.

The loadbearing capacity of existing elements can become a crucial consideration when a building is adapted, particularly for a change of use. Regulations may decree that old walls and joists are insufficient to meet modern requirements for offices or restaurants, potentially making any project economically unacceptable. Removing existing elements, particularly floors and beams, may affect the stability of a structure by reducing their bracing effect on walls. New loadings, especially on elements like columns that have little inherent lateral strength, may create unacceptable stresses that will lead to structural failure.

It is still useful to have knowledge of basic principles so that initial design work is realistic and will not need to be amended too dramatically or destructively when an engineer suggests final strategies. Knowledge of principles also allows a designer – the only person with a comprehensive vision of project – to discuss and assess options realistically and point towards a viable, and aesthetically acceptable, direction that an engineer, with a necessarily restricted perspective, may not see.

COMPRESSION
This occurs when a supporting element is compacted by the weight of the load it carries, such as a column resting on a firm foundation and carrying the weight of a floor above.

TENSION
This occurs when a supporting element, such as a suspension wire, is stretched by the load it carries.

Materials in compression and tension

All structural members – walls, columns, beams and floor and ceiling slabs – are in compression or tension or both, depending on their role and location. When elements under compression fail, they fracture and disintegrate. They tend to be bulky to spread the imposed load over a bigger area and to counteract bending.

When elements under tension fail, they tear apart. However, these elements can be very thin since they do not have to resist bending.

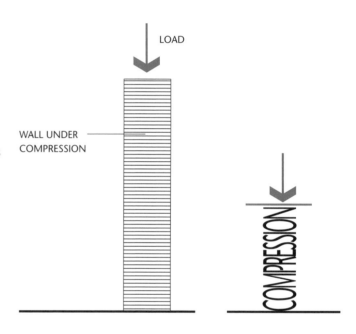

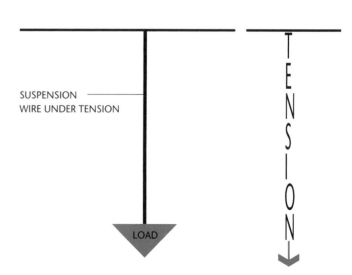

The combination of forces

Most structural members, even those only supporting their own weight, are subjected to both compressive and tensile forces. The clearest example of this is a horizontal beam spanning between columns or walls. The tendency of the beam to bend under loading means that the material on the upper edge will be compressed and the material on the lower edge will be tensioned. The intensity of both effects lessens towards the centre of the beam's cross-section, with the forces exerted in the exact centre neutralized. It is therefore good practice to form holes for the passage of services in the centre of beams.

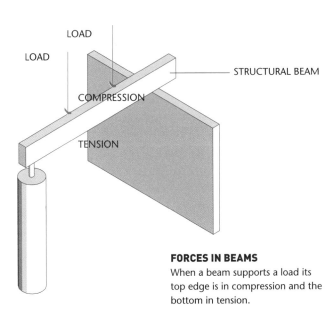

FORCES IN BEAMS
When a beam supports a load its top edge is in compression and the bottom in tension.

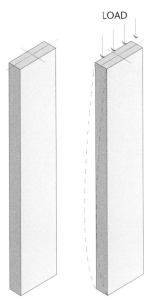

RESISTANCE TO BENDING
A column in which the dimension of one side is significantly greater than the other is liable to buckle under loading, even when that loading does not exceed the nominal capacity of the material used in the column's construction. The tendency towards buckling varies with materials.

Structural materials

Timber The comparative lightness of timber and the ease with which it may be cut and fixed make it the first choice for most structural work. The fibres that form its structure mean that it functions well in both compression and tension. Lengths of timber are cut so that fibres run lengthwise, helping provide a structural continuity.

In its simplest form, with a rectangular section, timber is quite adequate for floor and ceiling joists and for framing walls. Composite beams may be constructed using timber-based sheet materials for depth, and natural timber lengths for lateral rigidity. Laminate beams, which are composed of glued strips of timber, can rival steel and concrete for strength and, although they are liable to be greater in cross-section, are easily bent and curved.

Steel While excellent in tension, steel is comparatively poor in compression. However, it is malleable during manufacturing and is produced in a number of standard sections that counteract its tendency to bend under compression. The profiles, of which the best known are 'I', 'L' and 'C' sections, reduce the volume of steel required to add width to depth and provide lateral rigidity.

The loadbearing capability of each available section is set out in tables produced by the bodies responsible for approving structural work. These take into account not only dimensions but the thickness of metal used. This gives scope for varying dimensions to suit site conditions. Thicker cross-sections will allow smaller dimensions.

Concrete While extremely strong in compression, concrete is very weak in tension. Other than when it is used horizontally and supported over its entire area, as in ground-level floors, it is necessary to reinforce concrete with steel rods or mesh in columns, beams and suspended floor slabs. This steelwork is positioned in the mould into which the wet concrete will be poured, and if covered to a depth of 50mm will be protected against rusting. Rust will cause steel to swell, and this will fracture the concrete.

It is interesting, perhaps remarkable, that the thermal expansion rates of concrete and steel are the same, so both expand and contract at the same rate. Differential movement would result in fracturing of concrete.

Masonry Brickwork, blockwork or stone all function primarily as supporting elements. Shallow arches, supported on wooden or metal formwork while the mortar sets, can be an alternative to steel or concrete lintels, but are complicated to construct and inevitably have curved profiles so are only used for decorative effect.

Orientation of structural elements

Generally, the greater the size of a structural member the stronger it will be. For economical, and sustainable, solutions, the less material used the better. The calculation of the most efficient solution depends on finding the optimum relationship between the depth and width of structural elements – the strength of a beam or column is crucially affected by the relation between its longer and shorter dimensions.

Any element – whether a beam, slab or column – will be weakest at its midpoint because the effect of the load will be greatest and there will be less support against bending from lateral restraints.

While the depth of a beam, on the vertical X axis, will principally determine its loadbearing capacity, its width, on the horizontal Y axis, will determine its stability when loaded. In a beam the X dimension will normally be greater than the Y, but this has less significance in the design of an evenly loaded column, when there will be no variation in stresses over the cross-sectional area. Square and rectangular cross-sections will work equally efficiently.

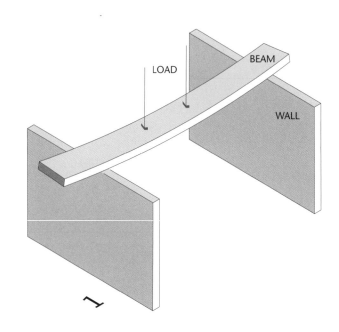

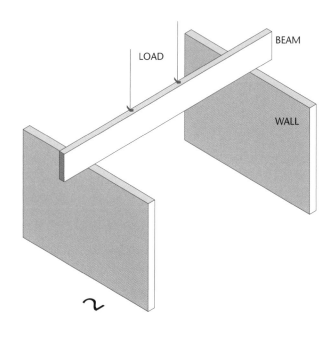

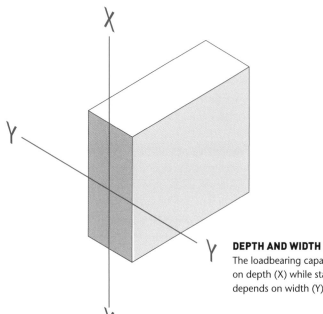

DEPTH AND WIDTH
The loadbearing capacity depends on depth (X) while stability depends on width (Y).

ORIENTATION AND LOADING
The depth of a material relates directly to its performance, and the same cross-section of the same material will perform quite differently if laid with its greater dimension horizontal (**1**) than vertical (**2**). Whether a beam, slab or column, it will be weakest at its midpoint.

The basic principles of creating a viable structure are simple, and most people will have an instinctive understanding of how they work. This knowledge, coupled with learning and experience, can suggest structural configurations that fulfil their functional obligations efficiently but also deliver a visual impact.

Depth and strength

The depth of a beam is the crucial factor in combating failure due to loading. Greater depth relates directly to greater strength, but lateral distortion can occur when a beam does not have sufficient width to resist buckling

under loading. As long as the structural component can withstand such lateral distortion, it is more economical (and sustainable) to reduce the volume of material used in manufacture if possible.

DEPTH AND LOADING
1 Lateral distortion: a beam needs width to resist buckling.
2 Rolled steel joist (RSJ) – the horizontal 'flanges' in this, the most common steel profile, resist lateral movement in the web (the vertical element of the joist).

3 To reduce the use of materials, holes may be cut from the web without affecting the strength that is gained from its depth.
4 Hollow box beam: composite timber board provides depth and lateral rigidity; lengths of natural timber reinforce glued joints.
5 I-section timber beam: composite timber board provides depth, and lengths of natural timber provide lateral rigidity.

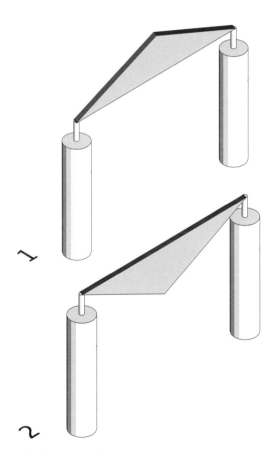

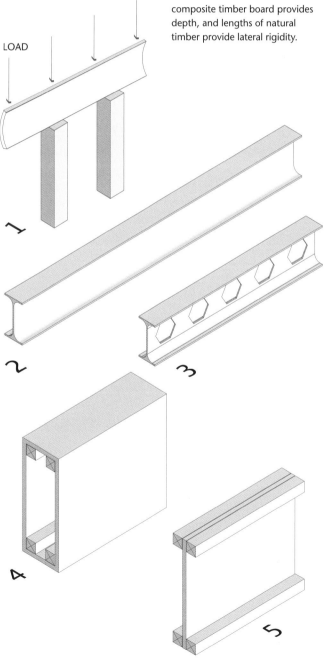

INCREASED DEPTH AT THE MIDPOINT
The profile of a beam may be shaped in response to the forces acting within it, with greater depth at its midpoint. The resulting triangular profile will be equally effective as a roof structure, with its apex above the points of support (**1**), or as a beam for long floor spans, with its apex below support points (**2**).

Cantilevers

A cantilever is a projecting element, usually a floor or canopy, that has structural support on only one side. It may be used for practical reasons but it is generally an aesthetic gesture.

Simple cantilevers It is feasible to attach a modest projecting element from a wall or line of columns if a sufficiently substantial connection can be made. The further a cantilever projects beyond its support point, the greater the strain on both the connection and the supporting element. It is unlikely that anything in excess of a metre is viable. Additional connection to a supporting structure can be provided by an angled strut in compression below the cantilevered element, or a tie in tension above it, so that loading on the front edge of the cantilever is transferred back to the supporting structure. The latter may be incorporated into a balustrade.

Counterbalanced structures For more substantial cantilevers it is more effective to build a counterbalanced structure in which a conventionally supported structure, whether timber joists or a concrete slab, is projected beyond one of its support points. The greater weight of the conventionally supported area should be sufficient to stabilize the cantilevered section. The counterbalancing effect can be increased by additional loading on the non-cantilevered section of a floor structure.

Tapering It is common practice to taper the underside of a cantilevered floor: since the area of the projection is normally less than that of the floor from which it extends, its depth can be less. The taper will emphasize the lightness of the cantilever and suggest that it is braced against the supporting structure. There is no reason why the angle of taper should not be exaggerated visually.

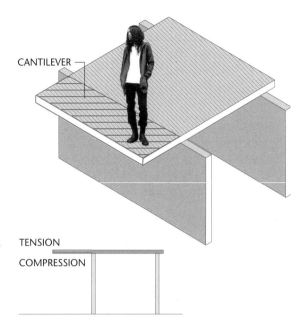

CANTILEVER

TENSION

COMPRESSION

SHIFTING FORCES
For the area of the slab that is conventionally supported on the walls, the top edge will be in compression and the bottom in tension, as usual. This will be reversed for the cantilevered section when the top is in tension and the bottom in compression.

TAPERING CANTILEVERS
A cantilevered beam or slab may be tapered away from the supporting point, allowing the depth of the beam or slab over the cantilever to be reduced, as it carries less weight.

STRUCTURE WITH COUNTERBALANCING WALL
As long as the weight of the cantilevered element is exceeded by the weight that is counterbalancing it, then the structure should remain stable.

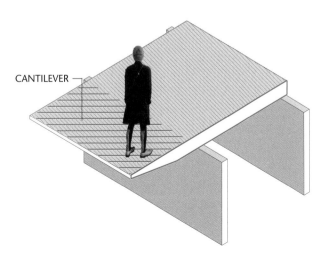

CANTILEVER

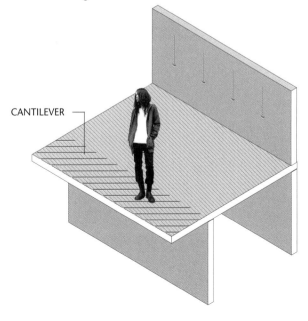

CANTILEVER

Beams

Disguising beams

Downstand beam A conventional 'downstand' beam projects below the floor it supports, so it is a visually significant element in the rooms below, unless concealed by a suspended ceiling. With restrictive floor-to-floor heights there may not be enough headroom to accommodate the beam, although a height of 2000mm to its underside will usually be acceptable, or to the underside of the suspended ceiling.

Upstand beam It is possible to introduce an 'upstand' beam, projecting above the floor it supports. This would have to be accommodated within a wall in the rooms into which it projects, or alternatively by a change of level, if it is not to form an obstruction. An upstand beam may also be contained within the thickness of a balustrade on the edge of a mezzanine floor.

Mezzanines It is also feasible to design a lightweight steel edge beam that will both support the edge of a floor and provide a safety barrier for the mezzanine.

Alternative beam sections

While the rectangle remains the most common cross-section, there is no reason – other than cost and possible delays in the manufacture – that other options may not be used.

Circles A circular steel section is reasonably easy to obtain. However, for clear expression of the purity of the circular section, the beam and the floor slab should be separated visually by spacing 'cleats'. An oval beam provides a section that responds more closely to structural width-to-depth ratios.

Triangle It is possible to produce a beam that has three solid faces, but it is more usual to exploit the inherent strength of a triangulated structure by reducing it to a skeleton of members in compression and tension. It may be used with the flat surface at the top or bottom. The latter has the advantage of visually separating the beam and the supported floor slab.

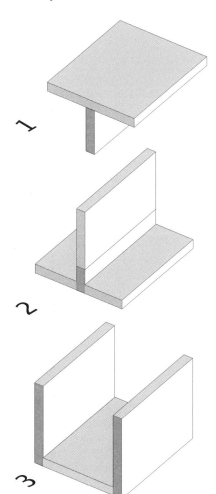

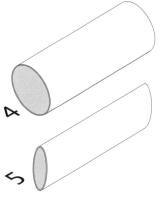

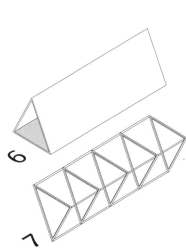

DISGUISING BEAMS
1 Downstand beam projecting beneath floor.
2 Upstand beam disguised in wall above.
3 Upstand beams can act as balustrades on the edge of bridges or mezzanines.

ALTERNATIVE SECTIONS
4 Circular beam.
5 Oval beam.
6 Triangular beam.
7 Triangular beam with skeletal members.

Stability

Allowance is frequently made for some limited, controlled, movement in the design of large-scale external structures, to allow response to short-term temperature and loading changes. Interior construction tends to be protected from environmental variations, and loadings are generally modest. However, the elimination of movement in interior construction is necessary to prevent damage to finishes. Construction techniques have evolved to minimize the amounts of material used and reduce construction time, and standard practice has adopted a number of stratagems to ensure an appropriate degree of rigidity.

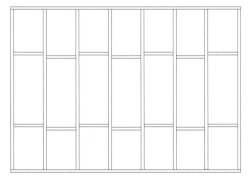

1

STRUCTURAL INSTABILITY
A frame with simple unreinforced corner joints that lack inherent rigidity will tend to distort under minimal pressure. A single nail or screw connection will act as a fulcrum, around which the connected elements will rotate. Two or more connections at a joint position will not eliminate the problem because they will be too close together to counteract each other.

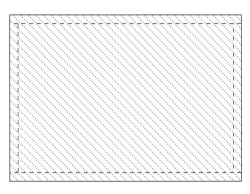

2

STUD PARTITION
The addition of extra vertical and horizontal members will reduce the tendency to distort. While the individual connections, of single nails or screws, will not themselves be rigid, the accumulative effect of elements within the whole reduces movement.

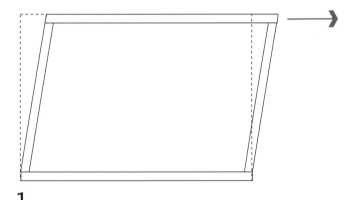

3

STUD PARTITION COVERED IN SHEET MATERIAL
Simple butt joints and fixings (often the result of economic priorities) will remain fragile, but this skeletal structure can be stabilized if clad with rigid sheet material. The most common example is the stud partition, in which plasterboard sheets are used to establish and retain right angles. Plasterboard is not particularly resistant to impact and is easily damaged by the nails or screws fixing it to the studs, but the frequency of fixing points spreads the strain evenly over the entire surface of the frame. The filling of gaps between sheets with plaster skim or drywall jointing compound makes the whole monolithic.

PARTIAL COVERAGE OF STRUCTURE

It is not necessary to cover the whole face of a frame to make it rigid, although the less area used for reinforcement the stronger the reinforcing material must be and the more secure the jointing techniques (**4**, **5**, **6**). When edges of panels are exposed, the sheeting material must be capable of withstanding damage to exposed and unsupported edges. Examples include composite timber board like plywood, fixed with secure screw fixings and glued to spread the contact surface, or metal sheets screwed to a timber frame or welded to a metal frame.

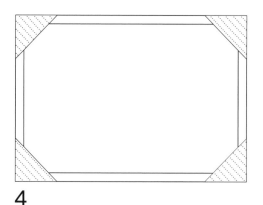

4

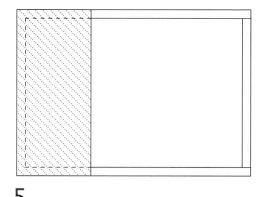

5

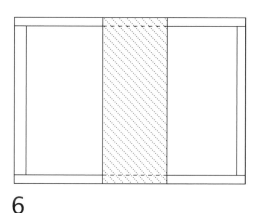

6

TENSION WIRES AND RODS

When a well-engineered and constructed skeletal frame is used, which may be timber but is more likely to be metal, any distorting effect may be counteracted by crossed tension wires, which will counteract a tendency in either direction. The angles of the frame to which the wires are attached need to be strong enough to contain the stress caused by the tensioning of the wires (**7**). In particular, a single wire can only counteract movement in one direction and will tend to destabilize the structure by allowing the distortion of the frame when tensioning is applied (**8**). A single rod that remains rigid in both compression and tension will be structurally effective but more visually obtrusive (**9**).

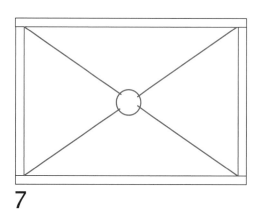

7

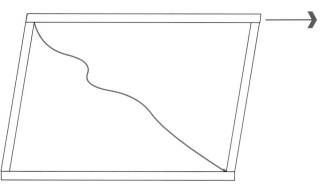

8

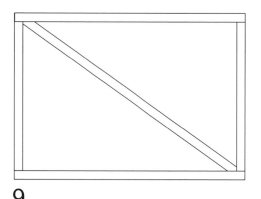

9

Rule-of-thumb sizing

While final sizes should be calculated by a structural engineer, it is valuable for the designer to have a realistic idea about the likely dimensions of structural elements in the initial stages of project development. This should ensure that proposals are essentially feasible and do not have to be abandoned when significant time has already been devoted to evolving them. The ratios here are rough guides only, and can be assumed to apply to all materials.

1

2

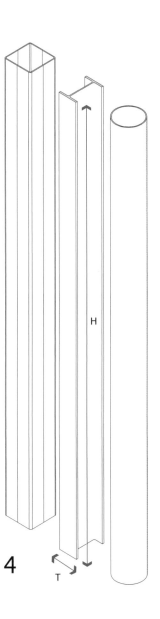

3

4

1 LOADBEARING MASONRY (BRICK, BLOCK OR STONE)

T (width) should not exceed $\frac{1}{12}$ of H (height).

2 IMPROVING STABILITY

Piers, or attached columns, bonded into, and therefore integral to, a brick wall at regular intervals effectively increase its width and therefore its stability. The same principle applies to construction in any material.

3 REINFORCED-CONCRETE COLUMNS

T (width) should not exceed $\frac{1}{15}$ of H (height).

4 STEEL COLUMNS

T (width) should not exceed $\frac{1}{30}$ of H (height).

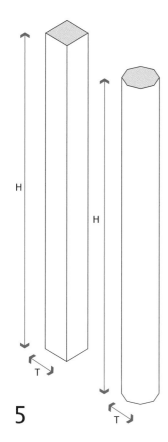

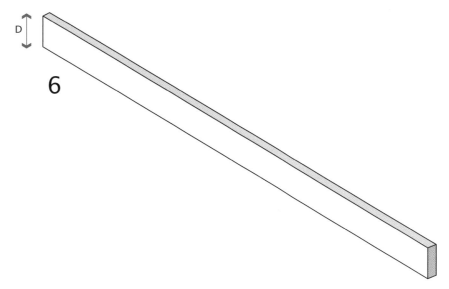

6

5

5 TIMBER COLUMNS OR POSTS

T (width) should not exceed $\frac{1}{20}$ of H (height) – this rule of thumb does, however, vary with the grade of timber used.

6 BEAMS

D (depth) should be at least $\frac{1}{15}$ of the span. However, with rigid braced corners this can be reduced to $\frac{1}{20}$.

7 FLOOR SLABS SUPPORTED ON TWO SIDES

When the floor slab is supported on two sides, the slab depth should be $\frac{1}{25}$ of the span.

8 FLOOR SLABS SUPPORTED ON FOUR SIDES

When the floor slab is supported on four sides, the slab depth should be $\frac{1}{30}$ of the span.

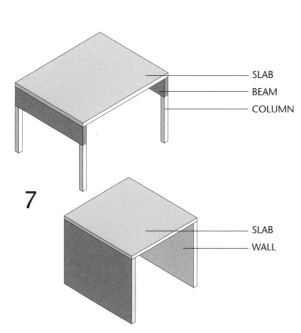

7

— SLAB
— BEAM
— COLUMN

— SLAB
— WALL

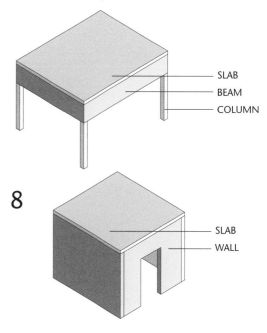

8

— SLAB
— BEAM
— COLUMN

— SLAB
— WALL

CHAPTER 11 A TO Z

GLOSSARY

A

Architrave : A strip – usually wood, sometimes metal or plastic, frequently decoratively moulded – that covers the junction of wall and frames for doors and windows. It may be fixed by nailing, screwing or gluing.

Arris : The sharp edge formed by the meeting of two planes, for instance a corner.

B

Baluster : The vertical member that supports the handrail in a balustrade (*see below*).

Balustrade : A protective vertical barrier on a stair or mezzanine.

Batch production : Limited production of the same artefact.

Bead : A thin strip of wood, metal or plastic, sometimes decoratively shaped or moulded, that secures panels or sheets of glass, or provides cosmetic cover for joints.

Biscuit : An elliptical composite-timber sliver inserted into both faces of a butt joint to improve adhesion.

Blockwork : Masonry constructed with concrete blocks – usually plastered, sometimes left fairfaced.

Butt joint : The simplest joint – two elements are clamped flat against each other and secured by nails, screws or glues.

C

Carcass : The basic structure that supports cladding panels in joinery work.

Carpentry : Structural and framing woodwork, usually using sawn timbers. A first-fix operation, liable to be encased behind finishing materials.

Chamfer : The angled trimming of an edge to reduce its visual bulk.

Chases : Channels cut in walls or floors to accommodate runs of wiring or piping and covered after installation.

Clear float glass : Glass, free of distortion or reflection, produced by pouring molten glass over a bed of molten tin.

Clout : A nail with a large round head, used where the area of contact needs to be spread to avoid damaging brittle materials, particularly plasterboard.

CLS : Abbreviation for 'Canadian Lumber Size', a standard sizing for roughly finished sawn timber.

Column : An isolated vertical element – circular, square or rectangular in cross-section – usually constructed of concrete, steel or brick, primarily used to support overhead structures but which can also serve to subdivide areas, when it may be non-loadbearing and constructed of plasterboard on a stud frame.

Conduits : Metal or plastic tubes – square or round in section – attached to the surface or embedded in walls or floors, through which service elements, usually electrical wiring, are circulated. Wire lies loose and may be pulled out and replaced without destroying finishes.

Contract : The formal, legal agreement between client and contractor that specifies the work to be carried out and the sum for which it will be completed.

Contractor : The individual or, more usually, the company who will carry out construction. They should have a contractual agreement with the client to carry out the work described by the designer in tender drawings and written documents. They may be responsible for all or part of the work but it is usual for specialized work, such as the installation of heating and ventilating equipment, to be carried out by subcontractors (*see below*).

Cornice : A strip – usually plaster, sometimes timber or plastic, often decoratively moulded – that covers the junction of wall and ceiling. It may be fixed by nailing, screwing or gluing.

Countersinking : The recessing of screw or nail heads to finish either flush or a few millimetres below a finished surface to allow filling and making good.

Course : A single-level stratum in masonry construction.

Cover strip : A strip – usually thin timber, frequently decoratively moulded – used to mask raw joints and junctions.

D

Dabs : Spots of plaster (75–100mm wide) added to an existing wall to provide adhesion for a plasterboard fixed directly on to the wall, minimizing making good.

Dead load : The total weight of building components that must be considered in the calculation of structure.

Dowel : A short cylindrical length of timber or of timber-composite material that is inserted into abutting faces of a timber joint in order to improve adhesion.

Door stops : Continuous strips, usually timber, which are nailed, screwed, glued or integral to the door frames against which the door leaf closes. They also serve to reduce draughts.

DPC (damp-proof course) : A strip of waterproof material inserted across the width of a wall, under sills or around door and window openings, to prevent water penetration to the interior.

DPM (damp-proof membrane) : A sheet of waterproof material laid over the total area of a floor or wall to prevent water penetration to the interior. It should be bonded to a damp-proof course to create a complete seal.

Dry-lining : The construction of an inner skin, usually plasterboard on a stud frame, against a solid outer wall to prevent water penetration to the interior.

Drywall : A method of constructing plasterboard partitions and ceilings that relies on specialist fixing and filling techniques to eliminate the need for a finishing skim coat of plaster.

E

Expanded metal : A mesh used to support and reinforce plasters and renders, made by cutting short slits in a flat aluminium or steel-alloy sheet that is then pulled in two opposing directions so that it distorts to form a three-dimensional lath.

F

Fairfaced : Masonry construction that is left exposed rather than plastered or otherwise concealed. It will normally require a more expensive product and more care and skill in construction to achieve a satisfactory standard.

'Finger' joints : Metal jointing mechanisms in which projecting 'fingers' secure adjacent corners of sheets in a glass wall.

First fix : The installation of, primarily, service elements such as plumbing and electricity that must be carried out before further building work makes access impossible.

Flange : A flat metal projection or extension formed during manufacture or added to a primary metal element to strengthen it or to provide a fixing device.

Flight : A single, unbroken run of stairs or steps.

Framed : A construction that relies on a skeleton structural support to provide fixing and stability for cladding panels.

G

Galvanize : To coat steel and steel alloys with a zinc alloy to protect against rusting.

Going : The horizontal length of a flight of stairs, the distance it covers on plan.

Grout : A fine mortar used to fill joints, particularly between floor and wall tiles.

H

Hanger : A timber or metal element that connects a suspended element to its structural support.

Header : A brick or block built into a wall so that its shorter edge is exposed.

I

In situ : Work carried out on site.

Intumescent strip : Material recessed into a door frame or door leaf that expands in heat to prevent the passage of smoke throughout a burning building.

J

Jamb : The vertical edge of a door or window opening.

Joinery : Visible finished woodwork, carried out on site but frequently partly pre-fabricated in workshops, and almost invariably using PAR timber (*see below*) and applied as a second fix (*see below*).

K

Key : A roughening of surface to improve cohesion for applied wet finishes, principally plaster.

L

Laminated glass : Sheets of glass sandwiched with layers of clear plastic to which the glass adheres when broken, improving safety.

Landing: The horizontal area between sloping flights of stairs or steps.

Lath : A perforated base to support and reinforce plaster, traditionally consisting of thin strips of timber and now of expanded metal (*see above*).

Live loads (also known as superimposed loads): The total weight of elements such as equipment, furniture and people that are not components of a built structure and must be considered in the calculation of the forces on a structure.

Lost head nail : A nail without a wider head that can be driven below the surface of timber.

M

Main contractor : The individual or company responsible for the greater part of construction on a project and also for liaison with, and support for, subcontractors (*see below*) to ensure efficient completion of the contract.

Masonry : Bricks, concrete blocks or stones, bonded with mortar.

MDF (medium density fibreboard) : A board made from wood fibres, glued together under heat and pressure. It may be machined with great precision.

Mitre : The angling of the edges of two abutting planes to ensure visual continuity of surface. The angle of each mitre should be half that of the angle of the corner.

Monolithic : Being, or appearing to be, constructed solidly of one material.

Mortice and tenon : A traditional joinery joint in which a slot (the mortice) is cut in one element to receive a compatible projection (the tenon) in the other. The two elements interlock tightly but the joint is normally glued for additional cohesion.

Multiple production : *See* batch production.

N

Nail : A metal pin that when hammered into timber forces fibres apart and is consequently gripped tightly by them as they try to return to their original state. Nails come in various sizes and cross-sections for various applications.

Nail punch : A metal device with a small flattened point that, when struck by a hammer, will drive nail heads below the surface of, usually, wood or wooden-composite materials, to allow for filling and sanding before painting.

Nosing : The projecting front edge of a stair tread.

O

One-off (production) : The making of a unique object.

Opaque : Cannot be seen through and will not allow light to pass through.

Oriented strand board (OSB; also known as strand board) : Composite board – made up of very thin slivers of wood, glued together under heat and pressure – that is stable and useful in carcassing work.

Oval wire nail : A nail with an oval cross-sectioned shaft and a slightly wider oval head that may be driven below the surface of timber.

P

Packing out : The insertion of timber slivers in localized gaps between new and existing elements to ensure a firm connection.

Padstone : A beam – usually reinforced concrete, but which may also be stone or steel – built into a masonry wall to spread the weight of a point load (see below).

Panel pin : A very thin, usually short, nail used for fixing sheet materials to a supporting frame. The small head may be driven below the surface of the sheet.

PAR : An abbreviation of 'planed all round', describing timber that has had an average of 3mm planed from all faces of its sawn lengths. It is used primarily in joinery work.

Partition : An internal wall, usually non-loadbearing and of lightweight stud framing and plasterboard construction.

Patina : The patterning or discolouring, usually accepted as decorative, that occurs when a material is subjected to ageing, weathering or both. Some effects may be artificially induced.

Permissible loading : The weight that a building element or material is designated capable of supporting by the statutory body responsible for approving building work.

Pier : A projection beyond the face of a wall to provide lateral bracing or support for a point load.

Plaster beads and stops : Expanded metal strips used as guides during plastering and as reinforcement for vulnerable plaster edges and angles. There are various profiles to suit various locations and plastering techniques.

Plate glass : A term now used primarily to describe high-quality glass but originally referring to a manufacturing process.

Point load : A concentration of the weight of a structure, the result of its being supported by a column or pier, that usually requires increased foundation provision.

Post : A wooden column, usually loadbearing.

Precast : A description of elements, typically of concrete or plaster, that are shaped and hardened in a mould before being brought to site. They may be one-off, batch or multiple production (see above).

Pre-fabricated : Refers to work, usually complex or delicate, that is shaped and assembled in a specialist workshop before being brought to site for installation.

Production information drawings (also known as production or working drawings) : Drawings made by a designer to instruct contractors and subcontractors (see below) about the extent and quality of work necessary to complete a project satisfactorily. Such drawings will be extensively annotated with dimensions, descriptions of materials and assembly methods.

Pugging : Loose material – stone chippings, sand or clinker – laid between joists to improve sound insulation by reducing reverberation and the passage of sound waves across voids.

R

Rise : The vertical height of a flight of stairs or steps.

Riser : The vertical element in a step.

Round wire nail : A nail with a circular cross-sectioned shaft and a wider circular head that finishes on the surface of timber.

Routing : The mechanical cutting of a channel into timber or timber-based boards to improve joint adhesion.

S

Sawn timber : Lengths of timber with the rough finish that results from the initial conversion of tree trunk to plank, used primarily in carpentry.

Screed : The smooth and level final coat on a concrete floor. It may be used as a finish in its own right or to provide a substratum for thin floor finishes.

Screw : A pointed fixing device with a raised thread or continuous helical ridge, which, when turned by a hand or electrically powered screwdriver, cuts into a material, usually wood, so that the areas between the threads are filled with the material, creating a fully integrated connection. This interlocking makes screws significantly more effective as a gripping device than nails.

Screw 'cups' : Raised circular metal collar for a screw, raising it slightly from the surface of the fixed element and masking any surface damage caused during fixing.

Scrim tape : A loosely woven jute fabric or paper strip used to bridge, and reinforce, joints in plasterboard construction.

Second fix : Final installation, primarily of fixtures and fittings, after building work has been effectively completed and further incidental damage is unlikely.

Self-tapping screws : Screws with a sharp raised thread, which penetrate and connect thin metal materials.

Shadow gap : The, usually narrow, space created by the physical separation of elements, which, in modern construction and assembly, replaces the traditional cover strip as a device for visually refining joints.

Sheet glass : Refers to thin sheets of glass.

Shuttering : A temporary mould for concrete during pouring and drying.

Skim : The final coat of plaster on a wall or ceiling, approximately 3mm thick, which is 'polished' to give a smooth surface. It may be applied to one or two undercoats on a masonry wall or as a single coat on plasterboard. It is usually finished with paint or paper.

Skirting : A strip – usually wood, sometimes metal or plastic – frequently decoratively moulded, that covers the junction of wall and floor. It is fixed by nailing, screwing or gluing.

Soffit : The visible underside of major elements such as floors and stair flights.

Sole plate : The base member in a timber or metal stud partition.

Specification : The written description, prepared by the designer, of the quality of materials and construction required to complete a project to an appropriate, acceptable standard. It may be contained on drawings, in a separate document, or in a combination of both.

Stairwell : The vertical space that contains a flight or flights of stairs. It need not be enclosed unless used as a fire escape route.

Stanchion : A steel column, usually loadbearing.

Stretcher : A brick or block built into a wall so that its longer edge is exposed.

String : The inclined structural support for the treads of a stair.

Studwork : The timber or metal framing that provides the support skeleton for lightweight partition walls.

Subcontractor : An individual, or company, with specialist skills, usually employed and supervised by the main contractor.

T

Tender : The price for which a contractor (*see above*) agrees to carry out the work necessary to construct a project in accordance with the tender drawings. It is normal for at least three contractors to be asked to submit tenders, and for the contract to be awarded to the lowest bidder. However, a designer must be satisfied that the work can be carried out satisfactorily for the sum. When a single contractor is chosen for the job – usually because of particular expertise in a specialist area of work, or previous successful collaboration with a client – a negotiated contract is entered into, in which contractor and designer collaborate to produce a contract that will ensure the mutually acceptable completion of the proposed work.

Tender drawings : These usually comprise the complete set of production information drawings, but it is possible to seek tenders on the basis of a representative selection of key drawings. This is acceptable as long as all contractors submitting a tender base their price on the same set.

Thermal movement : Expansion or contraction caused by temperature changes, which can lead to cracking in finishes.

Thread : A raised, helical ridge on a screw, nut, or bolt.

Timber ground : A length of timber, usually sawn, that contributes to the fixing of another element.

Tongue and groove : The traditional detail for timber products used in flooring and wall cladding, in which a projecting 'tongue' on one long face fits inside a compatible 'groove' on the other. Planks and boards interlock to ensure a level intersection. With composite boards, particularly flooring products, a development of the basic form locks units together and reduces the need for nail fixing.

Toughened glass : Glass with increased resistance to impact and tension loading made by rapid heating and cooling during manufacture.

Translucent : Cannot be seen through but will allow light to pass through, to varying degrees.

Transparent : Clear visibility through a material – even if colour-tinted.

Tread : The horizontal element in a stair, which users step on.

Trimmed joist : A joist cut short to form a floor opening.

Trimmer joist : A joist that supports the ends of trimmed joist (*see above*).

Trimming joist : A joist that supports the ends of trimmer joists (*see above*).

Turnbuckle : A device, integral to a tensioned structure, for carrying out the final tightening of wires on site.

W

Well (or stairwell) : The volume that contains flight(s) of stair(s) and landings.

Wired glass : Glass with a wire grid embedded in its core that provides improved security and fire resistance.

RESOURCES

FURTHER READING

1) A technical manual from first principles:

Ashcroft, Roland, *Construction for Interior Designers*, 2nd edition, Longman Scientific and Technical, 1992

2) Books aimed primarily at an architectural audience:
These contain information about interior construction and are also a source of background information about those exterior elements of buildings that may impact on interior proposals.

Ching, Francis D., *Building Construction Illustrated*, 4th edition, Wiley, 2008

Chudley, Roy and Roger Greeno, *Building Construction Handbook*, 8th edition, Butterworth Heinemann, 2010

Emmitt, Stephen and Christopher Gorse, *Barry's Introduction to Construction of Buildings*, 2nd edition, Wiley, 2010

Emmitt, Stephen and Christopher Gorse, *Barry's Advanced Construction of Buildings*, 2nd edition, Wiley, 2010

Fullerton, R.L., *Construction Processes: Level One*, Technical Press, 1983

Hall, Fred and Roger Greeno, *Building Services Handbook*, 5th edition, Butterworth Heinemann, 2009

McLean, Will and Pete Silver, *Introduction to Architectural Technology*, Laurence King Publishing, 2008

3) Building legislation:
Decisions about construction and detailing are often influenced by legislation.

The Building Regulations 2000: Complete Set of Approved Documents 2006, TSO (The Stationery Office), 2009

Billington, M.J., K.T. Bright and J.R. Waters, *Building Regulations: Explained and Illustrated*, 13th edition, Blackwell, 2007

4) Accepted standards for the configuration and dimensions of elements:
These will be crucial in assisting decision-making.

Baden-Powell, Charlotte, *Architect's Pocket Book,* 3rd edition, Architectural Press, 2008

Littlefield, David, *Metric Handbook: Planning and Design Data,* 3rd edition, Architectural Press, 2008

5) Specialist techniques and materials:
These require specialist research – those listed below are examples of such sources

Ballard Bell, Victoria and Patrick Rand, *Materials for Architectural Design,* Laurence King Publishing, 2006

Binggeli, Corky, *Materials for Interior Environments,* Wiley, 2007

Blanc, Alan and Sylvia, *Stairs,* Architectural Press, 2001

Brandi, Ulrike et al., *Lighting Design: Principles, Implementation, Case Studies,* Birkhäuser, 2006

Godsey, Lisa, *Interior Design: Materials and Specifications,* Fairchild Publications, 2008

Kaltenbach, Frank (ed.), *Translucent Materials: Glass, Plastics, Metals,* Birkhäuser, 2004

Reichel, Alexander, Anette Hochberg and Christine Kopke, *Plaster, Render, Paint and Coatings: Details, Products, Case Studies,* Birkhäuser, 2004

Riggs, J. Rosemary, *Materials and Components of Interior Design,* 2nd edition, Prentice Hall, 1989

Rupp, William, *Construction Materials for Interior Design: Principles of Structure and Properties of Materials,* Whitney Library of Design, 1989

Spens, Michael, *Staircases,* Academy Editions, 1995

White Book, British Gypsum, 2009
A trade publication that is available in printed form and for download at www.british-gypsum.com/literature/white_book. It provides comprehensive information about techniques and materials used in plasterboard construction.

Wilhide, Elizabeth, *Eco: The Essential Sourcework for Environmentally Friendly Design and Decoration,* 2nd edition, Quadrille Publishing, 2004

Wilhide, Elizabeth, *The Interior Design Directory: A Sourcebook of Modern Materials,* Quadrille Publishing, 2009

WEBSITES

Before the emergence of the Internet, interior designers were obliged to maintain a reference library of catalogues and brochures of products and materials, and to keep this up to date, adding new items and removing obsolete information. The use of search engines can avoid this, while introducing fresh specification options, as manufacturers and suppliers are now primarily putting their information online. This ensures continuous updating and, frequently, access to detailed drawings of components that may be downloaded and incorporated into designers' own production information drawings.

There are broadly two types of website:

1) Consortia of manufacturers and suppliers:
Below are examples of such sites.

British Glass Manufacturers Confederation
www.britglass.org.uk
Technical information and lists of specialist glass manufacturers.

British Gypsum
www.british-gypsum.co.uk
Information about plastering products and techniques – see also *White Book* above.

Matério
www.materio.com
A professional network and database devoted to innovative new materials and technologies.

Timber Research and Development Association
www.trada.co.uk
Technical information about timber, timber-based products and regulations; identification of species and their structural capacities.

2) Manufacturers' and suppliers' own websites
These usually give comprehensive information about individual manufacturers' products, and increasingly include advice about sustainability and details of installation techniques. Examples are some examples.

Expamet Building Products
www.expamet.co.uk
Manufacturer of expanded, metal materials, primarily for plastering and rendering.

Häfele
www.hafele.co.uk
Manufacturer of furniture fittings and architectural ironmongery.

National Building Specification
www.thenbs.com
Part of RIBA Enterprises Ltd, which produces specification products for building construction, engineering services and landscape design.

Pilkington NSG Group Flat Glass Business
www.pilkington.com
Technology datasheets and information about standard and specialist glass products.

INDEX

Numbers in *italic* refer to captions.

Picture Credits

All diagrams are by Olga Valentinova Reid and all photographs are by Drew Plunkett, except the following:

p.89   Kjeld Duits / FASHION JAPAN
p.156 top   Katsuhisa Kida / FOTOTECA
p.156 bottom Peter Paige Photography
p.165 left   Alexander Franklin Photography.
             Designers: Brinkworth

Acknowledgements

Thanks to:
Olga Valentinova Reid for converting my crude sketches into elegant drawings and diagrams – and then designing the book.
Alan Keane for demonstrating and explaining workshop practice.